Advances in

THE STUDY OF BEHAVIOR

VOLUME 39

Advances in
THE STUDY OF
BEHAVIOR

Edited by

H. JANE BROCKMANN

TIMOTHY J. ROPER

MARC NAGUIB

KATHERINE E. WYNNE-EDWARDS

JOHN C. MITANI

LEIGH W. SIMMONS

Advances in

THE STUDY OF

BEHAVIOR

Edited by

H. JANE BROCKMANN
Department of Zoology
University of Florida
Gainesville, Florida

TIMOTHY J. ROPER
School of Life Sciences
University of Sussex
Falmer, Brighton, Sussex
United Kingdom

MARC NAGUIB
Netherlands Institute of Ecology
(NIOO-KNAW)
Heteren, The Netherlands

KATHERINE E. WYNNE-EDWARDS
Department of Comparative
Biology & Experimental Medicine
Faculty of Veterinary Medicine
University of Calgary
HRIC, Calgary
Alberta, Canada

JOHN C. MITANI
Department of Anthropology
University of Michigan
Ann Arbor, Michigan

LEIGH W. SIMMONS
Center for Evolutionary Biology
The University of Western Australia
Crawley, Australia

VOLUME 39

AMSTERDAM • BOSTON • HEIDELBERG • LONDON
NEW YORK • OXFORD • PARIS • SAN DIEGO
SAN FRANCISCO • SINGAPORE • SYDNEY • TOKYO
Academic Press is an imprint of Elsevier

Academic Press is an imprint of Elsevier
525 B Street, Suite 1900, San Diego, CA 92101-4495, USA
30 Corporate Drive, Suite 400, Burlington, MA 01803, USA
32 Jamestown Road, London NW1 7BY, UK
Radarweg 29, PO Box 211, 1000 AE Amsterdam, The Netherlands

First edition 2009

Library of Congress Cataloging-in-Publication Data
A catalog record for this book is available from the Library of Congress

British Library Cataloguing-in-Publication Data
A catalogue record for this book is available from the British Library

ISBN: 978-0-12-374474-6

For information on all Academic Press publications
visit our web site at elsevierdirect.com

Printed and bound in USA
09   10   11   10 9 8 7 6 5 4 3 2 1

QL
750
.A38
v.39

Working together to grow libraries in developing countries

www.elsevier.com | www.bookaid.org | www.sabre.org

ELSEVIER   BOOK AID International   Sabre Foundation

Contents

The Dog as a Model for Understanding Human Social Behavior

JÓZSEF TOPÁL, ÁDÁM MIKLÓSI, MÁRTA GÁCSI,
ANTAL DÓKA, PÉTER PONGRÁCZ, ENIKŐ KUBINYI,
ZSÓFIA VIRÁNYI, AND VILMOS CSÁNYI

Strategies for Social Learning: Testing Predictions from
Formal Theory

BENNETT G. GALEF

Behavior of Fishes in the Sexual/Unisexual Mating System
of the Amazon Molly (*Poecilia formosa*)

INGO SCHLUPP

Alternative Mating Tactics in Acarid Mites

JACEK RADWAN

Contributors

Numbers in parentheses indicate the pages on which the authors' contributions begin.

FILIPPO AURELI (45), *Research Centre in Evolutionary Anthropology and Palaeoecology, School of Natural Sciences and Psychology, Liverpool John Moores University, Liverpool L3 3AF, United Kingdom*

DOROTHY L. CHENEY (1), *Departments of Biology and Psychology, University of Pennsylvania, Philadelphia, Pennsylvania 19104, USA*

VILMOS CSÁNYI (71), *Department of Ethology, Eötvös Loránd University, Pázmány P. S. 1/C, H-1117 Budapest, Hungary*

ANTAL DÓKA (71), *Department of Ethology, Eötvös Loránd University, Pázmány P. S. 1/C, H-1117 Budapest, Hungary*

MÁRTA GÁCSI (71), *Department of Ethology, Eötvös Loránd University, Pázmány P. S. 1/C, H-1117 Budapest, Hungary*

BENNETT G. GALEF (117), *Department of Psychology, Neuroscience and Behaviour, McMaster University, Hamilton, Ontario, Canada L8S 4K1*

ENIKŐ KUBINYI (71), *Department of Ethology, Eötvös Loránd University, Pázmány P. S. 1/C, H-1117 Budapest, Hungary*

ÁDÁM MIKLÓSI (71), *Department of Ethology, Eötvös Loránd University, Pázmány P. S. 1/C, H-1117 Budapest, Hungary*

PÉTER PONGRÁCZ (71), *Department of Ethology, Eötvös Loránd University, Pázmány P. S. 1/C, H-1117 Budapest, Hungary*

JACEK RADWAN (185), *Institute of Environmental Sciences, Jagiellonian University, UL. Gronostajowa 7, 30-387 Krakow, Poland*

GABRIELE SCHINO (45), *Istituto di Scienze e Tecnologie Della Cognizione, Consiglio Nazionale Delle Ricerche, 00197 Rome, Italy*

INGO SCHLUPP (153), *Department of Zoology, University of Oklahoma, Norman, Oklahoma 73019, USA*

ROBERT M. SEYFARTH (1), *Departments of Biology and Psychology, University of Pennsylvania, Philadelphia, Pennsylvania 19104, USA*

JÓZSEF TOPÁL (71), *Institute for Psychology, Hungarian Academy of Sciences, Victor H. U. 18–22, H-1132 Budapest, Hungary*

ZSÓFIA VIRÁNYI (71), *Department of Ethology, Eötvös Loránd University, Pázmány P. S. 1/C, H-1117 Budapest, Hungary*

Preface

Advances in the Study of Behavior has made "contributions to the development of cooperation and communication among scientists in the field" of animal behavior since 1965. The present volume continues to reflect the diversity of approaches that animal behaviorists use and the array of problems they address. The volume includes studies on social behavior (Cheney and Seyfarth, Schino and Aureli, Topál *et al.*), reciprocal altruism (Schino and Aureli), social learning (Galef), mate choice and conflict (Schlupp), and alternative mating tactics (Radwan). The trend in animal behavior toward more integrative and multidisciplinary studies is reflected in studies on the effect of stress on social behavior (Cheney and Seyfarth), the mechanisms of reciprocal altruism (Schino and Aureli), and both proximate and ultimate approaches to alternative mating tactics (Radwan). The studies in this volume include both laboratory and field research on a wide diversity of species including primates (papers by Cheney and Seyfarth, Schino and Aureli), dogs (Topál *et al.*), rats (Galef), fish (Schlupp), and mites (Radwan). The volume also reflects a continuing interest in applying our understanding of animal behavior to human behavior (Cheney and Seyfarth, Topál *et al.*). By highlighting particularly well-developed and original research programs, this volume continues to stimulate new, exciting advances in animal behavior.

With this volume, we welcome Dr. Leigh Simmons to our team of editors. His eclectic research interests and experience as an editor make him a particularly valuable addition. I remain the executive editor, and Tim Roper, Marc Naguib, Kathy Wynne-Edwards, and John Mitani continue as editors. Together we hope to maintain the intellectual diversity that has characterized this series since the beginning.

H. JANE BROCKMANN

Stress and Coping Mechanisms in Female Primates

Dorothy L. Cheney and Robert M. Seyfarth

DEPARTMENTS OF BIOLOGY AND PSYCHOLOGY,
UNIVERSITY OF PENNSYLVANIA, PHILADELPHIA,
PENNSYLVANIA 19104, USA

I. Introduction

Like pornography, stress is difficult to define but instantly recognizable. Everyone has felt stress, but not everyone suffers from chronic stress. Although our body's response to stress helps us to cope with physical and psychological challenges over the short term, over the long term it prevents us from dealing with the same challenges. A trigger for the stress response might be a physiological challenge, such as cold weather or a glucose imbalance, or an easily identifiable event, such as a traumatic incident or the death of a close companion. Other sources of stress, however, are more amorphous and difficult to specify.

In humans, two classes of causal agents interact to promote stress (defined below): physical agents, like smoking, excess alcohol, or a diet high in cholesterol, and psychological agents, like a catastrophic event, a death in the family, loneliness, or tension at work. Stress can also arise from subtle factors related to a lack of predictability, control, and support in daily life (e.g., Marmot, 2004). Bereavement, loneliness, and lack of social support are especially potent stressors that can compromise the immune system, lead to cardiovascular disease, and increase the risk of mortality (e.g., Cacioppo et al., 2000; Irwin et al., 1987; McCleery et al., 2000; reviewed in Segerstrom and Miller, 2004).

To what extent, however, are these causes of stress unique to humans? Humans have a wider variety of social relationships than other animals, our societies are much more stratified, our dependence on others for our material well-being is much greater, and our daily lives are much more multifaceted and complex. Furthermore, our ability to attribute thoughts, beliefs, and motives both to ourselves and others—our "theory of mind" (Premack and Woodruff, 1978)—drives us to dwell on our misfortunes and

1

0065-3454/09 $35.00
DOI: 10.1016/S0065-3454(09)39001-4

misconstrue and obsess about our relationships with others. We can perceive feelings of loneliness even when we are surrounded by others and feel loss of control even when we have dependable shelter and sustenance. It is very unlikely that any animal is capable of the same sort of introspection and mental state attribution that humans engage in routinely (reviewed by Cheney and Seyfarth, 2007; Tomasello et al., 2005). Similarly, it is well known that stress and feelings of loneliness in humans can be mitigated by friendship and social support (Rosal et al., 2004; Steptoe et al., 2004; Thorsteinsson and James, 1999). Such support seems to be particularly important for women's mental health (Kendler et al., 2005; Taylor et al., 2000). However, the empathy of friends does not require that the friends too be afflicted with feelings of grief or loneliness. Our ability to provide support and empathy is independent of our current emotional state. It is by no means clear whether animals—even apes—can empathize with others or recognize others' grief (Cheney and Seyfarth, 2007; Silk, 2007). As a result, the causes and amelioration of stress in humans may differ in subtle but fundamental ways from those in other species.

Like humans, animals suffer from stress when they are socially isolated or subjected to uncontrollable or unpredictable traumatic events. For example, monogamous rodents show physiological signs of stress when they are separated from their mates (reviewed by Carter, 1998; see below). Similarly, rats and dogs that are subjected to intermittent shocks experience more stress if they are unable to control the rate at which they receive shocks, or if they are unable to predict when shocks will be delivered (Sapolsky, 2002; Seligman, 1975; Weiss, 1970). Under natural conditions, however, animals are seldom subjected to social isolation or stressors such as shocks, so the ecological validity of these observations is unclear. Indeed, until the advent of Robert Sapolsky's pioneering research (e.g., Sapolsky, 1993a, 1998) on stress in wild male baboons (*Papio hamadryas anubis*), almost nothing was known about the causes and alleviation of stress in wild animals. And although there have now been numerous studies of stress and coping mechanisms in wild male nonhuman primates, female nonhuman primates have received very little attention (Adkins-Regan, 2005; Reeder and Kramer, 2005).

Here, we review the causes and alleviation of stress in wild female monkeys, focusing in particular on baboons. We should note at the outset that there have been surprisingly few studies of stress in female primates generally and wild female primates specifically, which is why our review is not as comprehensive as we would like it to be. In particular, nothing is known about the causes and amelioration of stress in female apes. Nonetheless, we believe that a review of stress in wild female primates is timely, in part because wild populations of primates offer a better model for human stress than captive ones. First, females in natural populations of monkeys typically live in large social groups that consist of both kin and nonkin, maintaining relationships that are both cooperative and competitive. These societies create a context for both increased social stress and opportunities for its alleviation. Second, females living under natural conditions are confronted with a variety of environmental stressors and traumatic events that not only present a challenge to reproduction and survival but also have the potential to damage an individual's social relationships. For example, a female baboon who sees a lion kills a close relative experiences not just a physiological but also a psychological stressor: her social network has now been damaged. Although some captive colonies approach wild groups in their size and social complexity, studies of stress in female monkeys have typically been conducted on individuals living either in newly established and unstable groups or in isolation from their companions—contexts that are highly stressful and very artificial.

We argue that many of the causes of stress in female monkeys—and its alleviation—are fundamentally social. Stress is influenced by events that threaten a female's survival and reproductive success, including in particular predation and the immigration of a potentially infanticidal male. Like humans, female monkeys rely on a stable social network to cope with stress. The presence of kin or close companions *per se* does not alleviate stress; rather it is the strength of a female's social bonds with a small number of specific companions. Females whose grooming networks are focused on a few individuals show lower levels of stress than females whose grooming networks are diffuse and relatively unselective. Females experience significant increases in stress when this network is damaged by the death of a close grooming partner, and they take active steps to seek out and identify new partners. The causes and amelioration of stress in female monkeys appear to be subtle and complex. It is the nature and quality of a female's social relationships, rather than sociality alone, that allows a female to cope with and manage stress.

II. THE STRESS RESPONSE

When the brain perceives a stressor, the hypothalamus responds by releasing corticotropin-releasing hormone, which in turn stimulates the adrenal gland to release glucocorticoids (GCs). GCs are secreted primarily by the adrenal glands within minutes following the onset of a physical or psychological stressor (reviewed by Adkins-Regan, 2005; McEwen and Wingfield, 2003; Nelson, 2000; Sapolsky, 1998, 2002). GCs increase the availability of glucose in the bloodstream by promoting glucose production and curtailing glucose uptake and storage (Nelson, 2000). Energy is mobilized, memory is sharpened, and immediately nonessential but energetically expensive functions like digestion, repair, growth, and reproduction are temporarily shut down. An increase in circulating GCs (cortisol and corticosterone in birds and mammals) is just one part of a cascade of neurological, hormonal, and immunological responses that characterize the "stress response" of the hypothalamic–pituitary–adrenal (HPA) axis.

Elevated GC levels enhance survival by mobilizing a suite of physiological and behavioral responses. The benefits of these behaviors may persist even when GC levels remain elevated over several weeks. For example, many species of birds and mammals show persistently elevated GC levels during winter and other periods of food scarcity, when environmental conditions demand an increase in metabolic rate (reviewed by Nelson et al., 2002). Similarly, although wild European rabbits (*Oryctolagus cuniculus*) that have temporarily been kept captive for several weeks experience both elevated GC levels and deterioration in body condition, they nevertheless survive at high rates after release (Cabezas et al., 2007).

However, although these anabolic processes are an essential and adaptive response to short-term challenges, they can be detrimental if sustained over long periods of time. Because elevated GC levels increase the immediate availability of energy from storage sites, increase cardiovascular activity, and suppress physiological activities that are not required for immediate survival, a chronic stress response can have harmful consequences, including loss of muscle mass, hypertension, immune and/or reproductive suppression, and even death (McEwen and Wingfield, 2003; Munck et al., 1984; Pride, 2005b; Sapolsky, 2002; Sapolsky et al., 2000). This is true of both physiological and psychological stressors. For example, social isolation and anxiety increase vulnerability to infections. Equally important, elevated GC levels over prolonged periods reduce the sensitivity of the HPA stress response to new challenges. Thus, chronic stress impedes the ability to mount future stress responses. For example, one function of GCs is to increase appetitive and food-seeking behavior—adaptive responses when food resources are scarce. Chronically elevated GCs, however, impede the ability of insulin to promote glucose uptake, leading to the accumulation of fat, obesity, and atherosclerotic plaques. Subordinate captive female rhesus macaques (*Macaca mulatta*) with chronically elevated GC levels show an increased preference for fatty, high calorie foods, in part perhaps because high calorie foods activate dopamine reward pathways (Wilson et al., 2008). Brain activity shows a similarly paradoxical reaction to stress. Emotionally salient events, facilitated by the sympathetic nervous system and the release of epinephrine, activate the hippocampus and the amygdala, aiding in the formation of memories that may prove useful in future dangerous or important encounters. Chronic stress, however, can result in neuronal atrophy and death, particularly in the hippocampus, impairing declarative, contextual, and spatial memory (McEwen and Wingfield, 2003).

As many have pointed out, however, stress is a vague, "ethereal concept" (Nelson et al., 2002) that often implicitly incorporates both the stressor and the stress response, each of which feeds back upon the other (e.g., Levine, 2005; Levine and Ursin, 1991; McEwen and Wingfield, 2003; Sapolsky, 2002). In its popular usage "stress" suggests a chronic, maladaptive challenge to homeostasis, even though the stress response is highly adaptive over the short term. Moreover, while there are obvious detrimental physiological and cognitive consequences of chronic stress, there is no definitive threshold for "bad," as opposed to "good," stress. It may be possible to determine when an individual's GC levels are above baseline, but it is far more difficult to define when an individual is "highly stressed," except after physiological damage has resulted. Finally, although it is relatively easy to identify the causal effects of a traumatic event on an individual's stress response, it is much more difficult to trace the more subtle causes and consequences of an individual's social status, support network, and daily social interactions on her "stress" hormones.

For many of these reasons, McEwen and Wingfield (2003; see also Goymann and Wingfield, 2004) have introduced the concept of "allostasis," which they define as "maintaining stability (homeostasis) through change." Whereas homeostasis refers to the systems that are essential for survival and reproduction, allostasis is the process that maintains those systems in balance, allowing individuals to adjust to social and environmental challenges. According to this reasoning all energetic challenges, including low temperatures, food deprivation, social isolation, and frightening events that activate the sympathetic nervous system prompt the secretion of GCs, which help to mobilize the energy required to restore homeostasis. And because restoring homeostasis requires more energy than maintaining it, exposure to stressors increases energetic demands. Functions that are energetically costly, like the reproductive and immune systems, are temporarily suppressed.

"Allostatic load" is the cumulative cost to the body as the individual attempts to adjust her physiology and behavior both to temporary events and to more permanent states, like social subordination (Goymann and Wingfield, 2004; McEwen and Wingfield, 2003). Over the short term, an increase in allostatic load is adaptive, because it helps the organism to cope with unpredictable events and results in behaviors that ultimately help to reduce GC levels. If, however, allostatic load increases dramatically, or if short-term responses to the increase fail to return the individual to homeostasis, chronically high levels of GCs may trigger a response that results in damage to organs essential for survival and reproduction.

McEwen and Wingfield argue that the concept of allostasis is useful because it combines the energetic demands of survival and reproduction with those associated with social and environmental challenges into a continuum. "Stress" now refers to those environmental, social, and psychological factors that disturb homeostasis, increase allostatic load (whether adaptive or not), and elicit both physiological and behavioral responses (McEwen and Wingfield, 2003; Nelson et al., 2002). Phrased somewhat differently, a stressor can be thought of as "any event that causes an individual to increase energy consumption above baseline." (Nelson et al., 2002: 157). Because GC levels are expected to rise as allostatic load increases, they can be used to assess allostatic load.

Throughout this chapter, we use the term "stress" as McEwen and Wingfield does, to refer to an increase in allostatic load, as indicated by an increase in GC levels. A stressor is an event or condition that increases GC levels. We use the term "coping mechanism" to refer to behaviors that occur after an increase in GC levels, and that are correlated with a subsequent reduction in GC levels.

III. STRESS AND SOCIAL ATTACHMENT

In both animals and humans, stressful experiences—including not only pregnancy and birth but also conflict, war, and other traumatic events—often precede and motivate the formation of close social bonds (reviewed by Bartz and Hollander, 2006; Carter, 1998; Panskepp, 1998; Tops et al., 2007). Some degree of stress may even be essential for the formation of strong emotional attachments (reviewed by Simpson and Rholes, 1994). The link between stress and social attachment occurs in part because stress prompts the release of the peptide oxytocin, a hormone that motivates attachment, trust, and pair-bonding behavior.

Oxytocin interacts with GCs bidirectionally: separation, loss, and other stressful psychological events initially act to reduce oxytocin levels and increase GC levels. The increase in GCs, in turn, prompts the release of oxytocin, which increases attachment-seeking behavior, ultimately effecting a decrease in GC levels and HPA axis activity. In humans, administration of cortisol increases plasma oxytocin levels (Tops et al., 2007). This effect appears to be particularly strong in women (Taylor et al., 2000).

Much of the research concerned with the relationship among GC levels, oxytocin, social attachment, and social isolation in animals has been conducted on rodents. In rodents generally, oxytocin promotes social affiliation and parental behavior and is essential for social recognition (reviewed by

Bartz and Hollander, 2006; Carter, 1998; DeVries et al., 2003; Lim and Young, 2006; Panskepp, 1998; Tamashiro et al., 2005; Uvnas-Moberg, 1997; Von Holst, 1998).

Rodents' stress responses to social contact and isolation vary according to the social environment in which they have evolved. For example, the wounds of socially monogamous mice (*Peromyscus californicus* and *P. eremicus*) heal more rapidly when they are pair-housed than when they are socially isolated (DeVries et al., 2007; Glasper and DeVries, 2005). In contrast, social contact does not facilitate healing in the closely related *P. leucopus*, a polygynous species that does not form pair bonds. Similarly, in an experiment conducted on three social and one solitary species of African mole rats (*Heterocephalus* spp.), only members of the solitary species showed a lack of social tolerance and an increase in GC levels when introduced to an unfamiliar conspecific (Ganem and Bennett, 2004).

In the monogamous prairie vole, separation from a social partner of the opposite sex causes an increase in GC levels in both males and females, while reunification results in a decrease. This effect holds only for familiar partners; GC levels remain elevated if the separated voles are placed with an unfamiliar animal (reviewed by Carter, 1998). Interestingly, in previously unpaired individuals, stressful experiences and the administration of corticosterone stimulate the formation of pair bonds in males but not in females, who are more motivated to develop preferences for other females (Carter, 1998; Tops et al., 2007). These differences in social attachment may again reflect adaptive responses to differences in each sex's grouping and dispersal patterns (Carter, 1998). Although prairie voles are monogamous, males typically disperse at sexual maturity and do not mate with members of their natal group. Females, in contrast, may produce litters in their natal nest and retain bonds with matrilineal kin throughout their lives. The importance of kin or other close female companions to successful reproduction is also seen in wild European rabbits, where females who have litter mates in their current social group are more affiliative and begin to breed at younger ages, apparently as a result of reduced stress (Rodel et al., 2008).

Most species of nonhuman primates are group-living; social isolation is rare and an artifact of captive experiments. When isolated from familiar companions, monkeys show all of the classic behavioral and physiological symptoms of depression, particularly if they were previously housed in a social group. For example, monogamous titi monkeys (*Callicebus moloch*) that have been separated from their partners experience a sharp increase in GCs (Mendoza and Mason, 1986). Similarly, marmosets (*Callithrix* spp.) and tamarins (*Saguinus* spp.) of both sexes show elevated GC levels when temporarily placed in isolation; GC levels return to baseline when they are reunited with their partners (Ginther et al., 2001; Johnson et al., 1996; Smith and French, 1997; Smith et al., 1998). The presence of a social partner also helps to dampen the stress response in novel physical environments (French and Schaffner, 2000). Finally, female rhesus macaques that are socially isolated or placed into a novel group exhibit elevated stress responses; this increase is dampened, however, by the presence of a pre-ferred grooming partner (Gust et al., 1994). Even the threat of isolation from offspring or familiar companions can be sufficient to trigger a stress response. Lactating female rhesus macaques that were captured and held overnight in an individual cage with their infants had significantly higher plasma GC levels than similarly treated nonlactating females (Maestripieri et al., 2008). The heightened stress response of lactating females may have reflected their perception of risk to their infants.

IV. OKAVANGO BABOONS

Much of the data described in this review are derived from a long-term study of one group of free-ranging chacma baboons (*Papio hamadryas ursinus*) living in the Okavango Delta of Botswana. Like many other species of Old World monkeys, including in particular the macaques (*Macaca* spp.), female baboons remain in their natal groups throughout their lives, maintaining close bonds with their matrilineal female kin (Cheney and Seyfarth, 2007). Females assume dominance ranks similar to their mothers and usually retain their relative ranks throughout their lives. The result is a conservative matrilineal dominance hierarchy in which all the members of one matriline outrank or are outranked by all the members of another (Cheney et al., 2004; Samuels et al., 1987; Silk, 2002; Silk et al., 1999). Although there is often a positive correlation between female rank and reproductive success, this correlation rarely reaches significance (reviewed by Cheney et al., 2004; Silk, 2002), and all females produce offspring. Close bonds are manifested primarily through grooming. In contrast, male Old World monkeys typically emigrate from their natal groups at sexual maturity and form comparatively unstable dominance hierarchies based largely on fighting ability.

The Okavango Delta has a wider diversity of plant and tree species than other African woodland savannahs, and a high density of predators, includ-ing leopards (*Panthera pardus*), lions (*Panthera leo*), crocodiles (*Crocodilis niloticus*), and spotted hyenas (*Crocuta crocuta*). The area is seasonally flooded, and the baboons forage over an area of roughly 4 km^2, fording or swimming from one wooded island to another at the height of the flood

(Cheney et al., 2004; Hamilton et al., 1976). During the period of study (1992–2007), group size ranged from approximately 70 to 85 individuals, including 19–26 adult females (>6 years), 3–12 adult males, and their offspring. The ages and matrilineal relatedness of all animals were known, and all individuals were fully habituated to humans on foot.

Behavioral samples on all adult females were conducted daily, using focal animal sampling (Altmann, 1974). In addition, weekly fecal samples were obtained from each adult female on a systematic basis (see, e.g., Beehner and Whitten, 2004; Beehner et al., 2005; Crockford et al., 2008; Engh et al., 2006b for details). There is a delay of 1–3 days between hormone secretion and detection in fecal steroids (Beehner and Whitten, 2004; Heistermann et al., 1993; Wasser et al., 2000; Ziegler et al., 1996); diet can also reduce or slow down steroid excretion. In contrast to hormones derived from blood or saliva, therefore, fecal hormones do not reflect physiological responses to specific single events, but rather "cumulative" hormone production over several days. Unless otherwise noted, all of the hormonal data on wild animals discussed below were derived from fecal samples.

V. Reproductive and Seasonal Influences

Studies of stress in nonhuman primates have tended to focus on males rather than females in part because of the confounding influences of reproductive state. Female mammals tend to have higher baseline GC levels than males, and a more robust stress response (Reeder and Kramer, 2005). Moreover, as in humans, basal GC levels in nonhuman primates increase steadily during pregnancy and decline rapidly postpartum (reviewed by Bowman et al., 2001; for baboons, see Altmann et al., 2004; Beehner et al., 2005, 2006; Crockford et al., 2008; Ramirez et al., 2004; Weingrill et al., 2004). As a result, all analyses of physiological and psychological stress in female primates and other animals must first control for reproductive state.

Elevation of the HPA axis during pregnancy may function in part to help females cope with the metabolic demands of gestation. Given the role of elevated GC levels in attachment formation, they may also prepare females to bond with their infants. Indeed, several studies of baboons have suggested that females with higher prepartum GC levels subsequently show higher levels of affiliative behavior toward their infants (Bardi et al., 2004; Nguyen et al., 2008; Ramirez et al., unpublished data). In contrast, higher postpartum GC levels can be associated with higher levels of infant rejection (Bardi et al., 2004; Ramirez et al., 2004).

GC levels are also strongly influenced by ecological variables. Numerous studies of birds and mammals have shown that GC levels are elevated during the winter, during times of food or water scarcity, and during periods of elevated metabolic and energetic demands (reviewed by, e.g., Nelson et al., 2002; Romero, 2002; Wingfield and Ramenofsky, 1999).

In ring-tailed lemurs (*Lemur catta*), females' mean GC levels are highest during months of low rainfall and fruit availability (Pride, 2005c). Elevated GC levels are associated with low daily food intake and high rates of aggressive intergroup encounters, but not with intragroup aggression or antipredator alarm calls (Pride, 2005a). Moreover, individuals in smaller groups tend to have higher GC levels than those in larger groups (Pride, 2005c). This association suggests that the acquisition and defense of food against other groups represent significant challenges to female survival, and that larger groups may have an advantage over smaller groups. Given the hypothesized importance of intergroup competition and resource defense to female reproductive success in nonhuman primates (Cheney, 1992; Isbell, 1991; Wrangham, 1980), it is unfortunate that no other studies have investigated the relationship between female GC levels and intergroup aggression.

Chacma baboons living at high latitudes in the Cape Peninsula of South Africa have elevated GC levels during the winter months, when they experience colder temperatures and shorter resting periods, both of which may increase metabolic rates (Weingrill et al., 2004). GC levels among gelada baboons (*Theropithecus gelada*) are similarly affected by cold temperatures (Beehner and McCann, 2008). In Amboseli, Kenya, an area of highly seasonal rainfall, female yellow baboons (*P.h. cynocephalus*) tend to exhibit higher GC levels during the dry season than during the wet season (Gesquiere et al., 2008; see also Sapolsky, 1986). Furthermore, GC levels are higher in hotter months and in months when females spend more time foraging than resting.

In contrast, in the Okavango Delta of Botswana seasonal effects on females' GC levels are less noticeable, at least in relatively normal years (Beehner et al., 2005; Crockford et al., 2008). This probably occurs because females in the Okavango have ready access to water throughout the year, as well as much greater diversity of tree and other plant species than do baboons in most other areas of Africa (Beehner et al., 2005; Cheney et al., 2004). GC levels do appear to rise in years when the annual flood arrives earlier than normal, before the fruits of the marula (*Sclerocarya birrea*) and jackalberry (*Diospyros mespiliformis*) trees have ripened (Cheney and Seyfarth, unpublished data). Even these increases, however, are overshadowed by the much greater increase in GC levels during periods of social instability (see below).

VI. Dominance Rank

When considering the relationship between GC levels and dominance rank in female mammals, it is useful to distinguish between species with high and low reproductive skew. In species with high reproductive skew, only one female usually breeds, while other females, who are often the offspring or siblings of the dominant breeding female, act as helpers. These cooperatively breeding species include meerkats (*Suricatta suricatta*), wolves (*Canis lupus*), wild dogs (*Lycaon pictus*), and, among the primates, tamarins and marmosets. Tamarins and marmosets live in small family groups composed of a breeding pair and varying numbers of adult helpers who are usually closely related to the breeding pair (Goldizen, 1987).

By contrast, in species with low reproductive skew all females breed, and there is little if any reproductive suppression. Although females may form a dominance hierarchy in which high-ranking females enjoy some reproductive advantages, there is usually no significant correlation between rank and reproductive success. Such species include spotted hyenas, lions, rabbits, and most species of nonhuman primates, including baboons and macaques (see above).

A. Species with High Reproductive Skew

In cooperatively breeding species with high reproductive skew, the single dominant breeding female often has significantly higher GC levels than the nonbreeding helpers (wolves: Sand and Creel, 2004; wild dogs: Creel, 2001; meerkats: Carlson et al., 2004; dwarf mongoose, *Helogale parvula*: Creel, 2005; reviewed by Creel, 2001; but see Hacklander et al., 2003 for a reverse effect in marmots, *Marmota marmota*). Some studies of tamarins and marmosets have also documented higher GC levels in dominant breeding females than in nonreproductive subordinates (common marmosets: Abbott et al., 1997; Saltzman et al., 1994, 1996, 1998; cotton-top tamarins (*S. oedipus*): Ziegler et al., 1995), although this pattern is not always found (common marmosets (*C. jacchus*): Sousa et al., 2005; Ziegler and Sousa, 2002; golden lion tamarins (*Leontopithicus rosalia*): Bales et al., 2005).

It appears, therefore, that reproductive suppression in helpers is not stress-related (Carlson et al., 2004; Creel, 2001). Indeed, a notable characteristic of subordinate females in all of these species is that they are usually closely related to the dominant breeding female. Although dominant females often kill any infants produced by subordinate females (e.g., Creel and Creel, 2002; Saltzman et al., 2008; Sousa et al., 2005), subordinate females receive generally low rates of aggression and enjoy high levels of social support from kin. This support may mitigate any stress that might otherwise result from subordination (Abbott et al., 2003). Conversely, high GC levels in the dominant breeding female probably reflect the metabolic demands of breeding rather than any costs associated with the maintenance of dominance. Dominant female wolves, for example, are not more aggressive than subordinate females (Sand and Creel, 2004).

B. SPECIES WITH LOW REPRODUCTIVE SKEW

There have been comparatively few studies of rank-related stress in nonprimate mammals with low reproductive skew. Goymann et al. (2001) found that lower-ranking nonlactating female hyenas had higher GC levels during months when their groups' territories were stable. During unstable periods, however, when females were forced to travel outside their groups' territorial boundaries to hunt, all females exhibited elevated GC levels. In contrast, Dloniak et al. (2006) reported no relationship between rank and GC concentrations in pregnant spotted hyenas living in the northern portion of the Serengeti ecosystem in Kenya. Instead, GC concentrations appeared to be more strongly influenced by instability in the female dominance hierarchy, with females exhibiting higher levels during period of rank instability (Van Meter et al., 2009).

The degree to which female monkeys exhibit rank-related stress seems to depend largely on whether subordinates are able to avoid aggression and derive support from kin and other companions. Under constrained captive conditions, and especially when living in unstable or newly formed groups, subordinate females often exhibit high levels of stress. When female long-tailed macaques (*M. fascicularis*) were randomly housed in groups of four individuals, females who acquired subordinate ranks developed many of the classic signs of physiological and behavioral depression, including hunched posture, low levels of activity, disturbed menstrual cycles, weight loss, higher heart rates, and increased mortality (Shively, 1998; Shively et al., 2005). The frequency of depression in subordinate females was higher than that in individually housed females. Similarly, female pig-tailed macaques (*M. nemestrina*) in a newly formed group exhibited higher GC levels and a significant decrease in T-helper cells than females housed in individual cages, despite the fact that their dominance hierarchy was established without serious fighting or wounding (Gust et al., 1996). Females who received a greater frequency of grooming showed a smaller decrease in T-helper cells, suggesting that social support played a role in mitigating the effects of social instability.

Other studies of female long-tailed (Stavisky et al., 2001) and rhesus macaques (Gust et al., 1993) living in newly established captive groups have failed to document a relationship between social subordination and elevated GC levels. In fact, in one comparison subordinate females had higher GC levels in an established group than in a newly formed one (Gust et al., 1993). This might have occurred because females in the newly established group reconciled with each other after aggression at high rates. However, it might also have been due to the fact that ranks in the newly formed group were unstable and difficult for human observers to determine.

Although there have been comparatively few studies of rank-related stress in wild female monkeys, current evidence suggests that low-ranking females do not typically exhibit high GC levels (long-tailed macaques: van Schaik et al., 1991; baboons: Nguyen et al., 2008; Weingrill et al., 2004, reviewed by Abbott et al., 2003; Sapolsky, 2005). Analyses of GC levels among females in the Okavango baboon population over three different time periods have also revealed no evidence of rank-related stress (Beehner et al., 2005; Crockford et al., 2008; Engh et al., 2006b). These observations are perhaps not surprising. Although high-ranking female baboon and macaques have priority of access to food, the correlation between rank and reproductive success is typically only weakly positive, and low-ranking females are as likely as high-ranking females to have close relatives available for social support. While high-ranking females can redirect aggression onto more targets than low-ranking females, the level of harassment they impose upon low-ranking females is moderate, and low-ranking females do not typically receive aggression at significantly higher rates than other females (Abbott et al., 2003; Cheney and Seyfarth, unpublished data; Walters and Seyfarth, 1987).

Despite the lack of evidence for chronically elevated GC concentrations in free-ranging subordinate female baboons, low-ranking individuals may nonetheless sometimes be subjected to nutritional and social stressors that exert other subtle physiological effects. In the Okavango baboon popula-tion, for example, the GC levels of all females rose dramatically during the week after a potentially infanticidal male immigrated into their group (Wittig et al., 2008). However, subordinate females maintained this increase for a longer period of time than dominant females, with the GC levels of high-ranking females beginning to decrease at least 1 week earlier than those of low-ranking females. This may have occurred because higher-ranking females were able to exert greater control over the timing and nature of their social interactions, allowing them to experience less stress during periods of instability. Whether there is any fitness advantage to being able to reduce GC levels more rapidly, however, remains to be determined.

Similarly, in one study of adolescent male baboons in Amboseli, Kenya, the sons of subordinate mothers were found to have significantly higher GC levels than the sons of dominant mothers (Onyango et al., 2008), even though subordinate females in this population do not generally appear to have elevated GCs themselves (Nguyen et al., 2008). This effect persisted beyond the age when males become larger than females, extending even beyond maternal death. These results suggest potential long-term organizational effects of maternal dominance status on offspring HPA axis, possibly related to nutritional stress, aggression, or lack of social support (Onyango et al., 2008).

Further complicating matters, dominant females living in multifemale groups of ring-tailed lemurs sometimes exhibit higher GC levels than subordinate females (Cavigelli, 1999; Cavigelli et al., 2003; but see Pride, 2005a,c). Dominant female ring-tailed lemurs tend to be more aggressive than lower-ranking females, and they are also more active participants in intergroup encounters (Cavigelli, 1999; Pride, 2005a,c). These observations suggest that occasional high GC levels in dominant females may result from high-energy expenditure during aggressive interactions and intergroup defense rather than from any inherent attribute of rank.

Taken together, these studies suggest that there is no simple correlation between dominance rank and GC levels in female primates. Although stress and depression can be induced in low-ranking females under confined, unstable captive conditions (e.g., Shively et al., 2005), under more natural conditions low-ranking females receive comparatively little aggression and show little evidence of rank-related stress or reproductive suppression (Cheney et al., 2004; Silk, 2002). Moreover, because the female dominance hierarchy remains stable for years at a time, females' stress responses are by definition usually unaffected by female rank instability.

This is not to say, however, that females' ranks are always immutable. Although upheavals in the female dominance hierarchy in species such as macaques and baboons are very rare, they do occasionally occur (Samuels et al., 1987; Silk, 2002). One such event occurred in the Okavango baboon group in 2003, when the members of a lower-ranking matriline initiated two attempts to overthrow a higher-ranking matriline (Engh et al., 2006b). The first period of upheaval, which lasted a week, was ultimately unsuccessful and resulted in the retention of all females' previous ranks. A second, successful challenge targeted a large, noncohesive, middle-ranking matriline composed of several sisters and aunts and only one mother–daughter pair. Eventually, three females from this matriline fell to the bottom of the dominance hierarchy. During these periods of instability, the targeted females received significantly higher rates of aggression than other females, and their GC levels also rose significantly. Interestingly, however, those females whose ranks eventually rose also experienced a significant increase in GC levels. In contrast, the GC levels of females at the top of the dominance hierarchy, whose ranks were not at risk, showed little change (Engh et al., 2006b).

These results are somewhat similar to those obtained in studies of female hyenas (Van Meter et al., 2009) and male baboons. In free-ranging groups of baboons, low-ranking males tend to have higher basal GC levels than high-ranking males when the dominance hierarchy is stable. When a dominant immigrant male enters the group and challenges the reproductive control enjoyed by high-ranking males, however, GC levels of high-ranking males are higher than those of low-ranking males (Bergman et al., 2005; Sapolsky, 1990, 1992, 1993a,b, 2005; Sapolsky et al., 1997). Thus, the loss of control and predictability associated with rank instability appear to be more stressful than low rank *per se*.

VII. BEHAVIORAL CORRELATES OF GC LEVELS DURING
PERIODS OF SOCIAL STABILITY

In addition to the seasonal and nutritional effects previously described, elevated GC levels in female primates appear to be correlated primarily with the loss of a close companion and events that directly jeopardize their survival and reproduction (see below). During periods of social and ecological stability, females' GC levels are generally low. This is true even of subordinates, as long as they have social support and opportunities to avoid the aggression of dominants.

We were able to examine females' GC levels in the Okavango baboon population during one-eight-month long period of social stability in 2004, when there was no male immigration and relatively few cases of predation (Crockford et al., 2008; see below). All females' GC levels were significantly lower than during a subsequent, more eventful period precipitated by the immigration of a dominant male (Fig. 1). Nonetheless, there was still some variation in females' GC levels, even after controlling for reproductive state. This variation was correlated with subtle behavioral attributes that varied between individuals and within individuals across time.

Interestingly, we could detect no relationship between females' GC levels and the number of close female kin (Crockford et al., 2008). This is perhaps not surprising. Although female baboons maintain their grooming relationships with a few close relatives (Silk et al., 1999, 2006a,b, 2009), when kin are not available they form stable grooming partnerships with nonrelatives. This may mitigate any detrimental effects on stress or GC levels associated with the lack of close kin.

The primary factors influencing females' GC levels during this stable period appeared to be related to the control and predictability that they were able to exert over their social interactions. Not surprisingly, pregnant and cycling females who received higher rates of aggression from other

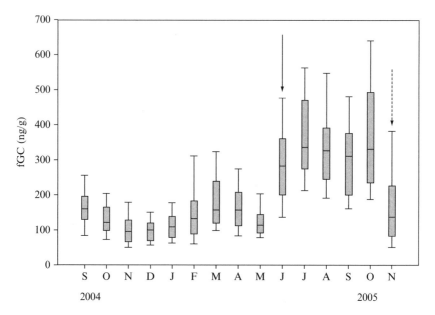

Fɪɢ. 1. The average monthly distribution of glucocorticoid levels (fGC) in 18 adult females between September 2004 and November 2005. The period from 15 October 2004 to 30 May 2005 was a period of relative social stability, when there were no changes in the alpha male position, no male immigration, no observed infanticidal attempts, no confirmed predation, and few disappearances. On 1 June (the week highlighted by the solid arrow), a new male immigrated into the group, and all females' GC levels increased significantly. The subsequent 5 months were marked by additional male immigration, instability in the male dominance hierarchy, infanticide, and the disappearance of several adult females. In the first week of November (highlighted by the dashed arrow), the male dominance hierarchy stabilized, and females' GC levels decreased significantly. Boxes show interquartile range with the median depicted by the internal line; whiskers indicate 95% confidence intervals.

females had higher GC levels than females who received lower rates of aggression. Conversely, pregnant and cycling females who received grunts at a high frequency from approaching dominant females had lower GC levels than those who received grunts at a lower frequency. Furthermore, pregnant females had lower GC levels in months when they received grunts at a higher than average frequency. Grunts are signals of benign intent and are reliably associated with a low probability of aggression (Cheney et al., 1995b; Silk et al., 1996). Grunts also function to reconcile opponents after aggression (Cheney and Seyfarth, 1997; Cheney et al., 1995b; Wittig et al., 2007a). Thus, grunts may mitigate the stress associated with aggression in part because they permit females to assess and predict the behavior of higher-ranking animals.

Lactating females' GC levels, however, showed the opposite pattern. This was probably a consequence of the intense attention that mothers with young infants receive from others. Infants are highly attractive to female baboons, and the mothers of young infants receive high rates of ostensibly friendly, but unsolicited, interactions from higher-ranking females (Altmann, 1980; Seyfarth, 1976; Silk et al., 2003a). These interactions are almost invariably accompanied by grunts. Because females with young infants seldom initiate these interactions and have little control over them, the close association between grunts and infant handling may weaken the otherwise placatory effects of grunts as signals of benign intent.

The relation between GC levels and females' level of control over their social interactions was most apparent, however, in their grooming relationships. Grooming appears to be the primary coping strategy adopted by female monkeys to reduce stress (Aureli et al., 1999; Boccia et al., 1989; Gust et al., 1993; Shutt et al., 2007). Little is known, however, about how and why grooming might function to alleviate stress. It is not clear, for example, whether social contact alone is sufficient to reduce stress, as opposed to social contact with a few select companions.

The grooming interactions of female baboons, like those of females in other monkey species, are highly differentiated. Although a female may groom with all other females in her group during the course of a year, most of her grooming is concentrated among a few predictable partners who are usually, but not always, close female kin (Silk et al., 2006a,b, 2009). These focused grooming interactions appear to be adaptive, because females who maintain the strongest bonds with other females experience higher offspring survival and longevity (Silk et al., 2003b, 2009).

Indeed, regardless of the number of close female kin they had, females in all reproductive states had lower GC levels in months when they concentrated their grooming among a few consistent partners than in months when their grooming was less focused and more equally distributed among partners (Fig. 2; Crockford et al., 2008). We used the Shannon–Wiener diversity index (Wilson and Bossert, 1971) to measure the diversity of a female's grooming partners. This index is a measure not of grooming network size but of grooming partner skew. For example, an individual who grooms with a large number of other females but restricts most of her grooming to one to two preferred partners will have a low grooming diversity index. Conversely, an individual who grooms with a large number of other females but distributes her grooming evenly among all her partners will have a high grooming diversity index. These results suggest that females may experience increased GC levels when their

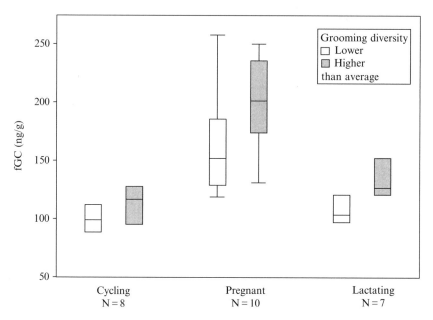

FIG. 2. Within-individual comparisons of females' GC levels between months when they had a higher diversity of grooming partners than average and months when they had a lower diversity of grooming partners than average. Females are separated by reproductive state. Females had significantly higher GC levels in months when they had a higher diversity of grooming partners than average. Legend as in Fig. 1.

grooming networks become less stable and discriminating. There was no correlation between GC levels and absolute grooming time, time spent grooming, or time spent being groomed.

For cycling females, the correlation between higher GC levels and an increased grooming diversity index was also associated with higher rates of aggression received and lower frequencies of grunting by approaching dominant females. Cycling females who are involved in sexual consortships are often the targets of aggression from adult females. It seems possible that they may attempt to mitigate this aggression by actively grooming potential aggressors. Indeed, cycling females' grooming was more diverse and less focused in months when they groomed more individuals than groomed them.

In contrast to cycling females, lactating females' grooming networks were more diverse in months when they were groomed by more partners than they groomed, indicating that the increase in their grooming diversity was unsolicited. The lack of control that lactating females were able to exert over their grooming partners, in combination with the attention given to their infants, may have contributed to their increased GC levels. In support of this argument, Shutt et al. (2007) found that GC levels in pregnant female Barbary macaques (*M. sylvanus*) were lower in individuals who groomed others at higher rates than they were groomed, and who groomed more partners than groomed them.

Taken together, the results suggest a complex relationship between GC levels, active as opposed to passive grooming initiations, and grooming network size. Unstable, diffuse grooming networks are associated with higher GC levels. Although these results do not distinguish between the cause and effect of this association, it seems probable that GC levels increase when the expansion of a female's grooming network is unsolicited and initiated by others. A diffuse grooming network may provide less support than a more focused and selective one because it is less controllable and predictable. On the other hand, active expansion of a grooming network by females who are receiving increased aggression may function as a mechanism to mitigate stress by reducing the likelihood of aggression.

Numerous studies have shown that loss of control and unstable social bonds can increase stress in animals and humans, even in the absence of any specific traumatic event (see Section I; see also Carter, 1998; Marmot, 2004; Panksepp, 1998; Sapolsky, 2004). Although GC levels in female baboons are most strongly influenced by events that directly affect their reproductive success (see below), these more subtle social factors also exert an effect. GC levels may be lower if a female is able to predict the intentions of other group members—for example, if dominant females grunt to her to signal their intent—and if she is able to express some preference over the timing and identities of her grooming partners. A focused grooming network may function to lower GC levels in part, because it provides females with a dependable and controllable number of social partners. In short, it may be better to have a few good friends than many acquaintances.

If these conjectures are valid, we would predict that, during periods of social or environmental instability, females who have more focused grooming relationships should experience less stress than those whose grooming relationships are diffuse and distributed more evenly among a wide variety of partners. Furthermore, females should attempt to alleviate stress by restricting their grooming interactions to a few preferred partners.

VIII. TRAUMATIC EVENTS AND GC LEVELS

As with humans, the greatest stressors affecting female primates are unpredictable, traumatic events over which they have little control. As we have discussed, rank instability appears to be more stressful than subordination itself. Events that threaten a female's survival or the survival of her infant are even more stressful.

A. MALE IMMIGRATION

The immigration of a dominant, potentially infanticidal male is a potent stressor for female baboons. The disruption caused by the immigration of a male who quickly rises to the most dominant (or alpha) position is typically reflected by a sharp elevation of GCs in both males and females (Alberts et al., 1992; Beehner et al., 2005; Engh et al., 2006b; Sapolsky, 1993a,b; Wittig et al., 2008). In some cases, this elevation is associated with increased aggression against females. Following the immigration of a highly aggressive male into one group of yellow baboons in Kenya, Pereira (1983) reported an increase in serious injuries for both males and females, an elevated rate of fetal loss, and one infant death. In a subsequent period, another male immigration event was similarly associated with significantly higher rates of aggression, marked elevations in GCs, and an increase in fetal loss (Alberts et al., 1992). These observations suggest that the arrival of an unfamiliar and aggressive male may result in early termination of pregnancy in baboons. While slightly elevated GCs are necessary to maintain a pregnancy, chronically elevated GCs exert an inhibitory effect on the female reproductive system (Bronson, 1989).

Frequently, however, the immigration of an aggressive dominant male does not result in increased attacks on females, and the event appears to function more as a source of psychological than physical stress. For example, female mantled howler monkeys (*Alouatta palliatta*) experience a significant rise in GC levels when a new male enters their group (Cristobal-Azkarate et al., 2007). This elevation appears to be associated primarily with the potential risk of infanticide and the social instability resulting from increased aggression among males, because female howlers do not aggressively defend their group against incursion by immigrant males, nor are they frequently attacked by immigrant males.

Among the Okavango baboons, the arrival of a high-ranking immigrant male has a particularly disruptive impact on lactating, and to a lesser extent pregnant females, because such males often commit infanticide (Bulger and Hamilton, 1987; Busse and Hamilton, 1981; Collins et al., 1984; Palombit et al., 2000; Tarara, 1987). Male mating activity in the Okavango population is strongly correlated with dominance rank, and the alpha male monopolizes most mating (Bulger, 1993). However, turnover in the alpha rank position is also high, and a male typically maintains alpha status for less than a year (Hamilton and Bulger, 1990; Palombit et al., 2000). Infanticide appears to be a sexually selected strategy that accelerates the return to fertility in lactating females, permitting the infanticidal male to mate with as many females as possible during his short tenure in the alpha position (see reviews in Ebensperger, 1998; Hausfater and Hrdy, 1984; van Schaik and Janson, 2000). In the Okavango, infanticide is the single most important cause of infant mortality (Cheney et al., 2004).

Examination of Okavango females' GC levels during two different time periods showed that lactating females experienced significant increases following the immigration of a dominant male, while cycling females showed no increase. Pregnant females' responses were more variable, and fell in between those of cycling and lactating females (Beehner et al., 2005; Engh et al., 2006b). Not surprisingly, lactating females' GC levels showed an even greater increase when an immigrant male began to commit infanticide (Engh et al., 2006b).

In another period, however, male immigration was associated with an immediate and dramatic increase in GC levels among females in all reproductive states, although lactating females showed the greatest increase (Fig. 1; Wittig et al., 2008). This heightened response may have occurred because the immigration event coincided with a period of frequent and aggressive encounters with other groups and the sudden death of the group's resident alpha male. The initial week of upheaval was followed by 5 months of additional immigrations and instability in the upper levels of the male dominance hierarchy. Most females' GC levels remained elevated for the next 20 weeks, until after one of the immigrant males finally established himself firmly in the alpha position (see also Beehner et al., 2005 for similar results).

Females' stress responses appeared to be specifically related to the threat of infanticide rather than to any increase in aggression associated with instability in the male dominance hierarchy, because females did not receive higher rates of aggression from males or other females during these periods (Beehner et al., 2005; Engh et al., 2006b). Furthermore, females' GC levels did not increase when a natal male, who posed little threat of infanticide, rose to the alpha position (Beehner et al., 2005). Indeed, the specificity of females' stress response can be compared with that of adult males in the same group during the same time periods. In contrast to females, the GC concentrations of males were significantly elevated during all periods of instability in the male dominance hierarchy, whether caused by the rise in dominance of a natal male or an immigrant (Bergman et al., 2005). Male–male rates of aggression showed a similar pattern, with elevated levels during all periods of male rank instability. Unlike females, males appeared to be responding to any instability in the upper ranks of the male hierarchy, not just to the arrival of an unfamiliar male, a result that has also been documented in other baboon populations (Sapolsky, 1993b).

In some respects, it seems surprising that lactating females' GC levels should return to baseline within several months after the immigration of a real or potentially infanticidal male, because females are at risk of infanticide until they resume sexual cycling, usually a year or more after their infant's birth. There appear to be a number of reasons for females' failure to maintain elevated GC levels throughout the period when their infants are at risk. First, because most infanticide occurs in the 3 or 4 months after the male's immigration and ascent to the alpha position, the threat of infanticide diminishes with time (Cheney and Seyfarth, unpublished data). Second, it may simply be too costly for females to maintain an elevated stress response for more than several months, particularly as the risk of infanticide declines. Third, although baboons seem to be able to anticipate the threat of infanticide over the short term, they may not have the cognitive capacity to recognize that a male remains a threat until they have resumed sexual cycling. We explore some of these questions in more detail below.

B. Predation and the Loss of Kin

In his 1905 study of baboons living in South Africa, Eugene Marais observed "It was not long before we came to realize that the life of the baboon is in fact one continual nightmare of anxiety" (Marais, 1939). The reason was predation. Predation is a ubiquitous, pervasive, and chronic threat to wild primates, and is presumed to have exerted strong selective pressure on the evolution of sociality (Kappeler and van Schaik, 2002; Sterck et al., 1997; van Schaik, 1983). Unfortunately, however, there are few extant populations of primates where predation still occurs at any significant rate (reviewed by Busse, 1982; Cheney and Wrangham, 1987; Cowlishaw, 1994), and few studies have examined the effects of predation on stress.

There is no consistent relationship between predation risk and GC levels in animals. Indeed, animals confronted with high rates of predation often exhibit low basal GC levels despite showing high levels of antipredator behavior. For example, in California ground squirrels (*Spermophilus beldingi*), animals living in areas of high predation risk exhibit more vigilance behavior but lower GC levels than animals living in areas of low predation risk (Mateo, 2007). Similarly, bank voles (*Clethrionomys glareolus*) that are experimentally exposed to weasel odor decrease their foraging efforts but show no increase in GC levels (Ylönen et al., 2006). There is also no relation between GC levels and rates of alarm calling in ring-tailed lemurs (Cavigelli, 1999; Pride, 2005a).

The lack of a positive relation between predation risk and GC levels, though perhaps counterintuitive at first glance, is doubtless adaptive, as chronically elevated GC levels would prevent individuals from mounting an acute stress response when actually attacked.

The Okavango baboons are some of the few primates still exposed to high rates of predation; they are preyed upon by lions, leopards, and to a lesser extent crocodiles, spotted hyenas, and other carnivores (Busse, 1982; Cheney et al., 2004). Predation is estimated to account for over 95% of adult female deaths. In 2002, 25% of the group's 28 females disappeared as a result of confirmed or suspected predation (Cheney et al., 2004). Eighteen month later, another 26% of the adult females disappeared over a 12-month period. Bulger and Hamilton (1987) report a similarly high proportion of deaths among adult females due to predation in 1984.

Not surprisingly, predator attacks are highly stressful for adult female baboons. Females' GC levels were significantly higher in the 4 weeks following a predation event than in weeks when there had been no predation (Engh et al., 2006a). Predation was particularly stressful when it caused group members to become separated. Lions often attack in coalitions of three or more, causing baboons to panic and scatter in different directions. The resulting subgroups often remain separated for several days before reuniting. GC levels were significantly higher in months when lion attacks resulted in the group's separation for several days compared to months when lion attacks did not separate the group.

Predation was especially stressful for females whose close relatives were killed. Females who lost a close relative experienced a significant increase in GC levels in the month following their relative's death compared with the month before. By comparison, the GC levels of control females matched for reproductive state showed no similar increase (Fig. 3; Engh et al., 2006a). The rise in GC levels among females who lost a close relative to predation was, however, transient. By the second month following the predation event, these females' GC levels had returned to baseline. The relatively transient effect of a relative's death on females' stress levels may have occurred in part because "bereaved" females seemed to attempt to cope with their loss by extending their social network and identifying new grooming partners (see below).

IX. Stress Alleviation and Social Bonds

Sapolsky's studies of stress in male baboons revealed a number of behavioral strategies that appeared to enable some individuals to cope with the vicissitudes of life better than others. These included grooming

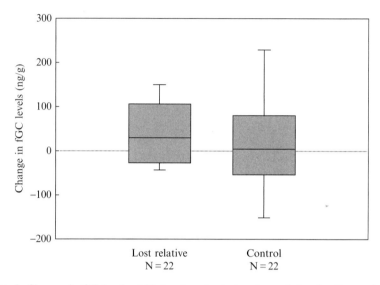

Fɪɢ. 3. Changes in GC levels of 22 females who lost a close relative (mother, maternal sibling, or offspring) to observed or suspected predation from the month before to the month after the predation event, compared with 22 control females who did not lose a close relative. Females who lost a close relative to predation experienced a significant rise. Legend as in Fig. 1.

relationships with females, the ability to distinguish between threatening and neutral interactions, the ability to recognize whether they had won or lost an aggressive interaction, and the tendency to redirect aggression onto a previously uninvolved third party when attacked (Ray and Sapolsky, 1992; Sapolsky and Ray, 1989; Virgin and Sapolsky, 1997). Thus, males who coped best had social support, social control, and were better able to predict the outcome of their interactions (Sapolsky, 1998). Most importantly, these coping strategies appeared to translate into higher reproductive success, because males who manifested these traits had lower GC levels and retained their high ranks for longer durations. Similar coping strategies can be found in females.

Although GCs extracted from feces provide a measure of the effects of an individual's social relationships on stress over days and weeks, they do not permit any evaluation of the immediate effects of specific behaviors on GC levels. Recent advances in techniques that permit the noninvasive assessment of GCs from saliva and urine, however, are beginning to make such short-term evaluations feasible, at least in captive animals. These studies suggest that specific behaviors can help to alleviate stress even within very short time periods. For example, saliva samples taken from common marmosets just after they had mobbed and alarm called at a snake model revealed that alarm calling resulted in a significant decrease in GC levels. In fact, there was a significant positive correlation between the number of alarm calls produced and the magnitude of the decrease in GC concentrations (Cross and Rogers, 2006). At a proximate level, alarm calls may help to reduce stress because they reduce the risk of predation. They may also provide the vocalizer with some control over the predator encounter.

In other contexts, too, vocalizations may serve to reduce stress over the immediate term. Marmosets that were temporarily isolated from their long-term mate showed a significant increase in urinary GCs. However, isolated marmosets who heard their mate's signature vocalization showed a significantly lower increase than individuals who heard an unfamiliar individual's vocalization or no vocalization (Rukstalis and French, 2005). Simply hearing the vocalization of a close companion, therefore, may exert a calming influence.

As we have discussed, the immigration of a potentially infanticidal dominant male is highly stressful to female baboons, particularly when they are lactating. In an apparent response to the threat of infanticide, lactating females in the Okavango Delta often form close, affiliative relationships, or "friendships," with specific adult males (Palombit et al., 1997, 2000, 2001; Weingrill, 2000). These males are always long-term residents of the group who are the infants' real or potential fathers (Moscovice et al., 2009). Observational and experimental data indicate that male friends are more likely than other males to aid females under attack, especially when the aggressor is a potentially infanticidal alpha male (Palombit et al., 1997, 2000).

Analyses conducted over two different time periods have shown that lactating females who have a male friend when an immigrant male enters the group have significantly lower GC concentrations than females without a male friend. Although GC levels rose significantly in lactating females without friends, GC levels in females with friends showed little change (Fig. 4; Beehner et al., 2005; Engh et al., 2006b). Females in the Okavango take a more active role than males in the formation and maintenance of friendships, and females with friends experience fewer attacks by potentially infanticidal males (Palombit et al., 1997, 2000). The comparatively lower stress levels manifested by lactating females with friends support the hypothesis that females recognize the risk posed by potentially infanticidal immigrants and actively attempt to compensate for this risk by forming friendships with long-term resident males.

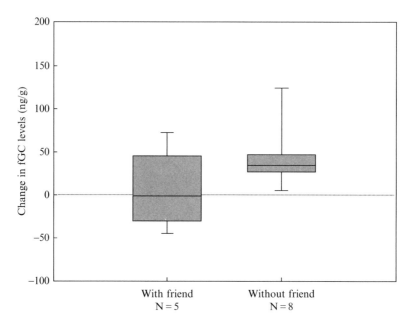

Fig. 4. Changes in GC levels in females with and without a male friend during a period of infanticidal attacks. Females without a male friend experienced a significant rise. Legend as in Fig. 1.

Baboons are a highly sexually dimorphic species, and although females actively defend their own and their relatives' infants against infanticidal attacks, if the infanticidal male is determined and relentless their efforts are usually fruitless. It is therefore interesting that female baboons also responded to the threat of infanticide by consolidating their relationships with other females. Because these relationships are relatively ineffective in preventing infanticide, their function may be primarily psychological.

As we have discussed, female baboons appear to have lower GC levels in months when their grooming networks are more focused. These observations led us to predict that, when confronted with an acute stressor like the immigration of a potentially infanticidal male, females with more focused grooming relationships would experience less stress than those whose grooming relationships were diffuse. We also predicted that grooming would function as a coping mechanism to alleviate stress, leading all females to reduce their grooming diversity and restrict their grooming interactions to a few preferred partners.

As we have mentioned, an 8-month period of relative social stability for the Okavango baboons ended abruptly when the resident alpha male died suddenly and a potentially infanticidal male immigrated into the group. Strikingly, all females reduced their grooming diversity in the weeks following the onset of the unstable period, to focus more strongly on a few preferred partners (Fig. 5). For most females, these partners were close kin. Two sorts of data suggest that this more focused pattern of grooming acted to reduce stress. First, for both females at high and low risk of infanticide, the change in grooming patterns preceded and was correlated with a decrease in GC levels 1 week later. Second, cycling and pregnant females whose grooming networks had been more focused during the previous stable period experienced a smaller increase in GC levels in the week after the onset of the unstable period (Fig. 6; Wittig et al., 2008).

Several studies have suggested that grooming functions in part to decrease stress and anxiety (e.g., Aureli et al., 1999; Boccia et al., 1989; Shutt et al., 2007). The Okavango baboon data suggest more specifically

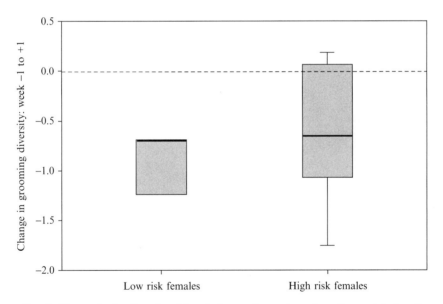

FIG. 5. Changes in the diversity of females' grooming partners from the week before the male immigration event to the week after his immigration. Females at "low risk" of infanticide were either cycling or in the early stages of pregnancy; females at "high risk" of infanticide were either lactating or in the last trimester of pregnancy. Females in both categories significantly decreased the diversity of their grooming partners in the week after the male's arrival. Legend as in Fig. 1.

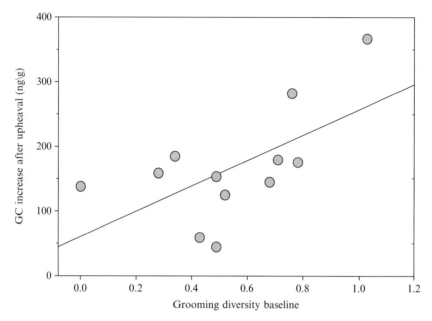

FIG. 6. The correlation between cycling and pregnant females' grooming diversity before the male immigration event and the increase in their GC levels in the following week (increase = GC levels$_{week\ 1}$–GC levels$_{week\ 1}$). Females who had a lower diversity of grooming partners experienced a smaller increase than females with a higher diversity of grooming partners.

that a concentrated grooming network focused on a few predictable partners is more important than grooming direction or grooming rate in reducing stress. During periods of social stability, female baboons had lower GC levels when their grooming network was more restricted (Crockford et al., 2008). During periods of instability, all females—regardless of their immediate risk—contracted their grooming network even further, and females whose grooming network had been more focused experienced smaller increases in GC levels (Wittig et al., 2008).

X. COPING WITH A DAMAGED SUPPORT SYSTEM

If a predictable, stable, and focused grooming network helps baboons to cope with stress, what do female baboons do when this network is damaged by the death of a close grooming partner? The loss of a close relative and grooming partner is highly stressful to female baboons, and "bereaved" females experience a significant rise in GC levels. This rise, however, is transient; by the second month after their relative's death, GC levels have returned to baseline. Apparently, stress is transitory because females attempt to cope with their loss by seeking out social contact.

Because females concentrate much of their grooming on close kin (Silk et al., 1999), females who lose a close female relative might be expected to experience a decrease in grooming diversity, number of grooming partners, and grooming rate. However, the opposite seems to occur. In one analysis of 14 females who lost a close adult female relative to predation, all females increased the number of female grooming partners in the 3 months following this loss, while 14 control females matched for reproductive state showed no similar increase (Fig. 7; Engh et al., 2006a). These control females had also witnessed the predation events, but they had not lost a preferred grooming partner and their social networks remained intact. Females who had lost a close relative also increased their grooming rates and the diversity of their grooming partners, while control females did not.

From a proximate, physiological standpoint, it is not surprising that females initiated bond formation with other females after the loss of a companion, and that this increase in social contact had a stress-reducing effect. As we

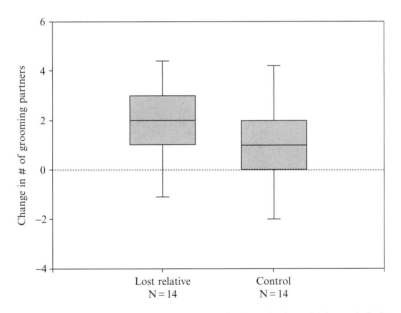

FIG. 7. Change in number of grooming partners of 14 females from the 3 months before to the 3 months after the loss of a close female relative, compared to matched controls. Females who lost a close female relative groomed significantly more females in the months after the loss. Legend as in Fig. 1.

have discussed, the stress response in both animals and humans can be mitigated by social contact and affiliation (Sapolsky et al., 1997; reviewed by Carter, 1998; Panskepp, 1998; see Section I). Increases in GC levels prompt the release of oxytocin, which motivates the urge for social bonding and physical contact (Uvnas-Moberg, 1997). Oxytocin both inhibits the release of GCs and promotes affiliative behavior, including not only maternal behavior but also an increased tendency to associate with other females (Carter, 1998; Taylor et al., 2000). From a functional perspective, this behavior may be adaptive because it enables females to identify and establish new social relationships. It may also provide females with the opportunity to bring some measure of control and predictability into their disrupted lives.

XI. COPING MECHANISMS IN MONKEYS AND HUMANS: SIMILARITIES

Stress in female monkeys appears to be driven primarily by real and anticipated threats to fitness: their own and their offspring's survival, unpredictable and uncontrollable events, and the loss of a close relative or companion. The stress associated with all of these events can be alleviated by the presence of close social companions. When captive female macaques are socially isolated or placed into a novel group, they experience increased stress. This stress can be dampened considerably, however, by the presence of a preferred grooming partner (Gust et al., 1994). Similarly, in the Okavango, female baboons with undamaged social networks appear to turn to their male friends and their closest female partners for support during periods of instability, in particular following the immigration of a potentially infanticidal male. Their grooming networks become correspondingly more focused and less diffuse.

These results complement those obtained in studies of humans. Women show a greater desire than men to seek social contact during times of stress, and they are also more likely to turn to smaller support groups (Taylor et al., 2000). In both sexes, the number of "core" individuals on whom people rely for support during times of crisis (3–5 individuals) tends to be significantly smaller than their circle of mutual friends (12–20) or regular acquaintances (30–50) (Dunbar and Spoor, 1995; Hill and Dunbar, 2003; Zhou et al., 2005). In the elderly, strong social networks enhance survival (Giles et al., 2005), and when humans perceive future social opportunities to be limited or at risk—either as they age or when they become ill—they tend to contract their social networks and become more selective in their social relationships (Carstensen, 1992, 1995).

One of the most potent stressors in both humans and other animals is the loss of a close companion. In humans, bereavement and feelings of loneliness are associated with increased GC production, decline in immune responses, and, in some cases, increased mortality (see Section I for references). These effects, however, can be mitigated by social support (Thorsteinsson and James, 1999). Social support seems to be particularly important for women's mental health (Kendler et al., 2005; Taylor et al., 2000). The same is true of female monkeys. Similarly, when female baboons in the Okavango Delta lose a close relative to predation, they attempt to compensate for this loss by temporarily expanding their grooming network and increasing the number of grooming partners.

The data on "bereavement" in baboons are especially interesting because most previous studies of stress and social isolation in animals have been conducted on individuals deprived of all social companions. In contrast, the Okavango baboons who lost a close companion were more akin to humans experiencing loss, because they were not separated from their social group and could still interact with other relatives and companions. Even in the presence of familiar group mates and relatives, however, these females experienced a stress response to the disappearance of a specific individual. They apparently sought to alleviate it by broadening and strengthening their social relationships. Similar behavior occurs in the Amboseli baboon population, where females who lose a close relative seek to establish relationships with more distant kin, and those who lack even distant kin seek to establish relationships with unrelated females (Silk et al., 2006a,b).

XII. COPING MECHANISMS IN MONKEYS AND HUMANS: DIFFERENCES

In addition to experiencing increased stress as a result of grief and anxiety in their own lives, humans often show stress in response to grief or anxiety in the lives of others. Health-care workers who attend to sick or traumatized patients often experience "compassion fatigue" and elevated stress profiles (Figley, 1995). Baboons have many opportunities to experience vicarious stress. There is little evidence, however, that they do so, even when their own fitness is affected. The reason for this may be related to their apparent inability to understand the beliefs, knowledge, and emotions of others.

As we have seen, both human and nonhuman species show physiological responses to the loss of close companions—what in humans we label as the emotion of grief. In a variety of animals ranging from rodents to primates, social isolation and separation from a close companion produce a stress response. Baboons experience the same kinds of physiological responses when they lose a preferred companion, even when they have other kin or close companions with whom they can still interact.

Grief, however, is an egocentric emotion, like fear; it does not require the attribution of mental states to others. It is certainly possible to feel grief or a sense of loss without recognizing that others might feel the same way. In contrast, empathy requires that an individual be able to recognize emotions like grief or fear in others even when she is not experiencing these emotions herself. It demands that she deliberately imagines herself in another individuals position while still dissociating her own mental states from her companions. In humans, the recognition of emotions like pain, disgust, and shame in others activates many of the same areas of the brain as those activated when we experience or imagine ourselves experiencing the same emotions. Other areas of the brain, including in particular the right inferior parietal cortex and the prefrontal cortex, allow us to detach our own emotions and knowledge from others (Decety and Jackson, 2004, 2006). Thus, although we use much of the same neural architecture to understand our own and others' mental states, we are nonetheless able to maintain a degree of separation between them. The same does not seem to be true of nonhuman primates, even of chimpanzees (Cheney and Seyfarth, 2007; Silk, 2007; Tomasello and Moll, 2009; Tomasello et al., 2005).

Chimpanzees are often described as showing compassion; in the wild, they have been reported to build nests and bring food to an injured relative (Goodall, 1986). But there is considerable disagreement about whether chimpanzees experience empathy for the anxiety, fear, or grief of others. Most examples are anecdotal (e.g., Preston and de Waal, 2002) and subject to a variety of interpretations. And for each anecdote that seems to demonstrate empathy there are several counterexamples. In fact, two experimental studies designed explicitly to test whether chimpanzees show concern and regard for others concluded that they do not (Jensen et al., 2006; Silk et al., 2005). In this respect, it is particularly unfortunate that there have been almost no studies of the causes and amelioration of stress in wild apes.

Baboons' apparent inability to feel empathy may prevent them from being able to understand the plight of others. For example, when most of the group's juveniles were separated from all of the adults for several days during a period of high flood in the Okavango, adult females showed no evidence of recognizing their offspring's dilemma. Despite being able to hear their offspring's agitation and distress on the adjacent island, none of the females showed any behavioral reactions to the calls, nor did they show elevated stress responses during the days of the separation (Cheney and Seyfarth, 2007). One explanation for their apparent lack of empathy is that they were incapable of recognizing that their offspring's fear of making a long and dangerous water crossing was greater than their own. Alternatively, it remains possible that the females' lack of concern simply reflected their knowledge, that their offsprings were in no immediate danger, and that they could easily return to them if necessary.

Similarly, when a potentially infanticidal male immigrates into a group of baboons, GC levels in cycling females are often unaffected. This is perhaps not surprising, because the offsprings of cycling females are not in danger. In many cases, though, these cycling females have daughters, mothers, or sisters who are lactating at the time and whose infants are at considerable risk. Because these infants are close relatives, their deaths would reduce the cycling females' own overall fitness. Although it could be argued that it is maladaptive for female baboons to respond to every indirect threat to their fitness, the relative lack of a stress response to the anxiety of a close relative is puzzling.

In sum, female baboons show stress responses primarily to events that directly affect themselves; the loss of a close relative, an infanticidal threat to their own infant, and rank instability that threatens their own dominance position. The indirect impact of a threat to their inclusive fitness, however, appears to be less important.

XIII. The Adaptive Value of Social Bonds, Social Knowledge, and the Stress Response

The stress response is adaptive over the short term in large part because it is self-correcting: it induces individuals to take active measures to alleviate it. But because it is harmful if maintained over long periods of time, the stress response is also selective and egocentric. Confronted with an array of potential stressors, female baboons exhibit elevated GCs primarily in response to those events that directly affect their own survival and reproduction. In the Okavango, a female's lifetime reproductive success is determined primarily by longevity (which depends largely on predation) and infant survival (which depends largely on infanticide). A female's rank is relatively unimportant in determining her reproductive success, though it may play a crucial role in years of drought or poor floods. Perhaps as a result, females exhibit a stress response primarily to predation and the threat of infanticide, and, to a lesser extent, rank instability. Conversely, females do not show a stress response to several events that do not directly affect them, even though they cause a general uproar in the group at large: instability in the ranks of natal and other resident males; the immigration of a potentially infanticidal male when the female does not have a vulnerable infant; and instability in the female dominance hierarchy if the female's own status is unaffected.

Baboons' stress responses also demonstrate that even environmental challenges like predation are inextricably linked with social ones. To survive and reproduce, baboons must not just avoid predation and find sufficient food to support themselves and their infants; they must also create, manage, and maintain the social relationships that buffer and support them in these endeavors. Marais (1939) may have been overstating matters when he described the life of a baboon as "one continual nightmare of anxiety." But however purple his prose, one thing is clear: in baboons, as in humans, many causes of stress—and its alleviation—are fundamentally social.

Although baboons lack a full-blown theory of mind, they have a rich and nuanced understanding of other individuals' social relationships. They recognize other individuals' relative dominance ranks and kinship relations, and they integrate this knowledge to recognize that the female dominance hierarchy is composed of a hierarchy of matrilineal families (Bergman et al., 2003; Cheney and Seyfarth, 1999; Cheney et al., 1995a). Their knowledge of other individuals' social relationships enables them to recognize that a "reconciliatory" grunt given by a close relative of a recent opponent can function as a proxy for direct reconciliation with the opponent herself (Wittig et al., 2007a). Conversely, it allows them to recognize that a threat grunt given by an opponent's close relative functions as an aggressive alliance (Wittig et al., 2007b). Knowledge of other individuals' social relationships may also permit baboons to identify new social partners when their social networks are damaged or threatened. Our data on Okavango baboons' stress responses suggest that females who have control over their social interactions and whose social relationships are focused and predictable experience the least stress. Ultimately, these focused social networks may also influence a female's reproductive success, because there is some evidence that females who maintain strong bonds with other females experience higher offspring survival and longevity (Silk et al., 2003b, 2009). It remains for future research to determine whether other populations of baboons and other species of monkeys show similar responses to real and perceived threats to fitness.

Reproductive success, at least in female baboons, appears to be related less to crude individual attributes like dominance rank or the number of close kin than to subtle behavioral attributes linked to the ability to create, manage, and sustain close social relationships. There appears to be a causal relationship between social skills, the stability of a female's social network, and reproductive success. It is as yet unclear whether some females, or some types of personalities, are better able than others to navigate this complex social world.

Finally, the data on wild female baboons also suggest that the causes of stress in humans, as well as its alleviation, are evolutionarily ancient and emerged long before language and a theory of mind. Like humans, baboons find a diffuse social network and the lack of a few reliable friends stressful. And, as for humans, the quality and strength of social bonds are much more important for female baboons than their number. Thus, the skills that allow individuals to identify and nurture friendships appear to have been under strong selective pressure for many millions of years.

References

Abbott, D.H., Saltzman, W., Schultz-Darken, N.J., Smith, T.E., 1997. Specific neuroendocrine mechanisms not involving generalized stress mediate social regulation of female reproduction in cooperatively breeding marmoset monkeys. Ann. N.Y. Acad. Sci. 807, 219–238.

Abbott, D.H., Keverne, E.B., Bercovitch, F.B., Shively, C.A., Mendoza, S.P., Saltzman, W., et al., 2003. Are subordinates always stressed? A comparative analysis of rank differences in cortisol levels among primates. Horm. Behav. 43, 67–82.

Adkins-Regan, E., 2005. Hormones and Animal Social Behavior. Princeton University Press, Princeton.

Alberts, S.C., Sapolsky, R., Altmann, J., 1992. Behavioral, endocrine, and immunological correlates of immigration by an aggressive male into a natural primate group. Horm. Behav. 26, 167–178.

Altmann, J., 1974. Observational study of behavior: sampling methods. Behaviour 49, 229–267.

Altmann, J., 1980. Baboon Mothers and Infants. Harvard University Press, Cambridge, MA.

Altmann, J., Lynch, J.W., Nguyen, N., Alberts, S.C., Gesquiere, L.R., 2004. Life-history correlates of steroid concentrations in wild peripartum baboons. Am. J. Primatol. 64, 95–106.

Aureli, F., Preston, S.D., de Waal, F.B.M., 1999. Heart rate responses to social interactions in free-moving rhesus macaques (*Macaca mulatta*): a pilot study. J. Comp. Psychol. 113, 59–65.

Bales, K.L., French, J.A., Hostetler, C.M., Dietz, J.M., 2005. Social and reproductive factors affecting cortisol levels in wild female golden lion tamarins (*Leontopithecus rosalia*). Am. J. Primatol. 67, 25–35.

Bardi, M., French, J.A., Ramirez, S.M., Brent, L., 2004. The role of the endocrine system in baboon maternal behavior. Biol. Psychiatr. 55, 724–732.

Bartz, J.A., Hollander, E., 2006. The neuroscience of affiliation: forging links between basic and clinical research on neuropeptides and social behavior. Horm. Behav. 50, 518–528.

Beehner, J.C., Bergman, T.J., Cheney, D.L., Seyfarth, R.M., Whitten, P.L., 2005. The effect of new alpha males on female stress in free-ranging baboons. Anim. Behav. 69, 1211–1221.

Beehner, J.C., McCann, C., 2008. Seasonal and altitudinal effects on glucocorticoid metabolites in a wild primate (*Theropithecus gelada*). Physiol. Behav. 95, 508–514.

Beehner, J.C., Whitten, P.L., 2004. Modifications of a field method for faecal steroid analysis in baboons. Physiol. Behav. 82, 269–277.

Bergman, T.J., Beehner, J.C., Cheney, D.L., Seyfarth, R.M., 2003. Hierarchical classification by rank and kinship in baboons. Science 302, 1234–1236.

Bergman, T.J., Beehner, J.C., Cheney, D.L., Seyfarth, R.M., Whitten, P.L., 2005. Correlates of stress in free-ranging male chacma baboons. Anim. Behav. 70, 703–713.

Beehner, J.C., Nguyen, N., Wango, E.O., Alberts, S.C., Altmann, J., 2006. The endocrinology of pregnancy and fetal loss in wild baboons. Horm. Behav. 49, 688–699.

Boccia, M.L., Reite, M., Laudenslager, M., 1989. On the physiology of grooming in a pigtail macaque. Physiol. Behav. 45, 667–670.

Bowman, M.E., Lopata, A., Wickings, J., Smith, R., 2001. Corticotropin-releasing hormone-binding protein in primates. Am. J. Primatol. 53, 123–130.

Bronson, F.H., 1989. Mammalian Reproductive Biology. University of Chicago Press, Chicago.

Bulger, J.B., 1993. Dominance rank and access to estrous females in male savanna baboons. Behaviour 127, 67–103.

Bulger, J.B., Hamilton, W.H., 1987. Rank and density correlates of inclusive fitness measures in a natural chacma baboon (Papio ursinus) population. Int. J. Primatol. 8, 635–650.

Busse, C., 1982. Leopard and lion predation upon chacma baboons living in the Moremi Wildlife Reserve. Botswana Notes Rec. 12, 15–21.

Busse, C.D., Hamilton, W.J., 1981. Infant carrying by male chacma baboons. Science 212, 1281–1283.

Cabezas, S., Blas, J., Marchant, T.A., Moreno, S., 2007. Physiological stress levels predict survival probabilities in wild rabbits. Horm. Behav. 51, 313–320.

Cacioppo, J.T., Ernst, J.M., Burleson, M.H., McClintock, M.K., Malarkey, W.B., Hawkley, L.C., et al., 2000. Lonely traits and concomitant physiological processes: the MacArthur social neuroscience studies. Int. J. Psychophysiol. 35, 143–154.

Carlson, A.A., Young, A.J., Russell, A.F., Bennett, N., McNeilly, A.S., Clutton-Brock, T., 2004. Hormonal correlates of dominance in meerkats (Suricata suricatta). Horm. Behav. 46, 141–150.

Carstensen, L.L., 1992. Social and emotional patterns in adulthood: support for socioemotional selectivity theory. Psychol. Aging 7, 331–338.

Carstensen, L.L., 1995. Evidence for a life-span theory of socioemotional selectivity. Curr. Dir. Psychol. Sci. 4, 151–156.

Carter, C.S., 1998. Neuroendocrine perspectives on social attachment and love. Psychoneuro-endocrinology 23, 779–818.

Cavigelli, S.A., 1999. Behavioural patterns associated with faecal cortisol levels in free-ranging female ring-tailed lemurs, Lemur catta. Anim. Behav. 57, 935–944.

Cavigelli, S.A., Dubovick, T., Levash, W., Jolly, A., 2003. Female dominance status and fecal corticoids in a cooperative breeder with low reproductive skew: ring-tailed lemurs (Lemur catta). Horm. Behav. 43, 166–179.

Cheney, D.L., 1992. Within-group cohesion and inter-group hostility: the relation between grooming distributions and inter-group competition among female primates. Behav. Ecol. 3, 334–345.

Cheney, D.L., Seyfarth, R.M., 1997. Reconciliatory grunts by dominant female baboons influence victims' behavior. Anim. Behav. 54, 409–418.

Cheney, D.L., Seyfarth, R.M., 1999. Recognition of other individuals' social relationships by female baboons. Anim. Behav. 58, 67–75.

Cheney, D.L., Seyfarth, R.M., 2007. Baboon Metaphysics: The Evolution of a Social Mind. Chicago University Press, Chicago.

Cheney, D.L., Wrangham, R.W., 1987. Predation. In: Smuts, B.B., Cheney, D.L., Seyfarth, R.M., Wrangham, R.W., Struhsaker, T. (Eds.), Primate Societies. Chicago University Press, Chicago, pp. 227–239.

Cheney, D.L., Seyfarth, R.M., Silk, J.B., 1995a. The responses of female baboons (*Papio cynocephalus ursinus*) to anomalous social interactions: evidence for causal reasoning? J. Comp. Psych. 109, 134–141.

Cheney, D.L., Seyfarth, R.M., Silk, J.B., 1995b. The role of grunts in reconciling opponents and facilitating interactions among adult female baboons. Anim. Behav. 50, 249–257.

Cheney, D.L., Seyfarth, R.M., Fischer, J., Beehner, J., Bergman, T., Johnson, S.E., Kitchen, D.M., et al., 2004. Factors affecting reproduction and mortality among baboons in the Okavango Delta, Botswana. Int. J. Primatol. 25, 401–428.

Collins, D.A., Busse, C.D., Goodall, J., 1984. Infanticide in two populations of savanna baboons. In: Hausfater, G., Hrdy, S.B. (Eds.), Infanticide: Comparative and Evolutionary Perspectives. Aldine, New York, pp. 193–215.

Cowlishaw, G., 1994. Vulnerability to predation in baboon populations. Behaviour 131, 293–304.

Creel, S., 2001. Social dominance and stress hormones. Trends Ecol. Evol. 16, 491–497.

Creel, S., 2005. Dominance, aggression, and glucocorticoid levels in social carnivores. J. Mammal. 86, 255–264.

Creel, S., Creel, N., 2002. The African Wild Dog: Behavior, Ecology, and Conservation. Princeton University Press, Princeton.

Cristobal-Azkarate, J., Chavira, R., Boeck, L., Rodriguez-Luna, E., Vea, J.M., 2007. Glucocorticoid levels in free-ranging resident mantled howlers: a study of coping strategies. Am. J. Primatol. 69, 866–876.

Crockford, C., Wittig, R.M., Whitten, P.L., Seyfarth, R.M., Cheney, D.L., 2008. Social stressors and coping mechanisms in wild female baboons (*Papio hamadryas ursinus*). Horm. Behav. 53, 254–265.

Cross, N., Rogers, L.J., 2006. Mobbing vocalizations as a coping response in the common marmoset. Horm. Behav. 49, 237–245.

Decety, J., Jackson, P.L., 2004. The functional architecture of human empathy. Behav. Cogn. Neurosci. Rev. 3, 71–100.

Decety, J., Jackson, P.L., 2006. A social neuroscience perspective on empathy. Curr. Dir. Psychol. Sci. 15, 54–58.

DeVries, A.C., Glasper, E.R., Detillion, C.E., 2003. Social modulation of stress responses. Physiol. Behav. 79, 399–407.

DeVries, A.C., Craft, T.K.S., Glasper, E.R., Neigh, G.N., Alexander, J.K., 2007. Social influences on stress responses and health. Psychoneuroendocrinology 32, 587–603.

Dloniak, S.M., French, J.A., Holekamp, K.E., 2006. Rank-related maternal effects of androgens on behaviour in wild spotted hyaenas. Nature 440, 1190–1193.

Dunbar, R.I.M., Spoor, M., 1995. Social networks, support cliques, and kinship. Hum. Nat. 6, 273–290.

Ebensperger, L.A., 1998. Strategies and counterstrategies to infanticide in mammals. Biol. Rev. 73, 321–346.

Engh, A.E., Beehner, J.C., Bergman, T.J., Whitten, P.L., Hoffmeier, R.R., Seyfarth, R.M., et al., 2006a. Behavioural and hormonal responses to predation in female chacma baboons (*Papio hamadryas ursinus*). Proc. R. Soc. Lond. B 273, 707–712.

Engh, A.E., Beehner, J.C., Bergman, T.J., Whitten, P.L., Hoffmeier, R.R., Seyfarth, R.M., et al., 2006b. Female hierarchy instability, male immigration, and infanticide increase glucocorticoid levels in female chacma baboons. Anim. Behav. 71, 1227–1237.

Figley, C.R. (Ed.), 1995. Compassion Fatigue: Coping with Traumatic Stress Disorder in Those Who Treat the Traumatized Brunner/Mazel Psychological Stress Series, Philadelphia.

French, J.A., Schaffner, C.M., 2000. Social modulation of reproductive behavior in monogamous primates. In: Wallen, K., Schneider, J. (Eds.), Reproduction in Context. MIT Press, Cambridge, MA, pp. 325–353.

Ganem, G., Bennett, N., 2004. Tolerance to unfamiliar conspecifics varies with social organization in female African mole-rats. Physiol. Behav. 82, 555–562.

Gesquiere, L.R., Khan, M., Shek, L., Wango, T.L., Wango, E.O., Alberts, S.C., et al., 2008. Coping with a challenging environment: effects of seasonal variability and reproductive status on glucocorticoid concentrations of female baboons (*Papio cynocephalus*). Horm. Behav. 54, 410–416.

Giles, L.C., Glonek, G.F.V., Luszcz, M.A., Andrews, G.R., 2005. Effects of social networks on 10 year survival in very old Australians: the Australian longitudinal study of aging. J. Epid. Comm.Health 59, 574–579.

Ginther, A.J., Ziegler, T.E., Snowdon, C.T., 2001. Reproductive biology of captive male cottontop tamarin monkeys as a function of social environment. Anim. Behav. 61, 65–78.

Glasper, E.R., DeVries, A.C., 2005. Social structure effects of pair-housing on wound healing. Brain Behav. Immun. 19, 61–68.

Goldizen, A.W., 1987. Tamarins and marmosets: communal care of offspring. In: Smuts, B.B., Cheney, D.L., Seyfarth, R.M., Wrangham, R.W., Struhsaker, T. (Eds.) Primate Societies. Chicago University Press, Chicago, pp. 34–43.

Goodall, J., 1986. The Chimpanzees of Gombe: Patterns of Behavior. Harvard University Press, Cambridge, MA.

Goymann, W., East, M.L., Wachter, B., Honer, O.P., Mostl, E., Van't Hof, T.J., et al., 2001. Social, state-dependent, and environmental modulation of faecal corticosteroid levels in free-ranging female spotted hyenas. Proc. R. Soc. Lond. B 268, 2453–2459.

Goymann, W., Wingfield, J.C., 2004. Allostatic load, social status, and stress hormones—the costs of social status matter. Anim. Behav. 67, 591–602.

Gust, D.A., Gordon, T.P., Hambright, M.K., Wilson, M.E., 1993. Relationship between social factors and pituitary–adrenocortical activity in female rhesus monkeys (*Macaca mulatta*). Horm. Behav. 27, 318–331.

Gust, D.A., Gordon, T.P., Brodie, A.R., McClure, H.M., 1994. Effect of a preferred companion in modulating stress in adult female rhesus-monkeys. Physiol. Behav. 55, 681–684.

Gust, D.A., Gordon, T.P., Wilson, M.E., Brodie, A.R., 1996. Group formation of female pigtail macaques (*Macaca nemestrina*). Am. J. Primatol. 39, 263–273.

Hausfater, G., Hrdy, S.B., 1984. Infanticide: Comparative and Evolutionary Perspectives. Aldine, New York.

Hacklander, K., Mostl, E., Arnold, W., 2003. Reproductive suppression in female Alpine marmots. Marmota marmota. Anim. Behav. 65, 1133–1140.

Hamilton, W.J., Bulger, J.B., 1990. Natal male baboon rank rises and successful challenges to resident alpha males. Behav. Ecol. Sociobiol. 26, 357–363.

Hamilton, W.J., Buskirk, R.E., Buskirk, W.E., 1976. Defense of space and resources by chacma (*Papio ursinus*) baboon troops in an African desert and swamp. Ecology 57, 1264–1272.

Heistermann, M., Tari, S., Hodges, J.K., 1993. Measurement of faecal steroids for monitoring ovarian function in New World primates, Callitrichidae. J. Reprod. Fert. 99, 243–251.

Hill, R.A., Dunbar, R.I.M., 2003. Social network size in humans. Hum. Nat. 14, 53–72.

Irwin, M.R., Risch, S.C., Daniels, M., Bloom, E., Weiner, H., 1987. Plasma-cortisol and immune function in bereavement. Psychosom. Med. 49, 210–211.

Isbell, L.A., 1991. Contest and scramble competition: patterns of female aggression and ranging behavior among primates. Behav. Ecol. 2, 143–155.

Jensen, K., Hare, B., Call, J., Tomasello, M., 2006. What's in it for me? Self-regard precludes altruism and spite in chimpanzees. Proc. R. Soc. Lond. B 273, 1013–1021.

Johnson, E.O., Kamilaris, T.C., Carter, C.S., Calogero, A.E., 1996. The biobehavioral consequences of psychogenic stress in a small, social primate (*Callithrix jacchus jacchus*). Biol. Psychiatr. 40, 317–337.

Kappeler, P.M., van Schaik, C.P., 2002. Evolution of primate social systems. Int. J. Primatol. 23, 707–740.

Kendler, K.S., Myers, J., Prescott, C.A., 2005. Sex differences in the relationship between social support and risk for major depression: a longitudinal study of opposite-sex twin pairs. Am. J. Psychol. 162, 250–256.

Levine, S., 2005. Developmental determinants of sensitivity and resistance to stress. Psychoneuroendocrinology 30, 939–946.

Levine, S., Ursin, H., 1991. What is stress. In: Brown, M.R., Koob, G.F., Rivier, C. (Eds.), Stress: Neurobiology and Neuroendocrinology. Marcel Dekker, New York, pp. 3–22.

Lim, M.M., Young, L.J., 2006. Neuropeptidergic regulation of affiliative behavior and social bonding in animals. Horm. Behav. 50, 506–517.

Maestripieri, D., Hoffman, C.L., Fulks, R., Gerald, M.S., 2008. Plasma cortisol responses to stress in lactating and nonlactating female rhesus macaques. Horm. Behav. 53, 170–176.

Marais, E.N., 1939. My Friends the Baboons. Human and Rousseau, Cape Town.

Marmot, M.G., 2004. The Status Syndrome: How Social Standing Affects Our Health and Longevity. Henry Holt, New York.

Mateo, J.M., 2007. Ecological and hormonal correlates of antipredator behavior in adult Belding's ground squirrels (*Spermophilus beldingi*). Behav. Ecol. Sociobiol. 62, 37–49.

McCleery, J.M., Bhagwagar, Z., Smith, K.A., Goodwin, G.M., Cowen, P.J., 2000. Modelling a loss event: effect of imagined bereavement on the hypothalamic–pituitary–adrenal axis. Psychol. Med. 30, 219–223.

McEwen, B.S., Wingfield, J.C., 2003. The concept of allostasis in biology and biomedicine. Horm. Behav. 43, 2–15.

Mendoza, S.P., Mason, W.A., 1986. Parental division of labour and differentiation of attachments in a monogamous primate (*Callicebus moloch*). Anim. Behav. 34, 1336–1347.

Munck, A., Guyre, P., Holbrook, N., 1984. Physiological actions of glucocorticoids in stress and their relation to pharmacological actions. Endocr. Rev. 5, 25–41.

Nelson, R.J., 2000. An Introduction to Behavioral Endocrinology. Sinauer, Sunderland, MA.

Nelson, R.J., Demas, G.E., Klein, S.L., Kriegsfeld, L.J., 2002. Seasonal Patterns of Stress, Immune Function, and Disease. Cambridge University Press, Cambridge.

Nguyen, N., Gesquiere, L.R., Wango, E.O., Alberts, S.C., Altmann, J., 2008. Late pregnancy glucocorticoid levels predict responsiveness in wild baboon mothers (*Papio cynocephalus*). Anim. Behav. 75, 1747–1756.

Onyango, P.O., Gesquiere, L.R., Wango, E.O., Alberts, S.C., Altmann, J., 2008. Persistence of maternal effects in baboons: mother's dominance rank at son's conception predicts stress hormone levels in sub-adult males. Horm. Behav. 54, 319–324.

Palombit, R.A., Seyfarth, R.M., Cheney, D.L., 1997. The adaptive value of "friendships" to female baboons: experimental and observational evidence. Anim. Behav. 54, 599–614.

Palombit, R., Cheney, D., Seyfarth, R., Rendall, D., Silk, J., Johnson, S., et al., 2000. Male infanticide and defense of infants in chacma baboons. In: van Schaik, C., Janson, C. (Eds.), Infanticide by Males and Its Implications. Cambridge University Press, Cambridge, pp. 123–152.

Palombit, R.A., Cheney, D.L., Seyfarth, R.M., 2001. Female–female competition for male "friends" in wild chacma baboons (*Papio cynocephalus ursinus*). Anim. Behav. 61, 1159–1171.

Panskepp, J., 1998. Affective Neuroscience: The Foundations of Human and Animal Emotions. Oxford University Press, New York.

Pereira, M.E., 1983. Abortion following the immigration of an adult male baboon (*Papio cynocephalus*). Am. J. Primatol. 4, 93–98.

Premack, D., Woodruff, G., 1978. Does the chimpanzee have a theory of mind? Behav. Brain Sci. 4, 515–526.

Preston, S.D., de Waal, F.M.B., 2002. Empathy: its ultimate and proximate bases. Behav. Brain Sci. 25, 1–72.

Pride, R.E., 2005a. Foraging success, agonism, and predator alarms: behavioral predictors of cortisol in *Lemur catta*. *Int.* J. Primatol. 26, 295–319.

Pride, R.E., 2005b. High faecal glucocorticoid levels predict mortality in ring-tailed lemurs (*Lemur catta*). Biol. Lett. 1, 60–63.

Pride, R.E., 2005c. Optimal group size and seasonal stress in ring-tailed lemurs (*Lemur catta*). Behav. Ecol. 15, 550–560.

Ramirez, S.M., Bardi, M., French, J.A., Brent, L., 2004. Hormonal correlates of changes in interest in unrelated infants across the peripartum period in female baboons (*Papio hamadryas anubis sp.*). Horm. Behav. 46, 520–528.

Ray, J.C., Sapolsky, R.M., 1992. Styles of male social behavior and their endocrine correlates among high-ranking baboons. Am. J. Primatol. 28, 231–250.

Reeder, D.M., Kramer, K.M., 2005. Stress in free-ranging mammals: integrating physiology, ecology, and natural history. J. Mammal. 86, 225–235.

Rodel, H.G., Starkloff, A., Bruchner, B., von Holst, D., 2008. Social environment and reproduction in female European rabbits (*Oryctolagus cuniculus*): benefits of the presence of litter sisters. J. Comp. Psychol. 122, 73–83.

Rosal, M.C., King, J., Ma, Y., Reed, G.W., 2004. Stress, social support, and cortisol: inverse associations. Behav. Med. 30, 11–21.

Romero, L.M., 2002. Seasonal changes in plasma glucocorticoid concentrations in free-living vertebrates. Gen. Comp. Endocrinol. 128, 1–24.

Rukstalis, M., French, J.A., 2005. Vocal buffering of the stress response: exposure to conspecific vocalizations moderates urinary cortisol excretion in isolated marmosets. Horm. Behav. 47, 1–7.

Saltzman, W., Schultz-Darken, N.J., Scheffler, G., Wegner, F.H., Abbott, D.H., 1994. Social and reproductive influences on plasma cortisol in female marmoset monkeys. Physiol. Behav. 56, 801–810.

Saltzman, W., Schultz-Darken, N.J., Abbott, D.H., 1996. Behavioural and endocrine predictors of dominance and tolerance in female common marmosets, *Callithrix jacchus*. Anim. Behav. 51, 657–674.

Saltzman, W., Schultz-Darken, N.J., Wegner, F.H., Wittwer, D.J., Abbott, D.H., 1998. Suppression of cortisol levels in subordinate female marmosets: reproductive and social contributions. Horm. Behav. 33, 58–74.

Saltzman, W., Liedl, K.J., Salper, O.J., Pick, R.R., Abbott, D.H., 2008. Post-conception reproductive competition in cooperatively breeding common marmosets. Horm. Behav. 53, 274–286.

Samuels, A., Silk, J.B., Altmann, J., 1987. Continuity and change in dominance relations among female baboons. Anim. Behav. 35, 785–793.

Sand, J., Creel, S., 2004. Social dominance, aggression and faecal glucocorticoid levels in a wild population of wolves, *Canis lupus*. Anim. Behav. 67, 387–396.

Sapolsky, R.M., 1986. Endocrine and behavioral correlates of drought in the wild baboons. Am. J. Primatol. 11, 217–226.

Sapolsky, R.M., 1990. Adrenocortical function, social rank, and personality among wild baboons. Biol. Psychiatr. 28, 862–878.

Sapolsky, R.M., 1992. Cortisol concentrations and the social significance of rank instability among wild baboons. Psychoneuroendocrinology 17, 701–709.

Sapolsky, R.M., 1993a. Endocrinology al fresco: psychoendocrine studies of wild baboons. Rec. Prog. Horm. Res. 48, 437–468.

Sapolsky, R.M., 1993b. The physiology of dominance in stable versus unstable social hierarchies. In: Mason, W.A., Mendoza, S.P. (Eds.), Primate Social Conflict. State University of New York Press, Albany, NY, pp. 171–204.

Sapolsky, R.M., 1998. Why Zebras Don't Get Ulcers. W.H. Freeman and Co., New York.

Sapolsky, R.M., 2002. Endocrinology of the stress response. In: Becker, J.B., Breedlove, S.M., Crews, M.M., McCarthy, M.M. (Eds.), Behavioral Endocrinology. MIT Press, Cambridge, MA, pp. 409–450.

Sapolsky, R.M., 2004. Social status and health in humans and other animals. Ann. Rev. Anthropol. 33, 393–418.

Sapolsky, R.M., 2005. The influence of social hierarchy on primate health. Science 308, 648–652.

Sapolsky, R.M., Ray, J.C., 1989. Styles of dominance and their endocrine correlates among wild olive baboons (Papio anubis). Am. J. Primatol. 18, 1–13.

Sapolsky, R.M., Alberts, S.C., Altmann, J., 1997. Hypercortisolism associated with social subordinance or social isolation among wild baboons. Arch. Gen. Psychiatr. 54, 1137–1142.

Sapolsky, R.M., Romero, L.M., Munck, A.U., 2000. How do glucocorticoids influence stress responses? Integrating permissive, suppressive, stimulatory, and preparative actions. Endocr. Rev. 21, 55–89.

Segerstrom, S.C., Miller, G.E., 2004. Psychological stress and the human immune system: a meta-analytic study of 30 years of inquiry. Psychol. Bull. 130, 601–630.

Seligman, M.E.P., 1975. Helplessness: On Depression. Development, and Death. Freeman, San Francisco.

Seyfarth, R.M., 1976. Social relationships among adult female baboons. Anim. Behav. 24, 917–938.

Shively, C.A., 1998. Social subordination stress, behavior, and central monoaminergic function in female cynomolgus monkeys. Biol. Psychiatr. 44, 882–891.

Shively, C.A., Register, T.C., Friedman, D.P., Morgan, T.M., Thompson, J., Laniera, T., 2005. Social stress-associated depression in adult female cynomolgus monkeys (Macaca fascicularis). Biol. Psych. 69, 67–84.

Shutt, K., MacLarnon, A., Heistermann, M., Semple, S., 2007. Grooming in Barbary macaques: better to give than to receive. Biol. Lett. 3, 231–233.

Silk, J.B., 2002. Kin selection in primate groups. Int. J. Primatol. 23, 849–875.

Silk, J.B., 2007. Empathy, sympathy, and prosocial preferences in primates. In: Dunbar, R.I.M., Barrett, L. (Eds.), Oxford Handbook of Evolutionary Psychology. Oxford University Press, Oxford, pp. 115–126.

Silk, J.B., Cheney, D.L., Seyfarth, R.M., 1996. The form and function of reconciliation among baboons, Papio cynocephalus ursinus. Anim. Behav. 52, 259–268.

Silk, J.B., Seyfarth, R.M., Cheney, D.L., 1999. The structure of social relationships among female baboons in the Moremi Reserve, Botswana. Behaviour 136, 679–703.

Silk, J.B., Rendall, D., Cheney, D.L., Seyfarth, R.M., 2003a. Natal attraction in adult female baboons (*Papio cynocephalus ursinus*) in the Moremi Reserve, Botswana. Ethology 109, 627–644.

Silk, J.B., Alberts, S.C., Altmann, J., 2003b. Social bonds of female baboons enhance infant survival. Science 302, 1231–1234.

Silk, J.B., Altmann, J., Alberts, S.C., 2006a. Social relationships among adult female baboons (*Papio cynocephalus*) I. Variation in the strength of social bonds. Behav. Ecol. Sociobiol. 61, 183–195.

Silk, J.B., Alberts, S.C., Altmann, J., 2006b. Social relationships among adult female baboons (*Papio cynocephalus*) II: variation in the quality and stability of social bonds. Behav. Ecol. Sociobiol. 61, 197–204.

Silk, J.B., Beehner, J.C., Bergman, T.J., Crockford, C., Engh, A.L., Moscvice, L.R., et al., 2009. The benefits of social capital: close social bonds among female baboons enhance offspring survival. Proc. Roy. Soc. Lond. B 276

Simpson, J.A., Rholes, W.S., 1994. Stress and secure base relationships in adulthood. In: Bartholmew, K., Perlman, D. (Eds.), Advances in Personal Relationships,Vol. 5. Jessica Kingsley Publisher, London, pp. 181–204.

Smith, T.E., French, J.A., 1997. Psychosocial stress and urinary cortisol excretion in marmoset monkeys (*Callithrix kuhli*). Physiol. Behav. 62, 225–232.

Smith, T.E., McGreer-Whitworth, B., French, J.A., 1998. Close proximity of the heterosexual partner reduces the physiological and behavioral consequences of novel-cage housing in black tufted-ear marmosets (*Callithrix kuhli*). Horm. Behav. 34, 211–222.

Sousa, M.B.C., Sales da Rocha Albuquerque, A.C., Albuquerque, F.D., Arauho, A., Yamamoto, M.E., Arruda, M.D., 2005. Behavioral strategies and hormonal profiles of dominant and subordinate common marmoset (*Callithrix jacchus*) females in wild monogamous groups. Am. J. Primatol. 67, 37–50.

Stavisky, R.C., Adams, M.R., Watson, S.L., Kaplan, J.R., 2001. Dominance, cortisol, and behavior in small groups of female cynomolgus monkeys (*Macaca fascicularis*). Horm. Behav. 39, 232–238.

Steptoe, A., Owen, N., Kunz-Ebrecht, S.R., Brydon, L., 2004. Loneliness and neuroendocrine, cardiovascular, and inflammatory stress responses in middle-aged men and women. Psychoneuroendocrinology 29, 593–611.

Sterck, E.H.M., Watts, D.P., van Schaik, C.P., 1997. The evolution of female social relationships in nonhuman primates. Behav. Ecol. Sociobiol. 41, 291–309.

Tamashiro, K.L.K., Nguyen, M.M.N., Sakai, R.R., 2005. Social stress: from rodents to primates. Front. Neuroendocrinol. 26, 27–40.

Tarara, E.B., 1987. Infanticide in a chacma baboon troop. Primates 28, 267–270.

Taylor, S.E., Cousino Klein, L., Lewis, B.P., Gruenewald, T.L., Gurung, R.A., Updegraff, J.A., 2000. Biobehavioral responses to stress in females: tend-and- befriend, not fight-or-flight. Psychol. Rev. 107, 411–429.

Thorsteinsson, E.B., James, J.E., 1999. A meta-analysis of the effects of experimental manipulations of social support during laboratory stress. Psychol. Health 14, 869–886.

Tomasello, M., Carpenter, M., Call, J., Behne, T., Moll, H., 2005. Understanding and sharing intentions: the origins of cultural cognition. Behav. Brain Sci. 28, 675–735.

Tomasello, M., Moll, H., 2009. The gap is social: human shared intentionality and culture. In: Kappeler, P., Silk, J. (Eds.), Mind the Gap: Tracing the Origins of Human Universals. Springer, Berlin.

Tops, M., van Peer, J.M., Korf, J., Wijers, A.A., Tucker, D.M., 2007. Anxiety, cortisol, and attachment predict plasma oxytocin. Psychophysiology 44, 444–449.

Uvnas-Moberg, K., 1997. Physiological and endocrine effects of social contact. In: Carter, S., Lederhendler, B., Kirkpatrik, B. (Eds.), The Integrative Neurobiology of Affiliation. MIT Press, Cambridge, MA, pp. 245–262.

van Schaik, C.P., 1983. Why are diurnal primates living in groups? Behaviour 87, 120–144.

van Schaik, C.P.,, Janson, C. (Eds.), 2000. Infanticide by Males and Its Implications. Cambridge University Press, Cambridge.

van Schaik, C.P., van Noordwijk, M.A., van Bragt, T., Blankenstein, M.A., 1991. A pilot study of the social correlates of levels of urinary cortisol, prolactin, and testosterone in wild long-tailed macaques (*Macaca fascicularis*). Primates 32, 345–356.

Virgin, C., Sapolsky, R.M., 1997. Styles of male social behavior and their endocrine correlates among low-ranking baboons. Am. J. Primatol. 42, 25–39.

Van Meter, P.E., Grench, J.A., Dloniak, S.M., Watts, H.E., Kolowski, J.M., Holekamp, K.E., 2009. Fecal glucocorticoids reflect socio-ecological and anthropogenic stressors in the lives of wild spotted hyenas. Horm. Behav. 55, 329–337.

Von Holst, D., 1998. The concept of stress and its relevance to animal behavior. Adv. Stud. Behav. 27, 1–131.

Walters, J.R., Seyfarth, R.M., 1987. Conflict and cooperation. In: Smuts, B.B., Cheney, D.L., Seyfarth, R.M., Wrangham, R.W., Struhsaker, T. (Eds.), Primate Societies. University of Chicago Press, Chicago, pp. 306–317.

Wasser, S., Hunt, K., Brown, J., Cooper, K., Crockett, C., Bechert, U., et al., 2000. A generalized faecal glucocorticoid assay for use in a diverse array of non-domestic mammalian and avian species. Gen. Comp. Endocr 120, 260–275.

Weingrill, T., 2000. Infanticide and the value of male–female relationships in mountain chacma baboons (*Papio cynocephalus ursinus*). Behaviour 137, 337–359.

Weingrill, T., Gray, D.A., Barrett, L., Henzi, S.P., 2004. Fecal cortisol levels in free-ranging female chacma baboons: relationship to dominance, reproductive state and environmental factors. Horm. Behav. 45, 259–269.

Weiss, J.M., 1970. Somatic effects of predictable and unpredictable shock. Psychosom. Med. 32, 397–408.

Wilson, E.O., Bossert, W.H., 1971. A Primer of Population Biology. Sinauer, Sunderland, MA.

Wilson, M.E., Fisher, J., Fischer, A., Lee, V., Harris, R.B., Bartness, T.J., 2008. Quantifying food intake in socially housed monkeys: social status effects on caloric consumption. Phys. Behav. 94, 586–594.

Wingfield, J.C., Ramenofsky, M., 1999. Hormones and the behavioral ecology of stress. In: Balm, P.H.M. (Ed.), Stress Physiology in Animals. Sheffield Academic Press, Sheffield, UK, pp. 1–51.

Wittig, R.M., Crockford, C., Wikberg, E., Seyfarth, R.M., Cheney, D.L., 2007a. Kin-mediated reconciliation substitutes for direct reconciliation in female baboons. Proc. Roy. Soc. Lond. B 274, 1109–1115.

Wittig, R.M., Crockford, C., Seyfarth, R.M., Cheney, D.L., 2007b. Vocal alliances in chacma baboons, *Papio hamadryas ursinus*. Behav. Ecol. Sociobiol. 61, 899–909.

Wittig, R.M., Crockford, C., Lehmann, J., Whitten, P.L., Seyfarth, R.M., Cheney, D.L., 2008. Focused grooming networks and stress alleviation in wild female baboons. Horm. Behav. 53, 170–177.

Wrangham, R.W., 1980. An ecological model of female-bonded primate groups. Behaviour 75, 262–300.

Ylönen, H., Eccard, J.A., Jokinen, I., Sundell, J., 2006. Is the antipredatory response in behaviour reflected in stress measured in faecal corticosteroids in a small rodent. Behav. Ecol. Sociobiol. 60, 350–358.

Zhou, W.X., Sornette, D., Hill, R.A., Dunbar, R.I.M., 2005. Discrete hierarchical organization of social group size. Proc. R. Soc. Lond. B 272, 439–444.

Ziegler, T.E., Sousa, M.B., 2002. Parent–daughter relationships and social controls on fertility in female common marmosets, *Callithrix jacchus*. Horm. Behav. 42, 356–367.

Ziegler, T.E., Scheffler, G., Snowdon, C.T., 1995. The relationship of cortisol levels to social environment and reproductive functioning in female cotton-top tamarins, *Saguinus oedipus*. Horm. Behav. 29, 407–424.

Ziegler, T.E., Scheffler, G., Wittwer, D.J., Schultz-Darken, N., Snowdon, C.T., Abbott, D.H., 1996. Metabolism of reproductive steroids during the ovarian cycle in two species of callitrichids, *Saguinus oedipus* and *Callithrix jacchus*, and estimation of the ovulatory period from fecal steroids. Biol. Reprod. 54, 91–99.

Reciprocal Altruism in Primates: Partner Choice, Cognition, and Emotions

Gabriele Schino* and Filippo Aureli[†]

*Istituto di Scienze e Tecnologie della Cognizione,
Consiglio Nazionale delle Ricerche, 00197 Rome, Italy
[†]Research Centre in Evolutionary Anthropology and Palaeoecology,
School of Natural Sciences and Psychology, Liverpool John
Moores University, Liverpool L3 3AF, United Kingdom

I. The Problem

Ever since Darwin, altruism has been a problem for evolutionists and animal behaviorists. Even after Hamilton (1964) and Trivers (1971) provided widely accepted explanations for its evolution, a continuing debate has been fueled by widespread semantic confusion. As a consequence of this sustained focus on the evolution of altruism, the problem of its proximate causation has been until recently completely neglected. In the last few years, however, it has come to be realized that an understanding of the proximate mechanisms underlying altruistic behavior is needed in order to obtain a more complete picture of the biology of altruism. Unfortunately, although adding the study of proximate mechanisms has generated interesting hypotheses and helped to elucidate possible constraints on the evolution of altruism, it has also added a new layer of confusion, as proximate and ultimate explanations are sometimes confused.

In this chapter, we review some of the recent work on altruism in primates with the aim of trying to clarify a sometimes confused field. We focus specifically on primates because much has been done on this taxon both theoretically and empirically. We also limit our treatment to altruism among nonkin, since kin selected altruism is less often questioned and has generated a less confused debate. We begin by reviewing semantic problems, then discuss the various ways of demonstrating the occurrence of reciprocal altruism, and argue that partner choice may have played a large role in the evolution of primate reciprocity. Finally, we show how failing to

45

0065-3454/09 $35.00
DOI: 10.1016/S0065-3454(09)39002-6

distinguish between proximate causation and ultimate function has led to questionable hypotheses about the mechanisms underlying primate reciprocity, and argue that a system of "emotional bookkeeping" (i.e., an emotionally based mechanism that allows to keep track of benefits exchanged) may be at the basis of the primates' ability to reciprocate over extended time periods.

A. SOCIAL SEMANTICS

Hamilton (1964) and then West et al. (2007) distinguished four classes of social behaviors depending on the individual (i.e., not inclusive) lifetime benefits and costs for the actor and the recipient: selfishness, spite, altruism, and mutual benefits. Note that this classification, being based on the benefits and costs of the behavior *and of its later consequences* as measured over the entire lifetime of an individual, includes what is classically termed reciprocal altruism under the heading of mutual benefits.

Behaviors that involve lifetime mutual benefits are favored by individual selection, but a complication arises due to the possible temporal decoupling of the benefits and costs for each of the individuals involved (Mesterton-Gibbons and Dugatkin, 1997; Stevens and Gilby, 2004). Since here we are specifically interested in reciprocal altruism, it is important to focus on the timing of the benefits and costs of behavior, and to separate immediate benefits and costs from those that may accrue at a later time. In fact, the heterogeneity in the timing of benefits and costs has created much of the semantic confusion surrounding altruism. Let us examine the various possibilities.

When both the actor and the recipient receive immediate benefits no particular problem arises. For example, male baboon A may help male B challenge consorting male C, and as a result both A and B increase their probability of gaining access to a fertile female. As long as for both males the benefits outweigh the cost of the challenge, their behavior is favored by individual selection, and the proximate mechanisms involved do not need to be particularly complex.

When the actor incurs immediate costs and receives future benefits that are the inevitable (though delayed) consequence of its action, again no particular problem arises. Examples include group augmentation effects for helpers of cooperative breeding species, which derive delayed benefits (e.g., in terms of increased survival) from the increase in group size that their presence brings about (Kokko et al., 2001).

When the actor incurs immediate costs (while the recipient gains immediate benefits) and receives delayed benefits that depend on the future behavior of the recipient, we have what is classically termed reciprocal altruism.

Note that here (and throughout this chapter) we are using the term altruism to indicate behaviors that have immediate costs for the actor and immediate benefits for the recipient *regardless of later consequences*. In so doing, we depart from Hamilton (1964) and West et al. (2007). We deem this necessary for the purposes of this review for two main reasons. First, the time lag between costs and benefits is the defining aspect of reciprocal altruism, and no discussion is possible without keeping immediate and later fitness consequences conceptually separate. Second, the time lag between costs and benefits, and especially their probabilistic relation (i.e., benefits are not an inevitable consequence of the actor's behavior), has important evolutionary consequences, as it selects for strategies and counterstrategies aimed at exploiting social partners, that is, at minimizing costs while maximizing benefits. Much of the debate about reciprocal altruism is about such strategies. What are the proximate mechanisms that allow (or constrain) reciprocal altruism? How do animals negotiate or exploit the uncertainty and time lag between costs and benefits?

B. Demonstrating (Low-Cost) Reciprocal Altruism

In the years after the formulation of reciprocal altruism theory (Trivers, 1971), an initial wave of studies reporting examples of reciprocal altruism was followed by difficulties in replicating these earlier findings (e.g., Bercovitch, 1988; Dugatkin, 1988; Milinski, 1987; Packer, 1977; Wilkinson, 1984). These difficulties led to a prevailing view that reciprocal altruism is less common than was originally thought, and indeed recent reviews (e.g., Hammerstein, 2003; Stevens and Hauser, 2004; Stevens et al., 2005b) have emphasized that reciprocal altruism is extremely rare among nonhuman animals. Often, a role for reciprocity is discounted on the grounds that the behavior under examination has little or no cost, the implication being that, if a behavior is not costly, then there is nothing that needs to be explained (e.g., Bercovitch, 1988).

Here, a distinction has to be made between how natural selection favors the existence of a given behavior and how natural selection shapes the distribution of such behavior among group members. Let us assume, for example, that coalition formation (specifically, aggressor support) is directly advantageous to the intervening individual because, for example, it reinforces the dominance position of the intervener at little or no cost (because the associated risk is minimal). Saying that individual selection will favor coalition formation (which is true under our assumptions) tell us nothing about how animals should distribute their help among group mates. The latter will depend on reciprocity. If receiving help is advantageous for the recipient, then selection will favor the deployment of coalitionary help toward those individuals that reciprocate most (i.e., partner choice), so that later (reciprocated) benefits will be added to the immediate benefits of reinforcing one own's rank. The selective role of partner choice has also been emphasized by Noë (2001) in the context of biological market theory.

The process described above, that we may call "reciprocal mutualism," is likely to have a significant influence on how group-living animals distribute behaviors that may benefit other individuals among group mates. In fact, reciprocity based on partner choice is expected to exert its role regardless of the immediate costs of the behaviors involved. In other words, we suggest that while the existence of a given behavior depends on its cost/benefit ratio (and thus classical reciprocal altruism implies immediate costs exchanged for later benefits), the distribution of such behavior among group members depends on reciprocal partner choice that acts regardless of the immediate costs involved (provided, of course, such costs are partner independent). Whenever a behavioral pattern that benefits other individuals (be it altruistic or mutualistic) is favored by individual selection (because of its delayed or immediate benefits), then selection will also favor the selective deployment among group members (i.e., partner choice) in relation to the extent of reciprocation.

Examples of primate behaviors that benefit other individuals at little cost for the actor are grooming, agonistic support, tolerance, and food sharing. We would like to argue that this kind of low-cost altruism is relatively common. Since costs are negligible anyway, there is little incentive for cheating (i.e., reaping the immediate benefits and failing to reciprocate later) and selection must have favored the maximization of received return benefits more than the minimization of immediate costs. Thus, we may expect selection to have favored the evolution of proximate mechanisms based on some form of partner choice ("groom most of the individuals who groom you most") more than mechanisms aimed at the immediate detection of cheating. Since individual episodes of failed reciprocation have negligible or no cost, it is more important to choose partners on the basis of their overall willingness to return benefits than to avoid being cheated. Under these conditions, long-term return benefits are more important than short-term costs (if any), and selection will favor partner choice (possibly based on the development of emotional bonds) rather than immediate reciprocation.

Note also that even behaviors that entail large and obvious immediate benefits for the actor may involve partner choice aimed at maximizing later added benefits. One example is mating. From the point of view of a female, mating implies immediate benefits in terms of conception. However, since the male also receives an immediate benefit, the female may be selected to exert partner choice in order to maximize later return benefits (e.g., agonistic support).

The above considerations about the role of partner choice in the evolution of reciprocal altruism have important implications for how we can demonstrate actual cases of reciprocal altruism. Demonstrating reciprocal altruism implies showing the existence of a contingency between action and reciprocation. In other words, it needs to be shown that if B is altruistic to A, then A will increase its probability of being altruistic to B. Also, if B fails to reciprocate, then A will stop being altruistic. Traditionally, this contingency has always being conceived as a (short-term) temporal contingency (Seyfarth, 1991; Seyfarth and Cheney, 1988). However, this is not necessary. If our reasoning about the role of partner choice is correct, then demonstrating contingency could also involve showing (longer-term) changes in partner choice in response to an increase or decrease in reciprocation. In this view, showing the existence of a group-wide correlation (e.g., a matrix correlation) between giving and receiving (Fig. 1) while controlling for any known confounding variable (e.g., kinship, availability) comes closer than has been generally assumed to demonstrating reciprocal altruism. In fact, group-wide correlations show that the probability of an animal (A, in the example above) being altruist to another is related to the amount of altruism received. It shows this, not by comparing the behavior of A at different times, but by comparing the behavior of A toward B and C (i.e., different individuals). As such, group-wide correlations constitute evidence of the first (A gives in relation to what is received), but not of the second

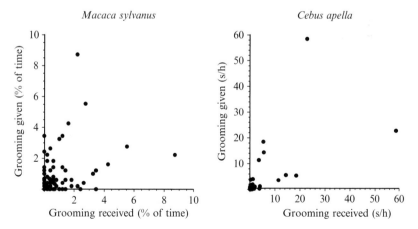

FIG. 1. Two examples of partner choice in grooming reciprocation (left: Barbary macaques, *Macaca sylvanus*; right: tufted capuchin monkeys, *Cebus apella*). The graphs show the amount of grooming given in relation to grooming received. Each point represents a different dyad. Unpublished data based on Aureli et al. (1997) and Schino et al. (2009b).

part (A stops giving if B fails to reciprocate) of the example above. Some form of experimental manipulation is probably necessary to provide evidence that failure to reciprocate causes a reduction in altruism received (e.g., Krams et al., 2008).

In summary, for group living animals such as primates, partner choice is likely to represent a critical aspect of reciprocity, as it allows the maximization of received benefits even when costs are small or absent. Animals are thus expected to direct their low-cost altruism preferentially to those group mates that reciprocate most. In the following section, we review some of the evidence supporting this hypothesis.

II. PARTNER CHOICE AS A WAY OF MAXIMIZING RECEIVED BENEFITS

Extensive evidence exists that primates direct their altruistic/mutualistic behaviors preferentially to those group members that reciprocate most. This kind of preference is generally tested using some sort of matrix correlation technique or, more recently, general linear mixed models. Since these tests aim at excluding the influence of kin selection, they typically have to control statistically for the effect of kinship, so as to make sure that the observed reciprocity is not an artifact due to a mutual preference among kin. Some of these tests also controlled for the amount of time spent in spatial proximity (e.g., de Waal and Luttrell, 1988; Romero and Aureli, 2008; Schino et al., 2007), based on the reasoning that reciprocity could occur as a by-product of interindividual proximity. It should be noted, however, that hypothesizing that reciprocation is a by-product of spatial proximity implies assuming that altruism is directed to neighbors unconditionally (i.e., with a fixed probability not dependent on amount of altruism received). This strategy, however, would not be evolutionary stable, as it would easily be invaded by a mutant that shows a reduced probability of being altruistic toward neighbors. Altruism would then collapse rapidly, since lower and lower levels of altruism would be selected for. We, therefore, believe symmetrical factors such as interindividual spatial proximity are unlikely to provide a general explanation for reciprocity.

"In kind" reciprocation, that is, reciprocal exchanges of a single "currency," has been shown for grooming, coalitionary support, and meat sharing (Fig. 1). Leinfelder et al. (2001, in captive hamadryas baboons, *Papio hamadryas hamadryas*), Mitani (2006, in wild chimpanzees, *Pan troglodytes*; see also Watts, 2002 for other data on the same population), Payne et al. (2003, in wild samango monkeys, *Cercopithecus mitis erythrarchus*), and Schino et al. (2003, 2009b, in captive Japanese macaques, *Macaca fuscata*, and tufted capuchin monkeys, *Cebus apella*) have all shown that primates groom preferentially those group mates that groom them most. De Waal and Luttrell (1988, in captive rhesus and stumptail macaques, *Macaca mulatta* and *Macaca arctoides*, and chimpanzees), Mitani (2006, in wild chimpanzees), Silk (1992, in captive bonnet macaques, *Macaca radiata*), Watts (1997, in wild gorillas, *Gorilla gorilla beringei*), and Widdig et al. (2000, in free-ranging *Macaca sylvanus*) have reported similar results for coalition formation: primates supported preferentially those individuals that supported them most. Mitani (2006) also observed reciprocal meat sharing in chimpanzees. Primate data on grooming reciprocation have been synthesized in a recent meta-analysis based on 48 primate groups belonging to 22 different species (Schino and Aureli, 2008a). This meta-analysis reported a relatively high weighted average correlation ($r = 0.468$) between amount of grooming given and received after controlling for the influence of maternal kinship, showing that primates, as a whole, recipro-cate the amount of grooming received (Fig. 2).

More controversial is the exchange of different altruistic behaviors ("currencies"). Mitani (2006) found that wild chimpanzees exchanged meat sharing for coalitionary support and grooming, while Gilby (2006) reported that grooming had only a limited influence on meat sharing and

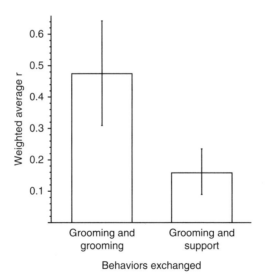

Fig. 2. A comparison of the results of two meta-analyses of primate reciprocation. Weighed average r values (and 95% confidence intervals) for the exchange of grooming for other grooming and of grooming for agonistic support. Data from Schino (2007) and Schino and Aureli (2008a).

suggested harassment and persistent begging were better predictors of the probability of meat sharing. Most of the published tests for the exchange of different currencies involved the exchange of grooming and support, as initially hypothesized by Seyfarth (1977). Henzi and Barrett (1999) have emphasized how, what originally was a hypothetical assumption underlying a theoretical model, was later uncritically accepted as a fact even if supporting evidence was scanty. These criticisms prompted renewed testing and the new evidence that is now accumulating suggests that, given the relative rarity of coalition formation, very large databases are needed to demonstrate a relation between grooming and agonistic support. Published reports remain contradictory; for example, Mitani (2006) and Schino et al. (2007) found reciprocal exchanges of grooming and support in Japanese macaques and chimpanzees, while Silk et al. (2004) found no significant effects in baboons (*Papio hamadryas cynocephalus*). The inconsistency of the available evidence constitutes an ideal case to test the usefulness of meta-analysis as applied to animal behavior. Summarizing the results of 36 independent tests involving 14 different species, Schino (2007) reported a weak but highly significant weighted average correlation between grooming and support ($r = 0.157$). Note that the strength of the relationship between grooming and support is considerably lower than that between giving and receiving grooming (Fig. 2). Besides helping solve a controversy that had raged through primatology for over 30 years, this latter study highlights the power of meta-analysis in tackling problems characterized by small effect sizes but large biological significance.

Having shown that grooming can indeed be exchanged for agonistic support, Schino (2007) also helped to solve the puzzle of primate preference for grooming high-ranking group mates. This preference was part of the predictions of Seyfarth's original model, and is indeed widespread among primates, as shown in the very first application of meta-analysis to the study of animal social behavior (Schino, 2001). However, in the absence of evidence that rank-related benefits (such as agonistic support) could indeed be exchanged for grooming, this widespread preference for high-ranking grooming partners was difficult to explain.

Recent experimental evidence also concurs in supporting the notion that primates use partner choice to maximize received benefits (Melis et al., 2006a). Chimpanzees were asked to solve a problem (pulling two ropes simultaneously in order to obtain a food reward) that required the collaboration of a group mate, and allowed to choose between two potential partners that differed in their ability to provide help. Chimpanzees consistently chose the best collaborator, thus maximizing success in the experimental task.

Partner choice is not limited to primates. Spotted hyenas (*Crocuta crocuta*) living in groups with high levels of fission–fusion dynamics (Aureli et al., 2008; Holekamp et al., 1997) preferentially joined subgroups containing higher-ranking animals in exchange for increased tolerance (Smith et al., 2007). In mobbing a predator, pied flycatchers (*Ficedula hypoleuca*) helped their reciprocating neighbors more than their nonreciprocating neighbors (Krams et al., 2008). Finally, Romero and Aureli (2008) showed that coatis (*Nasua nasua*) reciprocate agonistic support in a way similar to primates.

What is still missing in our understanding of reciprocal partner choice is how the relative value of the different currencies may vary across different species or populations. Overall, there is some evidence that within-species variation in the tendency to groom up the hierarchy is positively related to the steepness of the dominance hierarchy and negatively related to the tendency to reciprocate grooming (Barrett et al., 1999; Schino and Aureli, 2008b; Stevens et al., 2005a). It appears that steeper dominance hierarchies make rank-related benefits (such as tolerance or coalitionary support) more valuable and thus increase the amount of grooming that is directed up the hierarchy. We have, however, little understanding of the ecological underpinnings of variations in the steepness of dominance hierarchies (see Thierry, 2008 for a critical account) and we still know very little about interspecific variations (see Schino and Aureli, 2008b for a failed attempt). Furthermore, some primate taxa such as the genus *Cebus* are notoriously inconsistent in their relation between grooming and dominance rank (although in the case of capuchins small group size may be at the basis of the observed variability; see Schino et al., 2009a for a discussion of various hypotheses).

III. THE PROXIMATE MECHANISMS OF PARTNER CHOICE

A. DISTINGUISHING PROXIMATE CAUSATION AND ULTIMATE FUNCTION

Our understanding of the proximate mechanisms underlying reciprocation and partner choice has been hampered by a continuing confusion between proximate causation and ultimate function (de Waal, 2008). In terms of ultimate function, altruistic behaviors are maintained (i.e., favored by selection) because of the subsequent benefits they bring about. Consequently, there has been a tendency to erroneously assume that altruistic behaviors are also (proximately) motivated by their future benefits, that is, by the expectation of reciprocation. Sometimes this tendency has shown itself in the form of ambiguous language (Harcourt, 1992). In other cases, the assumption has been explicit (Koyama et al., 2006; Ramseyer et al., 2006; Tomasello and Call, 1997; Vonk et al., 2008).

Barrett et al. (2007) and Henzi and Barrett (2007) have highlighted this assumption and pointed out its weakness. Given the limited understanding that primates have of future events (Roberts, 2002), the assumption that they "plan" social interactions in order to gain future benefits may well be unwarranted. At about the same time, Stevens and colleagues (Stevens and Hauser, 2004; Stevens et al., 2005b) noted that reciprocation can be strongly constrained by temporal discounting (the tendency to devalue future rewards), and suggested cognitive limitations may explain the rarity of animal altruism. These suggestions were followed by experimental studies showing that primates are unable to wait more than a few minutes in an exchange task with a human experimenter, and this observation led to the conclusion that reciprocation of altruistic behavior, when it occurs, must necessarily be immediate (Dufour et al., 2007, in chimpanzees; Ramseyer et al., 2006, in tufted capuchin monkeys). In a naturalistic context, Barrett et al. (1999), Chancellor and Isbell (2009), Manson et al. (2004), Payne et al. (2003), and Port et al. (2009) observed that various primate species time-matched the grooming they had just received, although Gumert and Ho (2008) and Schino et al. (2003, 2009b) obtained different results and questioned the appropriateness of the analytical methods adopted by the previous studies.

It is interesting to note that critics of the assumption that primates can plan their social interactions in order to obtain benefits in the distant future also remained trapped by confusion between proximate causation and ultimate function. Having recognized that long-term reciprocation had been assumed to be based on a planning ability that is unlikely to exist, these authors did not challenge the assumption, but concluded that long-term reciprocation could not exist. In doing so, they again assumed that reciprocity could only be proximately motivated by the expectation of a future reward, the only difference from previous authors being the length of the temporal horizon available to the animals.

In contrast, we argue that hypotheses about proximate causation should not necessarily be modeled on ultimate functions. Altruistic behaviors are selected for because of the *subsequent* benefits they bring about, but what motivates animals to act altruistically are the *previous* benefits they received. This proximate mechanism is favored by natural selection because past behavior is generally predictive of future behavior.

If altruism is proximately motivated by the expectation of a future reward, then reciprocation should always be immediate, because of temporal discounting and the inability of animals to foresee future events. On the contrary, if altruism is proximately motivated by past altruism received, then reciprocation and partner choice can occur over much longer time frames, since what is needed is only a partner-specific "memory" of the receipt of altruism. Note here that episodic memory is not needed, since the simple formation of an emotional bond can suffice (see below). Thus, understanding the time frame of reciprocation and partner choice can provide critical information for testing whether past or future events motivate animal altruism. Before reviewing the results of studies that have addressed this topic, however, we will spend a few more words on the hypothesized role of temporal discounting.

B. THE ROLE OF TEMPORAL DISCOUNTING

Much has been said about the role of temporal discounting in constraining animal reciprocation. Animals heavily discount future rewards, that is, they are less and less willing to work for a reward that is progressively delayed. The curve describing temporal discounting is extremely steep, so that several species (from rats to monkeys) discount rewards by 50% in just 2–10 s (Stevens and Hauser, 2004; Stevens et al., 2005b). Temporal discounting is thought to be adaptive because of the uncertainty associated with future events (e.g., an external disturbance factor may prevent the animal from collecting the reward). It has been suggested that temporal discounting of future rewards strongly constrains the ability of animals to reciprocate. This suggestion, as mentioned above, is based on the assumption that animal altruism is proximately motivated by the expectation of a future reward (the reciprocation), and by a comparison between present costs and future benefits. Clearly, under this assumption, the inability of animals to wait for more than a few seconds should strongly limit their ability to reciprocate over long time periods. Reciprocation, in this view, is either immediate or impossible. More generally, this view of reciprocation implicitly assumes that nonhuman reciprocal altruism is governed by the rules of learning theory and operant conditioning. As noted by Noë (2006, p. 13), it seems that when it comes to reciprocation "the ghost of behaviorism still haunts the study of animal behavior." We argue that this view of reciprocation is untenable, and that temporal discounting and operant conditioning play almost no role in animal reciprocation (see below for possible exceptions).

We suggest that the adaptive function of temporal discounting is to help the animal deal with cause–effect relationships in the physical environment. Imagine, for example, a monkey that climbs a tree, steps onto a thin branch, and falls to the ground. It is adaptive, for the monkey, to associate stepping onto a thin branch with falling from the tree. If, however, the monkey yawned a few minutes before climbing the tree, it would not be adaptive to associate yawning with falling from the tree. Cause–effect physical relations are generally immediate, so that discounting the role of distant events is adaptive. In this view, temporal discounting is not so much about the value of future rewards, but rather about the association between an action and a future consequence. Note here that while animals cannot associate temporally distant events, they have no problem in probabilistic associations (i.e., they readily associate an action with its consequences even if those consequences have a relatively small probability of occurrence). Thin branches may or may not break but if they do, they do it immediately. That temporal discounting evolved in the context of dealing with cause–effect relations in the physical environment is also supported by recent evidence of its variation in relation to a species' foraging ecology (Stevens et al., 2005c).

Whatever its function, assigning a role to temporal discounting in regulating animal reciprocation assumes that animals have an overt cognitive representation of the immediate costs and future benefits associated with their altruistic behaviors, and that they calculate some sort of cost/benefit ratio. It also, more generally, assumes that animal altruism is governed by the rules of learning theory and operant conditioning. These assumptions have led to the view that animal reciprocation is necessarily short term. In the later text, we review evidence testing this hypothesis.

C. THE TIME FRAME OF RECIPROCATION AND PARTNER CHOICE

Until recently, studies of animal reciprocation were based on either of two different approaches. The majority looked for correlational evidence that giving was associated with receiving. These studies (that we have reviewed above and believe are important in that they demonstrate partner choice) are traditionally undervalued as they show "only correlations," which are interpreted as not providing evidence for causation. Other studies instead, examined the short-term temporal contingency between giving and receiving in a naturalistic context. Seyfarth and Cheney (1984) in their famous playback experiment on wild vervet monkeys (*Cercopithecus aethiops*) found that grooming increased the short-term willingness to attend to a request for help. In an equally ingenious experiment with captive long-tailed macaques (*Macaca fascicularis*), Hemelrijk (1994) showed that grooming increased the short-term probability of actual agonistic support. Koyama et al. (2006) obtained mixed results: the likelihood of receiving support from a chimpanzee increased if grooming was given to that individual the day before, but this was true for aggressor support and not for victim support. Finally, de Waal (1997a) observed that grooming during the previous 2 h increased the probability of partner-specific food sharing in captive chimpanzees.

Given the impact of these studies and the relevance of reciprocal altruism research in the last 30 years, it is surprising that so few studies have addressed the question of the temporal contingency between giving and receiving in a naturalistic context (see also above for the time matching of immediately reciprocated grooming, and below for data obtained in experimental "artificial" contexts). We suspect publication bias (the tendency not to publish negative results) may have played a role.

Recently, we argued that by combining the correlational and temporal contingency approaches important insights could be obtained. Schino et al. (2003, 2007) observed strong within-group correlations between grooming given and received and between grooming and support in Japanese macaques in the absence of short-term contingencies. Thus, over a period of a year, Japanese macaques groomed and supported preferentially those individuals that groomed them most, even if grooming had no immediate effect on the probability of grooming or of support. These studies were based on arbitrary definitions of what constitutes an immediate effect. For example, Schino et al. (2003) considered as immediately reciprocated those grooming episodes that occurred within 1 min of the receipt of grooming, and Schino et al. (2007) compared the probability of support in the presence versus absence of grooming in the previous 30 min. Schino et al. (2009b) improved over these earlier studies by quantifying the time frame of the effect of grooming received on the probability of grooming reciprocation. Having thus identified the time window of immediate reciprocation, they showed that even when cases of immediate reciprocation were excluded from analysis, tufted capuchins still preferred to groom those individuals that groomed them most. Again, immediate reciprocation was unable to explain partner choice, showing that monkeys base their social preferences on longer-term accounts of grooming received.

Melis et al. (2008) came to a similar conclusion on the basis of an elegant series of experiments aimed at testing whether chimpanzees reciprocate received favors. Although being helped increased the probability of helping, short-term effects were weak and unable to reverse preexisting social preferences. Finally, both Gomes et al. (2009, in wild chimpanzees) and Frank and Silk (in press, in wild baboons) reported that primates show a weaker time-match between grooming given and received when measured within a single bout or day than when measured over several months, while Gilby and Wrangham (2008), Mitani (2009), and Silk et al. (2006) provided evidence for the long-term stability of primate social preferences.

Taken together, these studies show that primates deploy their altruistic behaviors among group mates on the basis of long-term accounts of altruism received and not necessarily during short-term, immediate exchanges. It had been suggested that reciprocation should necessarily be immediate on the basis of the implicit assumption that what motivates the animal to act altruistically is the expectation of a future reward. The observation that reciprocation can occur over longer time frames provides evidence against this hypothesis. We need to explore alternative proximate mechanisms that are based on past, not future, events.

D. THE ROLE OF EMOTIONS

Our progress in understanding animal altruism may have been hindered by an unconscious equation between altruism and heroism. If animal altruism consisted of rare and very costly events, then selection would certainly favor the evolution of precise accounting methods aimed at the immediate detection of nonreciprocators. Most animal (and probably human) altruism, however, appears to consist of innumerable episodes of (almost) costless behaviors ("services" in de Waal's terminology). Among primates, these include grooming, food sharing, tolerance, and support. Under these conditions, selection can be expected to favor loose accounting mechanisms that guarantee the maximization of received benefits without necessarily being able to identify single episodes of failed reciprocation. The simplest way for evolution to build these mechanisms would have been to recruit the social bonding that (presumably) originally evolved in the context of mother–infant attachment. The recent application of the concept of "friendship" to nonhuman primates is coherent with this interpretation (Silk, 2002a,b).

What is known about the role of neuromodulators supports this view. Brain opioids are involved in social bonding (with both mothers and unrelated group mates; Barr et al., 2008; Schino and Troisi, 1992) as well as being modulated by grooming interactions (Keverne et al., 1989). Oxytocin underlies social bonding (both maternal and pair bonds; Insel and Shapiro, 1992a,b) and plays a role in modulating trust, an important component of the human capacity for altruism (Kosfeld et al., 2005).

The importance of social bonds is testified by the efforts primates make in ensuring their stability. For example, if two group members have an aggressive conflict that disturbs their cooperative relationship it is likely that they exchange a friendly contact to reconcile and restore their relationship (Aureli et al., 2002). It should be noted, however, that saying that animals put efforts into the stability of their social relationships does not imply that they are consciously striving for some optimal status (Henzi and Barrett, 2007). Emotions such as anxiety may motivate the animals' efforts without requiring any unrealistic cognitive complexity. Aureli and Schino (2004) in reviewing the role of emotions in primate social relationships noted that emotions may be part of a homeostatic mechanism of social regulation in which they act as both causes and consequences of social interactions. For example, anxiety is a consequence of the receipt of aggression, and appears also to play a role in facilitating reconciliation, thus reducing the probability of further aggression even in the absence of any cognitive understanding or estimate of the probability of future events (Aureli, 1997).

Emotions may play a similar role with regard to reciprocity. We have argued elsewhere (Schino et al., 2007, 2009b; see also Aureli and Schaffner, 2002; Melis et al., 2008; Romero and Aureli, 2008; van Hooff, 2001) that reciprocity and partner choice could be maintained by a system of emotionally based bookkeeping that allows the long-term tracking of reciprocal exchanges with multiple partners without causing an excessive cognitive load. Aureli and Schaffner (2002) and Aureli and Whiten (2003) suggested that emotions may often mediate primates' behavioral "decisions" (see also Damasio, 1996; McElreath et al., 2003). They construed emotions as intervening variables that are affected by previous social interactions and in turn affect subsequent interactions. As such, emotions may be part of a relatively simple mechanism that allows bookkeeping of social interactions and (importantly) conversion into a common currency. We thus suggest that the exchange of services triggers partner-specific emotional variations, and that animals make their behavioral decisions on the basis of the emotional states associated with each potential partner. The development of differential social bonds with individual group mates, thus, corresponds to an emotionally based bookkeeping system of received services in which emotions provide the basis for "rules of thumb" that guide social choices. This hypothetical mechanism is thus reminiscent of de Waal's (2000) attitudinal reciprocity, although we pose greater emphasis on comparative partner choice. However, while de Waal (2000) construed attitudinal reciprocity as based on short-term variations in emotional states depending on recent social interactions, we argue emotional mediation acts in a longer time frame, making it unnecessary to assume that attitudinal reciprocity is necessarily short term.

An important aspect of the emotional mediation hypothesis is that it incorporates a mechanism for the conversion of the different currencies that animals exchange. The receipt of the various forms of altruism (grooming, support, etc.) may have qualitatively similar emotional consequences and these, in turn, may have qualitatively similar effects on the probability of returning the various forms of altruism. It is possible to imagine that, although qualitatively similar, the emotional consequences of the receipt of various forms of altruism may differ quantitatively. This mechanism would thus allow for different "exchange rates" among the various currencies. Note, finally, that by modifying exchange rates natural selection or individual experience could allow flexibility in the value attached to the different currencies in relation to variations of ecological conditions or, in a biological market perspective, in the status of the marketplace. Determining how complex or simple this hypothetical mechanism of exchange rate is will depend on our understanding of the neural basis of social emotions and of how these are modulated by the receipt of different altruistic behaviors.

The hypothesis of an emotional mediation of reciprocity is consistent with recent evidence that primates are spontaneously altruistic in the absence of any immediate reward (Burkart et al., 2007; de Waal et al., 2008; Warneken et al., 2007; but see Silk et al., 2005; Vonk et al., 2008 for contrasting results). De Waal et al. (2008) suggested that some level of empathy could be at the basis of spontaneous altruism and noted that in both humans and animals empathy is biased toward familiar partners. If receiving altruistic behaviors such as grooming increases empathic responses this could provide a way for the emotional mediation of reciprocity. Fraser et al. (2008) observed that among chimpanzees, postconflict consolation (possibly involving some form of empathy) was more common toward close associates, and de Waal et al. (2008) showed experimentally that in capuchin monkeys spontaneous altruism increased with social closeness, being lowest toward strangers and highest toward kin.

These observations, together with the hypothesis of an emotional mediation of reciprocity, raise the issue of the emotional salience of the different altruistic behaviors. In discussing the limited effect of having just been helped to obtain some food on chimpanzee's willingness to reciprocate the favor, Melis et al. (2008) noted that behaviors that are outside of the normal repertoire of a species may lack the emotional salience needed to trigger reciprocity. The lack of emotional salience of the currency under study may explain the somewhat inconsistent results of attempts to experimentally demonstrate reciprocal altruism in laboratory settings (Cronin and Snowdon, 2008; Hattori et al., 2005; Hauser et al., 2003; Werdenich and Huber, 2002). It is possible that being helped to operate a mechanism in order to obtain a food reward does not have the same emotional consequences as does being groomed or being supported during an aggressive encounter. Under these experimental conditions animals have to learn (presumably by some form of operant conditioning) the consequences of their actions. They may thus be forced to rely on cognitive mechanisms of bookkeeping and expectation of future rewards, with the consequence that all of the constraints identified by Stevens and colleagues (Stevens and Hauser, 2004; Stevens et al., 2005b) come into play.

Admittedly, direct tests of the hypothesis of an emotional mediation of reciprocity are not easy to conceive. One possibility that comes to mind is the middle- to long-term pharmacological manipulation of emotional states. For example, given the role of endogenous opioids in regulating affiliative interactions (Keverne et al., 1989; Schino and Troisi, 1992), chronic administration of low doses of morphine would likely cause social withdrawal and a sustained decrease in the involvement in grooming interactions. This deterioration of social bonds is expected to affect, for example, the willingness of *untreated* group mates to provide agonistic support to the treated subject. The critical question would then be: how long would it take for the reduction in grooming induced by morphine to decrease the willingness of *untreated* group mates to provide agonistic support? Under the emotional mediation hypothesis we may predict that relatively long periods (weeks?) of social withdrawal by treated subjects would be needed before any reduction in the willingness to provide help is seen in untreated subjects.

The hypothesis that the various kinds of altruism differ in their emotional salience could be tested by neuroimaging studies of the neural correlates of the receipt of various kinds of altruism (Sanfey, 2007; van't Wout et al., 2006). We may predict that the emotional consequences of the receipt of grooming (a natural behavior presumably having a significant emotional salience) should be different from those of receiving food via the pressing of a lever by a group companion (an artificial situation presumably having little emotional salience). However, given our present limited knowledge it is difficult to make more precise predictions.

Indirect tests of the emotional mediation hypothesis may include comparative analyses of the role of short-term interactions in determining partner choice. It could be predicted that in those species characterized by stronger and more stable social bonds, short-term interactions should play a minor role in determining partner choice. Conversely, in those species characterized by more transient social interactions immediate reciprocation should be prominent. Similarly, it is also possible that, within species, immediate reciprocation would be more common in dyads having weaker social bonds than in those having stronger bonds. There is indeed limited supporting evidence for this prediction. Both de Waal (1997a) and Seyfarth and Cheney (1984) observed stronger short-term effects of grooming on reciprocation in less closely bonded dyads.

E.   THE DIFFERENT KINDS OF COOPERATION EXPERIMENTS

Before concluding this review, we need to spend a few words on laboratory cooperation experiments. Although these experiments are often discussed within the framework of reciprocal altruism theory, we believe they constitute a heterogeneous group that requires some clarification. Generally speaking, two kinds of cooperation experiments can be conducted in laboratory settings. These experiments ask fundamentally divergent questions, so it is important to highlight their differences. As we will show, they also differ in their relevance to our understanding of reciprocal altruism.

The first kind of experiment examines what we may call cooperation literally defined (i.e., coordinated action to reach a common goal). In these experiments animals have to act simultaneously to obtain a reward that cannot be obtained by a single individual (Chalmeau, 1994; Chalmeau et al., 1997; Cronin et al., 2005; Hattori et al., 2005; Melis et al., 2006b; Mendres and de Waal, 2000). These experiments aim at testing the animals' ability to perform coordinated action, and their capacity for understanding each other's role in the coordinated effort. As such, they offer little insight for our understanding of reciprocity since, as discussed above, a crucial component of reciprocal altruism is the time lag between action and reciprocation.

The second kind of experiment focuses on reciprocation. In these experiments each animal acts individually to deliver a reward to a partner, and the roles are then reversed. Note that there is no need for coordination, since the action of a single individual is sufficient to reach the goal (Hauser et al., 2003; Werdenich and Huber, 2002). While in principle experiments of this kind could provide important insights for our understanding of reciprocal altruism, we believe their relevance may be strongly limited by the artificiality of the experimental setup. As noted above, the emotional salience of receiving a piece of food as a consequence of the partner's pressing of a lever may be small. If emotions do play a role in facilitating reciprocal interactions, then these experiments may lack a crucial component of naturally occurring altruism. Note here that it is entirely possible to conceive laboratory experiments that capture the essential features of naturally occurring altruism, including retaining its emotional value (de Waal, 1997b, 2000).

In an intermediate experimental setup, animals are asked to make a coordinated effort, but the two partners receive different rewards. These experiments test the willingness of animals to tolerate the unfair sharing of a reward, and their ability to deploy their effort in relation to the projected return (Brosnan et al., 2006; de Waal and Davis, 2003). Again, they are of little interest in the context of this review.

Although these different kinds of experiments are sometimes all included during discussions on altruism (Noë, 2006), they ask fundamentally different questions and are, in our opinion, better kept separate. Problems of communication and coordinated action are irrelevant for reciprocal altruism. In fact, the animals' inability to understand a partner's role in a cooperation experiment does not in any way interfere with their ability, for example, to reciprocate grooming. On the other hand, experiments that test reciprocal interactions often fail to include the essential emotional aspects of naturally occurring altruism.

As noted above, demonstrating that failure to reciprocate causes a reduction in altruism is likely to require some experimental manipulation. Up to now, however, attempts in this direction have met with variable success (Krams et al., 2008; Melis et al., 2008). It is possible that the inconsistency of results is partly attributable to the lack of emotional salience associated to some of the experimental setups. It is left to the ingenuity of animal behaviorists to devise experimental settings that include the relevant features of naturally occurring altruism.

IV. CONCLUSIONS

Almost 40 years after its publication, the theory of reciprocal altruism still generates debate and new insights (Trivers, 2006). Although researchers have focused their attention mostly on the evolutionary aspects of altruism, in recent years a growing interest in its proximate causation is leading to a more balanced and complete view of the biology of altruism.

We have tried to contribute to this progress by suggesting two complementary hypotheses. First, we have noted that reciprocal partner choice may have played a significant role in the evolution of primate altruism, especially low-cost altruism. Second, we have argued that a system of emotional bookkeeping may be (possibly together with other mechanisms) at the basis of primate reciprocation. This system would allow comparative partner choice without the need for complex cognitive abilities.

Research conducted on human subjects has included emotions as a significant aspect of altruism (Rilling et al., 2002; Sanfey, 2007; van't Wout et al., 2006). Up to now, however, the interest of researchers has been mostly in investigating negative emotions associated with the detection of cheaters (Fehr and Gächter, 2002). As we believe cheating may have played a relatively minor role in the evolution of the most common low-cost altruistic behaviors, a greater attention to the positive emotions associated to the receipt of altruism (Güroglu et al., 2008; McCullough et al., 2008) and their possible role as a bookkeeping mechanism would be warranted.

In this picture, unfortunately, nonhuman primates are conspicuously absent (see de Waal et al., 2008 for a notable exception). It is hoped that this review may help stimulate new research aimed at investigating the role that emotions may play in the social life of nonhuman primates.

V. SUMMARY

This chapter reviews recent work on reciprocal altruism in primates with the aim of highlighting the roles that reciprocal partner choice may have had in the evolution of primate altruism, and that emotions may play in supporting primates' ability to exert such reciprocal partner choice.

Individual studies and meta-analyses show that primates reciprocate a variety of behaviors that benefit other individuals (be they altruistic or mutualistic). These behaviors include grooming, agonistic support, and food sharing. Analyses of the time frame of these reciprocal exchanges suggest primates deploy their altruistic behaviors among group mates on the basis of long-term accounts of altruism received, and are thus not constrained to immediate reciprocation. We argue that a system of emotional bookkeeping of benefits received may be at the basis of primate reciprocation. This hypothesis is consistent with behavioral data and with our current knowledge about primate cognitive abilities and the neurobiological correlates of affiliative behaviors. Investigations of the role that emotions play in the social life of primates may help us bridging the gap between the apparent complexity of their social life and the relative simplicity of their cognitive abilities.

Acknowledgments

We thank Tim Roper for inviting us to write this review, and Jane Brockmann, Tim Roper, and an anonymous reviewer for their comments on a previous version. During writing, G.S. was supported by a grant from the TECT Programme (The Evolution of Cooperation and Trading) of the European Science Foundation (SOCCOP Project, The Social and Mental Dynamics of Cooperation) and F.A. benefited from useful exchanges supported by the INCORE project (Integrating Cooperation Research across Europe; contract number 043318) funded by the European Community's Sixth Framework Programme.

References

Aureli, F., 1997. Post-conflict anxiety in nonhuman primates: the mediating role of emotion in conflict resolution. Aggress. Behav. 23, 315–328.

Aureli, F., Schaffner, C.M., 2002. Relationship assessment through emotional mediation. Behaviour 139, 393–420.

Aureli, F., Schino, G., 2004. The role of emotions in social relationships. In: Thierry, B., Sinsh, W., Kaumanns, W. (Eds.), Macaque Societies: A Model for the Study of Social Organizations, Cambridge University Press, Cambridge, pp. 38–55.

Aureli, F., Whiten, A., 2003. Emotions and behavioral flexibility. In: Maestripieri, D. (Ed.), Primate Psychology, Cambridge University Press, Cambridge, pp. 289–323.

Aureli, F., Das, M., Veenema, H.C., 1997. Differential kinship effect on reconciliation in three species of macaques (*Macaca fascicularis, M. fuscata* and *M. sylvanus*). J. Comp. Psychol. 111, 91–99.

Aureli, F., Cords, M., van Schaik, C.P., 2002. Conflict resolution following aggression in gregarious animals: a predictive framework. Anim. Behav. 64, 325–343.

Aureli, F., Schaffner, C.M., Boesch, C., Bearder, S.K., Call, J., Chapman, C.A., et al., 2008. Fission-fusion dynamics: new research frameworks. Curr. Anthropol. 49, 627–654.

Barr, C.S., Schwandt, M.L., Lindell, S.G., Higley, J.D., Maestripieri, D., Goldman, D., et al., 2008. Variation at the mu-opioid receptor gene (OPRM1) influences attachment behavior in infant primates. Proc. Natl. Acad. Sci. USA 105, 5277–5281.

Barrett, L., Henzi, S.P., Weingrill, T., Lycett, J.E., Hill, R.A., 1999. Market forces predict grooming reciprocity in female baboons. Proc. R. Soc. Lond. B 266, 665–670.

Barrett, L., Henzi, P., Rendall, D., 2007. Social brains, simple minds: does social complexity really require cognitive complexity? Philos. Trans. R. Soc. Lond. B 362, 561–575.

Bercovitch, F.B., 1988. Coalitions, cooperation and reproductive tactics among adult male baboons. Anim. Behav. 36, 1198–1209.

Brosnan, S.F., Freeman, C., de Waal, F.B.M., 2006. Partner's behavior, not reward distribution, determines success in an unequal cooperative task in capuchin monkeys. Am. J. Primatol. 68, 713–724.

Burkart, J.M., Fehr, E., Efferson, C., van Schaik, C.P., 2007. Other-regarding preferences in a non-human primate: common marmosets provision food altruistically. Proc. Natl. Acad. Sci. USA 104, 19762–19766.

Chalmeau, R., 1994. Do chimpanzees cooperate in a learning-task? Primates 35, 385–392.

Chalmeau, R., Visalberghi, E., Gallo, A., 1997. Capuchin monkeys, *Cebus apella*, fail to understand a cooperative task. Anim. Behav. 54, 1215–1225.

Chancellor, R.L., Isbell, L.A., 2009. Female grooming markets in a population of grey-cheeked mangabeys (*Lophocebus albigena*). Behav. Ecol. 20, 79–86.

Cronin, K.A., Snowdon, C.T., 2008. The effects of unequal reward distributions on cooperative problem solving by cottontop tamarins, *Saguinus oedipus*. Anim. Behav. 75, 245–257.

Cronin, K.A., Kurian, A.V., Snowdon, C.T., 2005. Cooperative problem solving in a cooperatively breeding primate (*Saguinus oedipus*). Anim. Behav. 69, 133–142.

Damasio, A.R., 1996. The somatic marker hypothesis and the possible functions of the prefrontal cortex. Phil. Trans. R. Soc. Lond. B 351, 1413–1420.

de Waal, F.B.M., 1997a. The chimpanzee's service economy: food for grooming. Evol. Human Behav. 18, 375–389.

de Waal, F.B.M., 1997b. Food transfers through mesh in brown capuchins. J. Comp. Psychol. 111, 370–378.

de Waal, F.B.M., 2000. Attitudinal reciprocity in food sharing among brown capuchin monkeys. Anim. Behav. 60, 253–261.

de Waal, F.B.M., 2008. Putting the altruism back into altruism: the evolution of empathy. Annu. Rev. Psychol. 59, 279–300.

de Waal, F.B.M., Davis, J.M., 2003. Capuchin cognitive ecology: cooperation based on projected returns. Neuropsychologia 41, 221–228.

de Waal, F.B.M., Luttrell, L.M., 1988. Mechanisms of social reciprocity in three primate species: symmetrical relationship characteristics or cognition? Ethol. Sociobiol. 9, 101–118.

de Waal, F.B.M., Leimgruber, K., Greenberg, A.R., 2008. Giving is self-rewarding for monkeys. Proc. Natl. Acad. Sci. USA 105, 13685–13689.

Dufour, V., Pele, M., Sterck, E.H.M., Thierry, B., 2007. Chimpanzee (*Pan troglodytes*) anticipation of food return: coping with waiting time in an exchange task. J. Comp. Psychol. 121, 145–155.

Dugatkin, L.A., 1988. Do guppies play tit for tat during predator inspection visits. Behav. Ecol. Sociobiol. 23, 395–399.

Fehr, E., Gachter, S., 2002. Altruistic punishment in humans. Nature 415, 137–140.

Frank, R.E., Silk, J.B. (in press). Impatient traders or contingent reciprocators? Evidence for the extended time course of grooming exchanges in baboons. *Behaviour*.

Fraser, O.N., Stahl, D., Aureli, F., 2008. Stress reduction through consolation in chimpanzees. Proc. Natl. Acad. Sci. USA 105, 8557–8562.

Gilby, C., 2006. Meat sharing among the Gombe chimpanzees: harassment and reciprocal exchange. Anim. Behav. 71, 953–963.

Gilby, C., Wrangham, R.W., 2008. Association patterns among wild chimpanzees (*Pan troglodytes schweinfurthii*) reflect sex differences in cooperation. Behav. Ecol. Sociobiol. 11, 1831–1842.

Gomes, C.M., Mundry, R., Boesch, C., 2009. Long-term reciprocation of grooming in wild West-African chimpanzees. Proc. R. Soc. Lond. B 276, 699–706.

Gumert, M.D., Ho, M.H.R., 2008. The trade balance of grooming and its coordination of reciprocation and tolerance in Indonesian long-tailed macaques (*Macaca fascicularis*). Primates 49, 176–185.

Güroglu, B., Haselager, G.J.T., Van Lieshout, C.F.M., Takashima, A., Rijpkema, M., Fernandez, G., 2008. Why are friends special? Implementing a social interaction simulation task to probe the neural correlates of friendship. Neuroimage 39, 903–910.

Hamilton, W.D., 1964. The genetical evolution of social behaviour. I & II. J. Theor. Biol. 7, 1–52.

Hammerstein, P., 2003. Why is reciprocity so rare in social animals? A protestant appeal. In: Hammerstein, P. (Ed.), Genetic and Cultural Evolution of Cooperation, MIT Press, Cambridge, pp. 83–94.

Harcourt, A.H., 1992. Coalitions and alliances: are primates more complex than non-primates? In: de Waal, F.B.M., Harcourt, A.H. (Eds.), Coalitions and Alliances in Humans and other Animals, Oxford University Press, Oxford, pp. 445–471.

Hattori, Y., Kuroshima, H., Fujita, K., 2005. Cooperative problem solving by tufted capuchin monkeys (*Cebus apella*): spontaneous division of labor, communication, and reciprocal altruism. J. Comp. Psychol. 119, 335–342.

Hauser, M.D., Chen, M.K., Chen, F., Chuang, E., Chuang, E., 2003. Give unto others: genetically unrelated cotton-top tamarin monkeys preferentially give food to those who altruistically give food back. Proc. R. Soc. Lond. B 270, 2363–2370.

Hemelrijk, C.K., 1994. Support for being groomed in long-tailed macaques, *Macaca fascicularis*. Anim. Behav. 48, 479–481.

Henzi, S.P., Barrett, L., 1999. The value of grooming to female primates. Primates 40, 47–59.

Henzi, S.P., Barrettt, L., 2007. Coexistence in female-bonded primate groups. Adv. Study Behav. 37, 43–81.

Holekamp, K.E., Cooper, S.M., Katona, C.I., Berry, N.A., Frank, L.G., Smale, L., 1997. Patterns of association among female spotted hyenas (*Crocuta crocuta*). J. Mammal. 78, 55–64.

Insel, T.R., Shapiro, L.E., 1992a. Oxytocin receptors and maternal-behavior. Ann. N.Y. Acad. Sci. 652, 122–141.

Insel, T.R., Shapiro, L.E., 1992b. Oxytocin receptor distribution reflects social-organization in monogamous and polygamous voles. Proc. Natl. Acad. Sci. USA 89, 5981–5985.

Keverne, E.B., Martensz, N.D., Tuite, B., 1989. Beta-endorphin concentrations in cerebrospinal-fluid of monkeys are influenced by grooming relationships. Psychoneuroendocrinology 14, 155–161.

Kokko, H., Johnstone, R.A., Clutton-Brock, T.H., 2001. The evolution of cooperative breeding through group augmentation. Proc. R. Soc. Lond. B 268, 187–196.

Kosfeld, M., Heinrichs, M., Zak, P.J., Fischbacher, U., Fehr, E., 2005. Oxytocin increases trust in humans. Nature 435, 673–676.

Koyama, N.F., Caws, C., Aureli, F., 2006. Interchange of grooming and agonistic support in chimpanzees. Int. J. Primatol. 27, 1293–1309.

Krams, I., Krama, T., Igaune, K., Mand, R., 2008. Experimental evidence of reciprocal altruism in the pied flycatcher. Behav. Ecol. Sociobiol. 62, 599–605.

Leinfelder, I., De Vries, H., Deleu, R., Nelissen, M., 2001. Rank and grooming reciprocity among females in a mixed-sex group of captive hamadryas baboons. Am. J. Primatol. 55, 25–42.

Manson, J.H., Navarrete, C.D., Silk, J.B., Perry, S., 2004. Time-matched grooming in female primates? New analyses from two species. Anim. Behav. 67, 493–500.

McCullough, M.E., Kimeldorf, M.B., Cohen, A.D., 2008. An adaptation for altruism? The social causes, social effects, and social evolution of gratitude. Curr. Dir. Psychol. Sci. 17, 281–285.

McElreath, R., Clutton-Brock, T.H., Fehr, E., Fessler, D.M.T., Hage, E.H., Hemmerstein, P., et al., 2003. The role of cognition and emotion in cooperation. In: Hemmerstein, P. (Ed.), Genetic and Cultural Evolution of Cooperation, MIT Press, Cambridge, MA, pp. 125–152.

Melis, A.P., Hare, B., Tomasello, M., 2006a. Chimpanzees recruit the best collaborators. Science 311, 1297–1300.

Melis, A.P., Hare, B., Tomasello, M., 2006b. Engineering cooperation in chimpanzees: tolerance constraints on cooperation. Anim. Behav. 72, 275–286.

Melis, A.P., Hare, B., Tomasello, M., 2008. Do chimpanzees reciprocate received favours? Anim. Behav. 76, 951–962.

Mendres, K.A., de Waal, F.B.M., 2000. Capuchins do cooperate: the advantage of an intuitive task. Anim. Behav. 60, 523–529.

Mesterton-Gibbons, M., Dugatkin, L.A., 1997. Cooperation and the prisoner's dilemma: towards testable models of mutualism versus reciprocity. Anim. Behav. 54, 551–557.

Milinski, M., 1987. Tit-for-tat in sticklebacks and the evolution of cooperation. Nature 325, 433–435.

Mitani, J.C., 2006. Reciprocal exchanges in chimpanzees and other primates. In: Kappeler, P.M., van Schaik, C.P. (Eds.), Cooperation in Primates and Humans, Springer–Verlag, Berlin, pp. 107–119.

Mitani, J.C., 2009. Male chimpanzees form enduring and equitable social bonds. Anim. Behav. 77, 633–640.

Noë, R., 2001. Biological markets: partner choice as the driving force behind the evolution of mutualism. In: Noë, R., van Hooff, J.A.R.A.M., Hammerstein, P. (Eds.), Economics in Nature, Cambridge Universtiy Press, Cambridge, pp. 93–118.

Noë, R., 2006. Cooperation experiments: coordination through communication versus acting apart together. Anim. Behav. 71, 1–18.

Packer, C., 1977. Reciprocal altruism in *Papio anubis*. Nature 265, 441–443.

Payne, H.F.P., Lawes, M.J., Henzi, S.P., 2003. Competition and the exchange of grooming among female samango monkeys (*Cercopithecus mitis erythrarchus*). Behaviour 140, 453–471.

Port, M., Clough, D., Kappeler, P.M., 2009. Market effects offset the reciprocation of grooming in free-ranging redfronted lemurs, *Eulemur fulvus rufus*. Anim. Behav. 77, 29–36.

Ramseyer, A., Pele, M., Dufour, V., Chauvin, C., Thierry, B., 2006. Accepting loss: the temporal limits of reciprocity in brown capuchin monkeys. Proc. R. Soc. Lond. B 273, 179–184.

Rilling, J.K., Gutman, D.A., Zeh, T.R., Pagnoni, G., Berns, G.S., Kilts, C.D., 2002. A neural basis for social cooperation. Neuron 35, 395–405.

Roberts, W.A., 2002. Are animals stuck in time? Psychol. Bull. 128, 437–489.

Romero, T., Aureli, F., 2008. Reciprocity of support in coatis (*Nasua nasua*). J. Comp. Psychol. 122, 19–25.

Sanfey, A.G., 2007. Social decision-making: insights from game theory and neuroscience. Science 318, 598–602.

Schino, G., 2001. Grooming, competition and social rank among female primates: a meta-analysis. Anim. Behav. 62, 265–271.

Schino, G., 2007. Grooming and agonistic support: a meta-analysis of primate reciprocal altruism. Behav. Ecol. 18, 115–120.

Schino, G., Aureli, F., 2008a. Grooming reciprocation among female primates: a meta-analysis. Biol. Lett. 4, 9–11.

Schino, G., Aureli, F., 2008b. Trade-offs in primate grooming reciprocation: testing behavioural flexibility and correlated evolution. Biol. J. Linn. Soc. Lond. 95, 439–446.

Schino, G., Troisi, A., 1992. Opiate receptor blockade in juvenile macaques: effect on affiliative interactions with their mothers and group companions. Brain Res. 576, 125–130.

Schino, G., Ventura, R., Troisi, A., 2003. Grooming among female Japanese macaques: distinguishing between reciprocation and interchange. Behav. Ecol. 14, 887–891.

Schino, G., Polizzi di Sorrentino, E., Tiddi, B., 2007. Grooming and coalitions in Japanese macaques (*Macaca fuscata*): partner choice and the time frame of reciprocation. J. Comp. Psychol. 121, 181–188.

Schino, G., Di Giuseppe, F., Visalberghi, E., 2009a. Grooming, rank, and agonistic support in tufted capuchin monkeys. Am. J. Primatol. 71, 101–105.

Schino, G., Di Giuseppe, F., Visalberghi, E., 2009b. The time frame of partner choice in the grooming reciprocation of *Cebus apella*. Ethology 115, 70–76.

Seyfarth, R.M., 1977. A model of social grooming among adult female monkeys. J. Theor. Biol. 65, 671–698.

Seyfarth, R.M., 1991. Reciprocal altruism and the limits of correlational analysis. J. Theor. Biol. 153, 141–144.

Seyfarth, R.M., Cheney, D.L., 1984. Grooming, alliances and reciprocal altruism in vervet monkeys. Nature 308, 541–543.

Seyfarth, R.M., Cheney, D.L., 1988. Empirical tests of reciprocity theory—problems in assessment. Ethol. Sociobiol. 9, 181–187.

Silk, J.B., 1992. The patterning of intervention among male bonnet macaques: reciprocity, revenge, and loyalty. Curr. Anthropol. 33, 318–325.

Silk, J.B., 2002a. Cooperation without counting: the puzzle of friendship. In: Hammerstein, P. (Ed.), Genetic and Cultural Evolution of Cooperation, MIT Press, Boston, pp. 37–54.

Silk, J.B., 2002b. Using the 'F'-word in primatology. Behaviour 139, 421–446.

Silk, J.B., Alberts, S.C., Altmann, J., 2004. Patterns of coalition formation by adult female baboons in Amboseli, Kenya. Anim. Behav. 67, 573–582.

Silk, J.B., Brosnan, S.F., Vonk, J., Henrich, J., Povinelli, D.J., Richardson, A.S., et al., 2005. Chimpanzees are indifferent to the welfare of unrelated group members. Nature 437, 1357–1359.

Silk, J.B., Alberts, S.C., Altmann, J., 2006. Social relationships among adult female baboons (*Papio cynocephalus*). II. Variation in the quality and stability of social bonds. Behav. Ecol. Sociobiol. 61, 197–204.

Smith, J.E., Memenis, S.K., Holekamp, K.E., 2007. Rank-related partner choice in the fission-fusion society of the spotted hyena (*Crocuta crocuta*). Behav. Ecol. Sociobiol. 61, 753–765.

Stevens, J.R., Gilby, C., 2004. A conceptual, framework for nonkin food sharing: timing and currency of benefits. Anim. Behav. 67, 603–614.

Stevens, J.R., Hauser, M.D., 2004. Why be nice? Psychological constraints on the evolution of cooperation. Trends Cogn. Sci. 8, 60–65.

Stevens, J.M.G., Vervaecke, H., De Vries, H., Van Elsacker, L., 2005a. The influence of the steepness of dominance hierarchies on reciprocity and interchange in captive groups of bonobos (*Pan paniscus*). Behaviour 142, 941–960.

Stevens, J.R., Cushman, F.A., Hauser, M.D., 2005b. Evolving the psychological mechanisms for cooperation. Annu. Rev. Ecol. Evol. Syst. 36, 499–518.

Stevens, J.R., Hallinan, E.V., Hauser, M.D., 2005c. The ecology and evolution of patience in two New World monkeys. Biol. Lett. 1, 223–226.

Thierry, B., 2008. Primate sociolecology, the lost dream of ecological determinism. Evol. Anthropol. 17, 93–96.

Tomasello, M., Call, J., 1997. Primate Cognition. Oxford University Press, Oxford.

Trivers, R.L., 1971. The evolution of reciprocal altruism. Q. Rev. Biol. 46, 35–57.

Trivers, R.L., 2006. Reciprocal altruism: 30 years later. In: Kappeler, P.M., van Schaik, C.P. (Eds.), Cooperation in Primates and Humans, Spinger-Verlag, Berlin, pp. 67–83.

van Hooff, J.A.R.A.M., 2001. Conflict, reconciliation and negotiation in non-human primates: the value of long-tem relationships. In: Noë, R., van Hooff, J.A.R.A.M., Hammerstein, P. (Eds.) Economics in Nature, Cambridge Universtiy Press, Cambridge, pp. 67–90.

van't Wout, M., Kahn, R.S., Sanfey, A.G., Aleman, A., 2006. Affective state and decision-making in the ultimatum game. Exp. Brain Res. 169, 564–568.

Vonk, J., Brosnan, S.F., Silk, J.B., Henrich, J., Richardson, A.S., Lambeth, S.P., et al., 2008. Chimpanzees do not take advantage of very low cost opportunities to deliver food to unrelated group members. Anim. Behav. 75, 1757–1770.

Warneken, F., Hare, B., Melis, A.P., Hanus, D., Tomasello, M., 2007. Spontaneous altruism by chimpanzees and young children. PLoS Biol. 5, 1414–1420.

Watts, D.P., 1997. Agonistic interventions in wild mountain gorilla groups. Behaviour 134, 23–57.

Watts, D.P., 2002. Reciprocity and interchange in the social relationships of wild male chimpanzees. Behaviour 139, 343–370.

Werdenich, D., Huber, L., 2002. Social factors determine cooperation in marmosets. Anim. Behav. 64, 771–781.

West, S.A., Griffin, A.S., Gardner, A., 2007. Social semantics: altruism, cooperation, mutualism, strong reciprocity and group selection. J. Evol. Biol. 20, 415–432.

Widdig, A., Streich, W.J., Tembrock, G., 2000. Coalition formation among male Barbary macaques (*Macaca sylvanus*). Am. J. Primatol. 50, 37–51.

Wilkinson, G.S., 1984. Reciprocal food sharing in the vampire bat. Nature 308, 181–184.

The Dog as a Model for Understanding Human Social Behavior

József Topál,* Ádám Miklósi,† Márta Gácsi,† Antal Dóka,†
Péter Pongrácz,† Enikő Kubinyi,† Zsófia Virányi,† and Vilmos Csányi†

*INSTITUTE FOR PSYCHOLOGY, HUNGARIAN ACADEMY OF SCIENCES, VICTOR H. U.
18–22, H-1132 BUDAPEST, HUNGARY
†DEPARTMENT OF ETHOLOGY, EÖTVÖS LORÁND UNIVERSITY, PÁZMÁNY P. S. 1/C,
H-1117 BUDAPEST, HUNGARY

I. Introduction

One of the important and controversial questions for cognitive science is "What makes human behavior and cognition unique in the animal kingdom?" From an empirical viewpoint, not denying the widely accepted premise that the evolution of human behavior rests crucially on uniquely human abilities, this question could be raised either from an evolutionary or from a developmental perspective. While the first approach focuses on the question, "What kind of specific changes took place during hominization?," the second approach points to the role of human social environment in the emergence of human behavior.

In searching for answers to these questions, different disciplines argue for different approaches suggesting theoretical and/or experimental analyses of human behavioral evolution and its underlying cognitive processes. At present, comparative social cognition is widely believed to be the most relevant discipline to deepen our understanding of the evolutionary origins of human behavior. Comparative social cognition looks for the presence or absence of human-like skills in animals that are often directly comparable at the behavioral level and suggests that the issue of human uniqueness can be addressed by asking about the specific behaviors of our species with respect to cognitive functioning.

The empirical answer to this question is, however, complex because behavioral traits and their underlying cognitive mechanisms develop as a result of epigenetic processes consisting of interactions between the social

71

0065-3454/09 $35.00
DOI: 10.1016/S0065-3454(09)39003-8

and nonsocial environment and the genetic makeup of the organism. According to the traditional ethological approach (Tinbergen, 1963), we must first understand the function of a behavioral trait before speculating about its underlying cognitive processing, that is, one must first separate functionally distinctive components of the observable behavioral "phenotype."

One widely used paradigm is the comparative analysis of human and nonhuman primate behavior, aimed at tracing the evolutionary origins of uniquely human skills (e.g., Povinelli et al., 1999; Tomasello and Call, 1997). This paradigm utilizes the homologous evolutionary relationship between extant nonhuman primates and humans who shared a common ancestor at some time in the distant past. Such comparative research programs are centered around the problem of whether the origin of some behavioral traits or cognitive skills can be traced back in time, that is, whether they can be assumed to have been present in the common ancestor or, alternatively, whether they have evolved after the "split" and thus are possibly adaptive (see Gould and Vbra, 1982) human-specific traits in *Homo sapiens*.

Comparative work, for example, has revealed an array of social behavioral traits which appear to have a common origin in *Homo* and apes (e.g., de Waal, 1996). The differences between humans and nonhuman great apes are of great importance because they call for specific hypotheses about the selective nature of ecological and social environments that provided the evolutionary scenario(s) since our lineage split from the other great apes (Hermann et al., 2007).

However, chimpanzees and humans not only are separated by 6 million years of evolution but they also occupy and are adapted to different niches. Species specific ecological niches can be characterized by different levels of social complexity and involve different "social problems" to solve (Humphrey, 1976). In principle, therefore, any of the social-cognitive abilities of these species could have been formed by specific adaptational demands. These selective forces were either shared for the two species (i.e., acted before the split of Pan-Homo lineage), or were different (i.e., emerged after the Pan-Homo split).

It seems that many of the specific features of human social cognition have emerged after the pan-Homo split, and therefore, we cannot explore these by the traditional human–ape comparisons. Accordingly, novel approaches may contribute a lot to exploring the evolutionary origins of the uniquely complex human cognition and behavior.

II. The Human Behavior Complex

During evolution, humans adopted a set of species-specific skills that influenced critically their social life, allowing them, for example, to form large, closed individual groups (Csányi, 2001). These include advanced cognitive skills as well as other behavioral traits which have evidently played a role in the manifestation of human-specific cognitive skills. It is unlikely that the separate effect of a single or a few behavioral features determined human evolution (see, e.g., Csányi, 2000 arguing against this approach). Most probably a wide horizon of social behaviors changed in parallel, and had a joint and synergistic effect of behavioral changes. The assembly of these traits is referred to as the "Human Behavior Complex" (Csányi, 2000).

According to Csányi (2000), during human evolution social behavior has changed in three important aspects: sociality, synchronization, and constructive activity. These can be used as broad collective groups of social behavior traits.

A. Sociality

The first one refers to those components of social behavior that contributed to marked changes in sociality. After socialization, individuals in human groups express strong attachment to each other (Bowlby, 1972). At the group level, this is manifested as loyalty, and presents a sharp contrast to the agonistic attitudes toward strange groups (xenophobia; LeVine and Campbell, 1973). Decreased aggressive tendencies and increased self-control facilitate the emergence of complex cooperative interactions, which are characterized by the subdivision of joint tasks into a set of complementary actions (Reynolds, 1993). Switching the role of the initiator in executing collaborative activities seems to be a unique feature of our species. Finally, humans have the ability to form groups that have their own identity (Csányi, 2001).

B. Synchronization

Synchronizing activities have a facilitating effect on the interaction of group members. Such synchronization is achieved by the employment of different means, such as the ability for emotional contagion (Hatfield et al., 1993), empathy or reliance on rhythms, dance and music. In addition, synchronization can be also increased by behavioral mimicry ("blind" imitation), and activities involving teaching (Csibra and Gergely, 2006) and other disciplining behaviors. The spontaneous human tendency to follow social rules (de Waal, 1996) is especially advantageous in organizing the behavior of humans living in large groups. It is assumed that through a process of internalization, social rules are incorporated in the representational system of dominance–submission relationships, and consequently humans possess a hybrid rank order system consisting of relative rankings of both individuals and particular social rules. This trait paved the way for the emergence of complex and variable social structures in human communities. At the same time, individuals are often members of different groups, follow different rules, and live in parallel and divergent rank orders. Moreover, humans in general are able to extract social rules by experiencing and observing actions and the interactions of others, similar to how a child extracts the rules of language when overhearing linguistic interactions.

C. CONSTRUCTIVE ACTIVITY

The third group of traits is concerned with the constructive character of social behavior. In contrast to animal communication systems that transmit mainly the inner motivational state of the signaler, human language enables the transfer of complex mental representations involving past, present, and future states, such as plans and desires. Being an open system, it is in principle suited for transmitting an infinite number of messages. The language system is able to represent actors, actions, and phenomena as events occurring in the environment. In addition they can be combined into novel representations as a reconstruction of reality (Brown, 1973). Importantly, such categorical representations do not presuppose the presence of language, and are very likely present in many nonhuman species (Bickerton, 1990).

Humans are not exceptional among animals in using tools, although nonhuman tool use is highly restricted for solving special tasks. Human tool use can be considered as an open constructive system that is isomorphic with linguistic competence and conceptual thinking. Humans can construct novel objects based on planning, can combine different tools, and can use them to make further tools. Objects are integrated parts of social interactions and their use and construction is heavily dependent on and influenced by, social rules, enabling the creation of machines and technologies.

The closed social system based on increased sociality together with synchronization, constructing, and conceptual abilities, has provided the basis for rich variation in individual action plans. This in turn has resulted in rapid cultural evolution. Most of the activities of these closed groups are directed upon themselves; so as a result, the group continuously reconstructs itself over time (Csányi, 1989).

The decomposition of the Human Behavior Complex into traits that can be investigated separately (see relevant parts of Table I), offers a descriptive framework for making behavioral comparisons between human and nonhuman species. The value of this comparative model depends on the degree to which the tallies of this complex can be experimentally tested and evaluated in the animal species under study.

III. COMPARATIVE APPROACHES FOR THE UNDERSTANDING OF HUMAN UNIQUENESS

Having been summarized those features of human social behavior that are assumed to have undergone marked changes after the *Pan-Homo* split, in the following sections of this review we point to the limitations of human–ape comparisons and provide arguments for developing convergent models. We propose that domestic dog (*Canis familiaris*) is a promisful candidate for convergent modeling as this species not only illustrates a single aspect of human behavior but there is a complex level of similarity in a set of functionally shared behavioral features.

Then we offer a step-by-step procedure on how to identify and utilize functionally analogous behaviors between dogs and humans and we apply the proposed approach to the case of dog–human attachment.

Finally, we summarize experimental evidence showing behavioral parallels between dogs and humans and define Dog Behavior Complex as a set of components that makes the dog compatible with human social environment.

A. LIMITATIONS OF HUMAN–APE COMPARISONS

In spite of the indisputable advantages for using homolog models in scientific investigations, human–ape comparisons also have clear limitations. Although the homologue model has a natural appeal to most scientists, recent reviews suggest that this approach is constrained both from theoretical and practical points of view (Boesch, 2007). Space constraints allow us to discuss only three of the most important constraints.

1. Problems in Verifying the Key Factor of the Evolution of Human Uniqueness

While searching for the "crucial difference" between human and nonhuman behavior and the underlying cognitive mechanisms, many researchers have focused on a single causal chain of events involving the effect of

TABLE I

A FUNCTIONAL COMPARISON OF THE HUMAN BEHAVIOR COMPLEX AND THE DOG BEHAVIOR COMPLEX

Category/dimension	Distinctive and shared components of social behavior	
	Human[a]	Dog–human mixed groups
Sociality	Attachment	Attachment to humans (Gácsi et al., 2001; Nagasawa et al., 2009; Palmer and Custance, 2008; Prato-Provide et al., 2003; Topál et al., 1998, 2005a)
	Food sharing and inequity avoidance	Inequity avoidance (Range et al., 2009)
	Group loyalty	
	Group individuality	
	Duality of intraspecific aggression	
	• Low level of intragroup aggression	Low level of intragroup aggression (Gácsi et al, 2005)
	• High level of intergroup aggression	
Synchronization	Emotional synchronization	Emotional synchronization (Odendaal and Meintjes, 2003)
	Behavioral synchronization	
	• Social learning	Social learning (McKinley and Young, 2003; Pongrácz et al., 2001a,b, 2003a,b; Topál et al., 2006a)
	• Rule following	Obeying behavioral rules (Kubinyi et al., 2003a; Topál et al., 2005b)
	• Complementary cooperation	Complementary cooperation (Naderi et al., 2001)
	• Ritual behavior	
	• Pedagogical receptivity	Pedagogical receptivity: "blind" replication of the human's behavior (Erdöhegyi et al., 2007; Szetei et al., 2003)
	• Selective imitation	Selective imitation (Range et al., 2007)
	• Teaching	

Constructive activity	
Constructing communication	
• Recognizing communicative intent of others	Selective responsiveness to human attention (Call et al., 2003; Gácsi et al., 2004; Schwab and Huber, 2006; Virányi et al., 2004)
• Initializing communication	Pointing behavior (Miklósi et al. 2000), initializing eye contact (Miklósi et al. 2003)
• Comprehension of the referential character of the gestures	Utilizing human directional gestures (Miklósi et al., 1998; Riedel et al., 2008; Soproni et al., 2002)
• Linguistic skills	Linguistic skills: fast mapping, learning by exclusion (Kaminski et al., 2004), using lexigrams to communicate requests (Rossi and Ades, 2008)
Tool use	
Tool construction	

The former consists of important behavioral traits (components) that are assumed to have played an important role in Hominine evolution (only the main components are listed; modified after Csányi, 2000). In the case of the later, we provide a list of functionally convergent behavioral features that have gained some experimental support in recent research.

[a]For detailed references in the case of the Human Behavior Complex see Csányi, 2000.

environmental factors and adaptive behavioral responses or they have argued for a restricted set of cognitive skills gaining significance during our evolution.

In line with this approach, several theorists have developed specific proposals about human uniqueness. Tomasello et al. (1993), for example, pointed out the importance of complementary cognitive mechanisms (e.g., linguistic skills, theory of mind) that make someone able to learn "culturally." In a more recent study, Tomasello et al. (2005) have argued that the crucial difference between human and nonhuman cognition is in the ability of "shared intentionality" based on construction of dialogic cognitive representations and mind reading. Other key features of hominization are supposed to be the emergence of identification-based imitative learning (Tomasello et al., 2003), or the evolution of the ability to teach and to learn from teaching (pedagogical receptivity—Csibra and Gergely, 2006). Regarding the human specificity of imitative abilities it has been shown, for example, that humans but not chimpanzees tend to copy even when it is not obvious how the action will bring about a desired result (Horner and Whiten, 2005).

Others suggest that as a result of hominization the importance of direct aggression in the maintenance of partnership and rank order within the group has gradually diminished, while within group interactions have been increasingly influenced by cooperative tendencies (Hare and Tomasello, 2005). These specific changes in temperament might have freed sociocognitive abilities from situational limitations in humans. For example, visual perspective taking is a highly generalizable skill among humans and has especial importance in the development of understanding communicative referential acts in infants (e.g., Flom et al., 2004). Chimpanzees, however, show this ability only when competing for food and not in cooperative tasks (Hare et al., 2000; Povinelli et al., 1990). The fact that apes usually underperform in cooperative tasks suggests that their social competence is biased toward competitive situations (Hare, 2001). In line with this assumption recent experiments seem to provide evidence that apes (Melis et al., 2006), unlike humans (Warneken and Tomasello, 2007), show limitations in cooperation.

The general problem with such ideas is that due to a lack of historical data there are problems in verifying the evolutionary scenario. Also, the emphasis on a single "main" cognitive feature obscures the real complexity of sociocognitive behavior. Such sequential approaches to human behavioral evolution can be contrasted with system theoretical models (Csányi, 1989) emphasizing the parallel nature of changes that have taken place in the process of human behavioral evolution. Accordingly, parallel emergence of some behavioral alterations and their simultaneous presence might provide a more plausible hypothesis for human-specific behavior.

In line with these, human evolution is best viewed as a process that affected many features of social behavior in a complex interacting way (Byrne, 2005; Hermann et al., 2007).

2. Concerns with the Sample Size, Rearing Condition, and Differences in Social Experience

In contrast to the large number of human subjects who have been involved in experimental studies of social-cognitive abilities, most nonhuman ape studies were conducted on a few human-reared subjects. The traditional technique has been to bring wild-caught animals to the laboratory and/or socialize captive born individuals with humans. However, this has introduced a complicating factor because these apes or monkeys are variously constrained in getting species-specific experience and, in addition, they are exposed to a variable extent to some aspects of the human social environment. Therefore, behavioral resemblances or similarities in performance could often be dismissed as peculiarities of the subjects' exposure to humans, while any differences could be explained by the lack of either familiarization with the human environment and/or social behavior or the lack of species-specific experiences (e.g., Bering, 2004). The high variability in environmental experience and the low number of individuals studied raise problems of external validity including the reproducibility of the research. This is most striking when a few "arbitrarily chosen" apes are compared to a large number of children. What is more, adult apes are often compared to human infants without controlling for external variables including previous experience and experimental/developmental factors.

3. Welfare Problems

The maintenance of apes and monkeys in captivity for experimental purposes creates an unsolvable welfare problem because these artificial environments cannot fulfill the natural needs of the species. The paradox here is that the more we know about the apes' complex social and mental skills, the less we become entitled to keep them under artificial conditions. Even if there are possibilities that could offer partial solution for the problems raised above (e.g., studying apes at habituated sites in their natural environment; Boesch et al., 1994), it is time to look for alternative and complementary paradigms.

B. CONVERGENT MODELING

While the evolutionary reasoning behind homologue models seems to be simple and straight forward, the argument for developing convergent models is more complicated. Convergent evolution is assumed when similarities between evolutionarily unrelated characters of species are attributed to their independent adaptation to similar environments. Thus, the detection of phenotypic convergence in different species lies at the heart of the evolution-ary argument because it provides critical evidence for the operation of adaptive processes. However, adaptation is a complex process that may involve single traits, correlated traits, or even a set of complex changes (Gould and Vbra, 1982). For example, to adapt to living in water, Cetaceans underwent a series of changes including morphological (e.g., skin, limbs, and body form), physiological (e.g., brain functioning, breath regulation), and behavioral (e.g., communication) modifications (see also Marino, 2002).

From our point of view, the most interesting question is whether such changes are single isolated convergent adaptations or whether they should be viewed as a complex set of traits emerging in concert. This is particularly important in the case of human evolution where one tries to separate homologous traits from those that emerged under neutral conditions or are adaptations to certain environmental challenges. In the case of behavior, the only possible solution seems to be to look for other organisms that evolved under similar adaptational challenges. Studies on a wide range of species seem to suggest that convergent approaches would be useful (e.g., dolphins: Herman, 2002; corvids: Emery and Clayton, 2001), but these are functionally restricted in the sense that they model only a narrow aspect of human behavior.

Alternatively, the development of human-like behaviors can be facili-tated by raising individuals of evolutionarily distant species in the human social environment. Such an example comes from the "Alex project" in which an African gray parrot provided evidence for conceptual quantitative ability (Pepperberg, 1987), social learning, and communicative abilities (Pepperberg and McLaughlin, 1996), in addition to remarkable linguistic skills (Pepperberg, 1991, 1992). These studies clearly argue that tamed animals are being shaped (in the psychological sense of the word) by their human environment. Human handling ensures very complex stimulation which may lead to the development of such complex behavioral and/or cognitive skills that are unobserved in natural environment (Bering, 2004). However, since the captive environment is ecologically irrelevant for the subject's individual development, it is unclear how the process of socializa-tion (enculturation) affects cognitive development and the emergence of different cognitive skills in these cases (Gomez, 2004).

Although many different species have been used for human–animal comparisons to model one or another aspect of the "hominization" process, there seems to be no perfect solution. For analyzing a wide spectrum of interacting phenotypic features a "multifunctional" species would be needed that shares an evolutionary and developmental history with humans by living in a similar environment.

C. THE DOG AS A CANDIDATE FOR COMPARATIVE STUDIES

On the basis of recent experimental evidence (for reviews, see Miklósi, 2007; Miklósi et al., 2004) it has been argued that the dog presents a useful subject for the comparative study of human social evolution (Hermann et al., 2007) and this species may be the "new chimpanzee" for studies of comparative social cognition (Bloom, 2004). There are several reasons for why dogs and not other species, including other domestic animals could be a primary target for convergent modeling (Table II).

1. The Dog Is Unique Among Domesticated Species

Although a handful of animal species have come into contact with humans through the process of domestication, the dog is unique. The dog's origin dates back earlier than that of any other domestic species (Savolainen et al., 2002) and dogs have survived in various niches provided by humans. Many argue that in the last 15,000–20,000 years dogs invaded the human niche by displaying traits which enhanced their survival in human groups (e.g., Paxton, 2000; Schleidt and Shalter, 2003). Unlike other domestic species, dogs are used and probably have been selected for many different functions in human groups including such "ancient" roles as hunting or guarding (Clutton-Brock, 1995)

TABLE II

A POSSIBLE UTILIZATION OF DOGS IN COMPARATIVE INVESTIGATIONS (BASED ON MIKLÓSI, 2007; TIMBERLAKE, 1993)

		Genetic relatedness	
		Low	High
Ecological relevance	High	Dog versus human (e.g., communicative behavior) *Convergence*	Among subspecies of wolf or wolf versus coyote and jackal *Microevolution*
	Low	Dog versus human (e.g., manipulating ability) *Classification*	Wolf versus dog (e.g., territorial behavior) *Homology*

The table shows that the nature of comparisons depends on the behavioral trait in question but will in many cases provide complementary information.

and more "novel" ones like assisting disabled people (James and MacDonald, 2000). They provide also emotional support (Wells, 2004) and participate in therapeutic programmes (Odendaal, 2000).

Although little is known about how early stimulation affects the development of dog–human relationship, dogs seem to be predisposed to develop close contact with humans (Gácsi et al., 2005) and human social environment seems to provide a natural niche for dogs (Miklósi, 2007). This is true, despite the fact, that the levels of socialization among dog and human populations are highly variable, ranging from stray dogs that fend for themselves in or around villages and live in very loose contact with humans to others that spend their life as pets in homes with their human owners. Even if some dog populations have lost most of their direct contact with humans, living as feral animals for many generations, the interspecific contact can be reestablished rapidly because the genetic variability between pet dogs and stray or feral dogs is smaller than the environmental variability causing behavioral differences in these phenotypes (Boitani et al., 1995). Since pet dogs can revert to feral life within a few generations (Daniels and Bekoff, 1989), the reverse is possibly also true for feral animals. The lack of an appropriate social environment can also cause irreversible effects on social behavior toward humans in the case of both dogs (Scott and Fuller, 1965) and humans (Candland, 1993).

Evolutionary parallels can be observed in cats or horses, where the domestication process has contributed to their adaptation to the human environment. However, in these noncanine cases, the transition from the wild to the domesticated is likely to represent an earlier state of domestication than is the case for dogs (Bradshaw and Cook, 1996; Bradshaw et al., 1999).

2. Comparison with the Ancestor Is Important for Convergent Modeling and the Dog Has a Living Ancestor, the Wolf (Canis lupus)

Dogs offer a unique opportunity for making behavioral comparisons not only with the "niche mate," the human, but also with the living ancestor, the wolf. The wolf provides a very useful comparative background, because we assume that the convergent skills of extant dogs are derived from homologous traits of the wolf (Kubinyi et al., 2007). For example, wolves show complex social behavior involving cooperation in hunting and parental care, expressive means of communication, and context-dependent dominance relationships (Mech and Boitani, 2003). Presumably, the presence of these skills facilitated the successful adaptation of the dogs' ancestor to the human social environment and served as the basis for the emergence of specific social behaviors. In our view, the divergence of dogs and wolves involved a process in which the emergence of the dog was accompanied by increased sociality, cooperativeness, and communicability in the anthropo-genic environment analogous to the changes that took place during hominization (i.e., the divergence of the *Pan-Homo* clade).

3. The Dog Represents a Natural Experimental Model and They Are Less Exposed to Risk of Welfare and Sample Size Problems

Apart from the evolutionary and developmental arguments elaborated above, this model has many practical advantages. Dogs sharing our life as companions are not only exposed to an environment that shares many physical and social factors that influence human life but observing free-ranging dogs in their natural environment allows for setting up situations in which the subjects can be tested in a rigorous manner. This includes the possibility of comparing directly the behavior of dogs and humans using similar experimental protocols without removing the subjects from their natural environment (e.g., Lakatos et al., 2009). This method has the potential to achieve higher external validity owing to a theoretically unlimited number of subjects.

In addition, the life history of dogs reveals important parallels with humans, which makes the dogs a valuable subject also for applied disciplines of biology. For example, recent studies have advocated the use of dogs as natural models of human psychiatric conditions (Overall, 2000) or aging (Milgram et al., 2002). These approaches rely heavily on the evolutionary convergence of the two species in combination with proximate causal factors such as unnatural (or lack of) social experiences causing malformation of social behavior or the extension of life expectancy in some dog populations due to increased protection from environmental challenges.

IV. STUDYING DOG–HUMAN PARALLELS

Human–dog comparisons have already been initiated long ago (e.g., Scott, 1992; Scott and Fuller, 1965), especially with regard to social behavior. However, these authors did not make explicit whether the comparisons were built upon a presumed homologous or convergent relationship. Based on evidence pointing to temporal and geographical coincidence between the emergence of mankind and dogkind, others have also noted that the evolution of the dog–human relationship was "closely woven" (Paxton, 2000; Schleidt and Shalter, 2003), and analogies have been argued for in the case of social-communicative skills (Hare and Tomasello, 2005) and personality models (Jones and Gosling, 2005).

A. A NEW APPROACH

Either explicitly or implicitly, recent enthusiasm for studying dogs reinforces the view that this animal species can provide a unique possibility for
modeling human behavior. The significance of identifying evolutionary
convergence between dogs and humans is that this makes it possible to
draw inferences from dog evolution to human evolution regarding the
factors that contributed to the rise of human-specific behaviors. However,
whilst the aforementioned dog–human comparisons focus on single behavioral traits, here we propose a system theoretical approach. This aims at
finding out whether and how the interaction between separate behavioral
changes leads to the accumulation of social skills that could resemble in
many respects the human social behavioral system. We suggest that the
comparative study of social cognition in dogs has the potential to answer
questions regarding the functionality of human behavioral components and
the following hypothesis could provide an operational framework for this.

1. The Working Hypothesis

The three main dimensions of the Human Behavior Complex (sociality,
behavioral synchronization, and constructive skills) are assumed to have
undergone changes after the *Pan-Homo* split. Taking a behavioral evolutionary perspective, the divergence of the dog from the wolf represents
steps taken in the same direction of increased sociality, cooperability, and
communicability as has been observed in the case of the *Pan-Homo* clade.
As a result of this evolutionary parallel, dogs possess a set of functionally
analogous skills corresponding to that of humans, which can be derived
from homologous traits of the wolf. Although the time scale is evidently
different (i.e., wolf–dog separation took place a few tens of thousands of
years ago, whilst the *Homo*-line diverged 6 million years ago), in our view
the evolution of dogs mirrors some aspects of hominization. It follows from
this that many social skills in dogs have undergone convergent evolutionary
changes (Miklósi et al., 2004) and the study of the behavioral convergences
between dogs and humans offers a comprehensive framework for understanding the evolutionary emergence of human social behavior (Fig. 1).
Naturally, we are aware that dogs cannot fully mirror the Human Behavior
Complex because of a number of evolutionary constraints including differences in anatomy and cognitive processing. Convergent behavior modeling
emphasizes the surface similarity of the behavior, and investigates the
extent of the functional resemblance between humans and dogs, without
making specific assumptions regarding the underlying cognitive capacities
and physiological mechanisms controlling these skills.

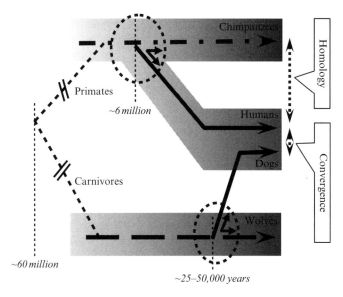

Fig. 1. Divergent and convergent evolution in the Canidae and Hominidae. Although at different time scales it is assumed that behavioral evolution in both cases was subjected to similar selective pressures which resulted in the emergence of convergent social features shared by humans and dogs, which distinguish them from chimpanzees and wolves, respectively. Accordingly, the wolf–dog split can be regarded as a model for early behavioral divergence in the *Pan-Homo* clade (based on Miklósi, 2007).

V.   How to Identify and Utilize Convergent Behaviors Between Dogs and Humans?

On the basis of the above working hypothesis, we offer a step-by-step procedure by using examples from different aspects of social behavior because, at present, no single trait has yet been subjected to sufficiently detailed analysis.

A.   Decomposition of Dog Behavior into Discrete, Functionally Separated Components

To identify convergent behaviors between dogs and human first we need to decompose the behavior of dogs into separate traits patterned after the Human Behavior Complex, and evaluate these behavioral components in comparison to humans. Functional correspondence of dog and human social behaviors cannot only be expected based on their shared evolution and development, but has already been confirmed by empirical evidence in cases of some behavioral traits.

For example, the Human Behavior Complex indicates that increased sociality has led to behavioral scenarios in which intensive gestural communication both facilitates joint collaborative group actions and ensures effective knowledge transfer in the form of teaching. Humans, even in early infancy, show special sensitivity to such "ostensive" cues that signal the teacher's communicative intention and are able to fast learn the contents of communicative interactions through a human-specific social learning system called natural pedagogy (Csibra and Gergely, 2006). Such a disposition prepares infants to efficiently learn from adults in wide range of situations (Gergely et al., 2007; Topál et al., 2008). There is accumulating evidence that dogs are also able to display some of the abilities required by the receptive side of teaching interactions: sensitivity to the human's communicative intent (e.g., Kaminski, 2009; Pongrácz et al., 2004) and to the referential character of human cuing (e.g., Riedel et al., 2008; Soproni et al., 2001). In line with these observations, those skills that makes the dog able to show relevant responsiveness to human communicative gestures, could be regarded as a functionally separated component of the dog behavior repertoire that is comparable to that of human's skills. Future research could find out what are the shared and distinctive traits in comparison with wolves and human infants?

B. INTRASPECIFIC COMPARISON OF FUNCTIONALLY CORRESPONDING
    BEHAVIOR BETWEEN DOGS LIVING IN A HUMAN ENVIRONMENT
    AND WOLVES LIVING IN THEIR NATURAL HABITAT (OR UNDER
    SEMINATURAL CONDITIONS)

The ethological approach holds that species comparisons should be based on natural behavior, which is by definition displayed under natural conditions. Behavioral differences that could be the result of evolutionary/ functional and/or developmental origin could provide the starting point for further investigations. Notwithstanding the fact that such research projects have a considerable history in ethology (Fentress, 1967; Fox, 1971; Frank and Frank, 1982), systematic comparisons are lacking because in the case of both wolves and dogs, the ideal circumstances for data collection are difficult to establish. The shyness of wolves and their long traveling distances prohibit close observation in nature and captive observation often produces behavioral artifacts. Similarly, with a few exceptions intraspecific observations on dogs are simply lacking. Nevertheless, the few relevant studies that exist provide a good starting point in the case of play (Bekoff, 1974), vocalization (Feddersen-Petersen, 2000), or agonistic behavior (Goodwin et al., 1997). Comparing the human-related social behavior of dogs to intraspecific wolf behavior would be necessary to investigate whether dog–human similarities reflect indeed convergences or rather homologous traits shared by wolves, dogs, and humans (and probably other social mammals).

C. INTERSPECIFIC BEHAVIORAL COMPARISONS OF HAND-REARED WOLVES AND DOGS

Raising wolves and dogs identically in human environment, and comparing their human-related behavior is crucial to account for possible environmental effects. It has been often argued (e.g., Udell et al., 2008) that the behavior of dogs is mainly the result of environmental influences dominated by human intervention. If the environment of wolves and dogs is equalized then the remaining behavioral differences could be explained in terms of inherited factors (and/or maternal prenatal influences). Although there have been a number of attempts for interspecific comparisons (e.g., Frank and Frank, 1982; Hare et al., 2002; Udell et al., 2008), there has been huge variability in the socialization of both the wolves and the dogs. This could have confounded the observed differences.

In a recent series of studies using extensively socialized hand-reared wolves and dogs, behaviors were compared in a divergent array of contexts involving humans and dogs, including social preferences (Gácsi et al., 2005), attachment to humans (Topál et al., 2005a), interspecific gestural communication (Udell et al., 2008; Virányi et al., 2008), and interaction with humans in problem solving situations (Miklósi et al., 2003). These studies point to important species-specific differences that can be attributed, at least in part, to the dogs' evolutionary adaptation to the human niche.

D. COMPARING DOGS AND HUMANS IN FUNCTIONALLY SIMILAR SITUATIONS

Based on behavioral differences between dogs and wolves found in steps 2–3, one could predict functional similarities between humans and dogs. In search for evolutionary convergent behaviors in dogs and humans the direct comparison of the two species is indispensable. There are various possibilities for comparing human and dog behavior because of the close similarity in the developmental environments and the relative absence of experimental or technical limitations for both observational and experimental work (in comparison with apes). One can also control for assumed cognitive skills and/or durations of social experience and utilize human children for comparison, or one can compare directly the behavior and performance of adults in both species.

For example, the dogs' ability to rely on various forms of human directional gestures can be directly compared with corresponding skills of human
infants at various ages. The results show that dogs' performance can be
equated with that of 1.5–2-year-old children (Lakatos et al., 2009). Also,
like 3-year-old children, dogs can discriminate between behaviorally very
similar visual cues when they differ in referential function only and not in
their effectiveness as discriminative cues (Povinelli et al., 1999; Soproni
et al., 2001). Moreover, pet dogs and 2.5-year-old children show functionally similar behaviors in tailoring their communication to others' state of
knowledge in an "out-of-reach reward" task (Virányi et al., 2006).

E. COMPARISON OF UNDERLYING CONTROLLING FACTORS AT THE
    BEHAVIORAL, PHYSIOLOGICAL, AND GENETIC LEVELS

Once a reasonable level of functional convergence has been established,
one might search for underlying causal factors (Miklósi et al., 2007). Dogs
provide a very interesting model for such an approach because they come in
genetically partially isolated populations and also because, within limits,
there is the possibility of manipulating their physical and social environment. This provides a natural scenario for testing interactions between both
genes and genetic background or genes and environment. Such investigations could reveal that the controlling factors behind convergent traits can
be different even while sharing some basic features. Such a case has been
revealed recently where activity/impulsivity in dogs (measured by an application of a human ADHD questionnaire, Vas et al., 2007) seems to be
influenced by similar genetic factors (a gene coding for dopamine receptor,
DRD4) while very probably the precise underlying genetic mechanism is
different (Héjjas et al., 2007a,b, 2009). These results and the recent publication of the dog genome (Lindblad-Toh et al., 2005; Parker et al., 2004) offer
new opportunities for the utilization of dogs in the understanding of causal
factors in human diseases and phenotypic malformations (Sutter et al., 2007).

VI. USING THE APPROACH: ATTACHMENT AS A CASE FOR
     CONVERGENT BEHAVIOR

Wickler (1976) defined attachment as a long-lasting attraction to a particular set of stimuli, which manifests itself as particular behaviors directed
toward or performed in the presence of these stimuli ("objects of attachments") in addition to maintaining proximity to the relevant stimuli over a
period of time. This operational description is consistent with Bowlby's
(1972) assumptions that attachment is a behavior-controlling structure,

which evokes a particular set of actions in stress situations (e.g., separation from the object of attachment). In practice, the existence of attachment-systems is usually decided upon fulfillment of certain behavioral criteria (Rajecki et al., 1978). In general, the organism should display separation stress in the absence of, seek proximity and contact with, and show specific greeting behavior in the presence of the object of attachment, which is at least quantitatively different from similar actions performed toward a stranger. In the following, we argue for behavior convergence in dogs and humans in the case of attachment. However, the lack of extensive research in this area means that many questions still remain to be answered.

Step 1: Is attachment a separable component of dog behavior?

It has often been assumed that humans live in a natural relationship with dogs which can be interpreted in the framework of social attachment (e.g., Serpell, 1996). A range of questionnaire studies has established that owners regard pet dogs as family members (e.g., Albert and Bulcroft, 1987). Owners attribute cognitive and emotional skills to their dogs that are in many respects similar to a 6-year-old child (Rasmussen and Rajecki, 1995) and owners are inclined to describe the relationship with their dog in terms of attachment (Poresky et al., 1987). This anthropomorphic attitude gains some support from observational studies revealing analogies in child–human and dog–human interaction (Prato-Previde et al., 2006) including verbal communication, such as the use of "motherese" and "doggerel," respectively (see Hirsch-Pasek and Treiman, 1981; Mitchell, 2001). Finally, at the behavioral level, Topál et al. (1998) were the first to reveal child–dog analogies in the pattern of attachment, which have since been replicated in other laboratories (e.g., Marston et al., 2005; Prato-Previde et al., 2003). Results show a characteristic selective responsiveness to the human caregiver (owner) in both dog puppies and adult ones, and this supports the view that attachment is a functionally distinct component of the social behavior of the dog.

Step 2: Is there evidence for intraspecific attachment behavior in dogs or wolves?

Very few studies reflect on the attachment-like relationships among wolves in their natural habitat or among feral dogs. For example, LeBoeuf (1967) describes a group of dogs reared together and associations between pairs of dogs but this was related to the sexual context, and the presence of attachment relationship was not implicated. It seems that, except for the relatively early phase of individual development, neither dog puppies nor wolf cubs show specific attachment to their mother. Mech (1970) reported that proximity and contact seeking behavior toward the mother gradually decreases after weaning in gray wolf cubs at 6–8 weeks of age, and attachment is observed mainly toward the pack as a whole rather than a specific individual (Rabb et al., 1967). Experimental studies revealed that in 2-month-old dog puppies the bitch plays only a minor role in reducing the effect of separation stress (Elliot and Scott, 1961; Ross et al., 1960) and in choice situations puppies do not show preference for the mother in comparison with an unfamiliar bitch (Pettijohn et al., 1977). In sum, although well-designed comparative studies are lacking, both dogs and wolves seem to fulfill the operational criteria for intraspecific attachment toward their mother only in early puppyhood.

Step 3: Are there interspecific behavioral differences in attachment behavior of hand-reared wolves and dogs toward humans?

Wolf puppies that are socialized by humans show species-specific affective behaviors toward their caregivers. However, unlike dogs, gray wolves exposed both to conspecifics and humans showed a preference for the canid partner if they were offered a choice (Frank and Frank, 1982; Gácsi et al., 2005). In a recent study (Topál et al., 2005a) we have argued that if the emergence of attachment is based exclusively on social experience during early exposure to humans then wolves reared in extensive human social contact should show attachment behavior toward their human caregivers that is similar to that observed for dogs. Results show, however, that in contrast to 4-month-old dog pups, gray wolf cubs of the same age did not fulfill the criteria for attachment (Topál et al., 2005a). Despite being hand-raised and socialized to an extreme level (in contact with their owners 20–24 h/day for the first 3–4 months of their life), these hand-reared gray wolf pups did not seem to discriminate between their caregiver and a stranger greeting them when left alone in an unfamiliar enclosure. It seems that unlike dogs, the human caregiver does not act as a "secure base" for wolves in stressful situations.

These observed differences between wolves and dogs provide little support for dogs' attachment to humans being either exclusively the outcome of extensive human socialization or resulting from species-specific differences in the rate at which the development of attachment system operates (heterochrony, see Coppinger and Coppinger, 2001; Goodwin et al., 1997). This is so because even very young wolves do not show attachment behavior toward their human caregivers. Moreover, this is in contrast to widely held views since both processes have hitherto been implicated heavily in explaining the development of dog–human attachment. Such theories have assumed that the behavior of dogs shown toward the owner is derived directly from the puppy–mother relationship in wolves, supposing a behavioral homology between dog and wolf behavior.

It is not yet clear whether the development of attachment toward humans is the result of a general mechanism with low specificity for accepting social stimuli/objects as group mates, or whether the continuous selection in the human environment might have resulted in more specific changes. Regarding the genetic aspects of attachment, recent research based on comparisons of closely related species (prairie vole vs mountain vole) has suggested that small and well-defined changes at the neurogenetic level (i.e., alteration in the oxytocin and vasopressin receptor genes) can lead to marked alteration in social affiliative behavior (for a review, see Insel and Young, 2000). One may assume that similar changes should be occurring in dogs leading to the "evolutionary" emergence of attachment to humans. In the lack of experimental evidence, however, we can only speculate about this hypothesis.

Step 4: To what extent do dogs and humans show functionally similar patterns of attachment behavior?

An experimental method for studying behavioral criteria of human infant–parent attachment has been developed by Ainsworth (1969) (Strange Situation Test). She found that separation from the caregiver in an unfamiliar environment evokes anxiety in infants which is behaviorally manifested in proximity seeking. Moreover, the activated attachment system upon reunion with the mother manifests in different forms of contact seeking behaviors. This method has also been utilized to test attachment behavior in dogs (Topál et al., 1998) offering direct comparisons between the behavioral manifestation of attachment behavior in dogs and human children.

Results have confirmed functional behavioral similarities between dogs and children. Dogs displayed a specific reaction toward their owners, but not toward a stranger, by looking for them in their absence and making rapid and enduring contact upon their return. They also preferred to play with the owner, and decreased play activity in the absence of the owner (Prato-Previde et al., 2003; Topál et al., 1998). Follow-up work provided evidence that this pattern of attachment is stable over at least 1 year and is independent of the peculiarities of the testing location (Gácsi, 2003).

An important further analogy to the human case has been revealed by observing the emergence of attachment behavior in shelter dogs. These observations suggest that dogs that have been deprived of human contact (adult shelter dogs) are able and motivated to initiate a new relationship rapidly after a short duration of social contact with humans (Gácsi et al., 2001). In a similar experiment, Marston et al. (2005) found that physical contact (massage) was more effective than obedience training as a form of handling in evoking patterns of attachment toward humans.

Other observations suggest that similar to the case of human infants (Matas et al., 1978), dog–human attachment provides a kind of scaffolding for the emergence of various social behaviors in cooperative and

communicative interactions (Topál et al., 1997). In contrast to the autonomous problem-solving behavior of the wolf (Frank, 1980), dogs show a
predisposition toward engaging in joint activities with human members of
their group (see also Miklósi et al., 2003).

In summary, compared to human children, pet dogs show functionally
similar attachment behaviors toward their caregiver. Moreover, unlike
other nonhuman species, dogs retain "infant-like" attachment behavior
and are able to reestablish novel attachment relationships in their
adulthood.

*Step 5: Is there evidence for similarity in the underlying genetic and/or
physiological controlling factors of dog and human attachment behavior?*

Attachment behavior is usually evoked by situational stress which
has evident physiological correlates. In human infants, separation from
the attachment figure results in elevated levels of cortisol and heart rate
(Spangler and Grossmann, 1993). Similarly, separation from the owner
induces emotional stress in dogs (Maros et al., 2008; Palestrini et al.,
2005), which is indicated by increased heart rate frequency. Interestingly,
these changes can be reversed by specific effects. For example, Tuber et al.
(1996) found that in novel environments the increased level of cortisol can
be reduced by the presence of a familiar human but not by a familiar dog.
In a similar vein, petting by a familiar human has a relaxing effect (release
of beta-endorphin, oxytocin, and prolactin, reduction of heart rate) on both
parties (Odendaal and Meintjes, 2003) and gazing at the owner and other
social interaction initialized by the dog can increase the owner's urinary
oxytocin concentration as a manifestation of attachment behavior
(Nagasawa et al., 2009).

Moreover, one might suppose that convergence in attachment behavior
could explain similarities in behavior problems that were described both for
infants and dogs (Fox, 1975; Overall, 2000), although the only study
conducted so far did not find a direct link between attachment to owners
and separation anxiety (Parthasarathy and Crowell-Davis, 2006).

Human attachment studies have shown that different allelic variations of
human dopamine D4 receptor (DRD4) gene are associated with different
patterns of attachment in infants (Lakatos et al., 2000). Recent molecular
genetic investigations have revealed the presence of an analogue polymorphism in the dog DRD4 receptor gene (Inoue-Murayama et al., 2002),
which implies the potential for similar gene-behavior associations in this
species (Héjjas et al., 2007a,b).

Taken together, our scattered evidence suggests that changes in genetic
and physiological mechanisms might have accompanied the emergence of
human-like attachment behavior in dogs.

VII. BEHAVIORAL PARALLELS BETWEEN DOGS AND HUMANS: THE DOG BEHAVIOR COMPLEX

On the basis of evidence suggesting that dogs' behavior became to some extent functionally similar to the most important aspects of the human behavior, we propose that the model developed for the description of human behavior traits (Human Behavior Complex, see above) might provide a useful framework with which to conceptualize evolutionary changes in dogs. The Dog Behavior Complex defines those components of dog behavior for which there is evidence that they have contributed to the species' success in the human social niche. Obviously, dogs cannot fully mirror the Human Behavior Complex because of evolutionary constraints (e.g., lack of linguistic skills in dogs). In spite of this, behavioral research so far has provided ample evidence that there is a parallel between the human and Dog Behavior Complex. In the following, we provide a short summary of the available evidence concerning human-oriented social behavior in dogs, presented within the framework of the human behavioral complex.

A. SOCIALITY

Anyone who has raised wolves and developed a close relationship with them has noticed major differences between human-oriented social behavior in dogs and wolves (e.g., Fox, 1971; Frank and Frank, 1982). These differences include both affiliative and agonistic aspects of social behavior that emerge during the early stages of development and become more pronounced during adult life. So far, three main factors have been studied which influence dog–human social relationships: attachment (see above, Section VI), social attraction, and agonistic behavior.

1. Social Attraction

The behavioral manifestation of group cohesiveness and intragroup attraction that holds groups together can be defined as social attraction (Oakes et al., 1998). In contrast to attachment, which can be regarded as individual personal attraction, social attraction is based on "liking of each other as group members," not as unique individuals. For both human and nonhuman species, attraction to conspecifics is a prerequisite for forming complex social groups.

While there is an array of possible mechanisms to achieve mutual attraction among conspecifics, the situation is more complex if such attraction is expressed toward heterospecifics. The idea that dogs might have some predisposition to be attracted to humans has been around for a long time. Earlier it had been observed that dog puppies develop preferences toward humans after only a brief exposure (Stanley and Elliot, 1962) and despite being punished for social contact (Fisher, 1955). Comparative experiments provided various types of evidence that overall dogs show a stronger attraction toward humans than wolves show toward humans (Frank and Frank, 1982; Zimen, 1987).

2. Agonistic Behavior

Wolves are often portrayed as being fiercely aggressive animals, in contrast to the gentle manner of "man's best friend." Both classic studies (Scott and Fuller, 1965) and recent accounts (Hare et al., 2005) have assumed that selection has led to reduced aggressive behavior in dogs (see also Price, 1999). In contrast, other observations on dog and gray wolf puppies does not provide support for a generally lower level of aggression in the former, as dog puppies have been found to display agonistic behavior more frequently than wolves of similar age (Feddersen-Petersen, 1986). However, even wolves with extensive socialization history were more likely to growl at or bite the caretaker who handled them during the experiment (Gácsi et al., 2005). This could have been a manifestation of increased defensive aggression in wolves indicating a lower threshold for socially inflicted constraints.

With regard to the sociality component of the Dog Behavior Complex, then, we argue that both the generally lower level and increased controllability of aggression, and the more intensive social relationships, contribute to the development of closer interspecific ties between humans and dogs.

B. SYNCHRONIZATION

Synchronization can be defined as processes leading to behavioral or motivational/emotional conformity. Achieving behaviors related in time (synchrony) is essential for group cohesion (Engel and Lamprecht, 1997). Thus, the ability for behavioral synchronization probably enhanced the ability of dogs to maintain close relationships with humans. Scant research on these issues has revealed so far four aspects of dog behavior: emotional synchronization, social learning, rule following, and complementary cooperation.

1. Emotional Synchronization

Although evidence is very limited, it is likely that dogs have the ability to show emotional synchronization by attending to various visual or acoustic social signals emitted by humans. For example, a recent study provided some evidence of synchronization during heterospecific play when various play signals seemed to have the potential to evoke play behavior from the other, probably through change in mood (Rooney et al., 2001). Similarly, when approached by an unfamiliar person showing definite signs of friendliness and threat in succession, dogs show rapid changes of emotional and behavioral response in accordance with the human's attitude (Vas et al., 2005). Such emotional synchronization is a bidirectional process. There is a growing literature indicating that the mere presence of dogs or interaction with them has an effect on the emotional state of humans (see Hart, 1995 for a review; Friedmann, 1995; Wilson, 1991). As bodily contact in the form of "social grooming" is a dominant behavior for expression empathy in humans, dogs could have been selected for similar tendencies (e.g., the mutual relaxing effect of petting in Odendaal and Meintjes, 2003).

2. Behavioral Conformities Achieved by Social Learning

a. Learning from conspecifics   Social learning is potentially an efficient method of obtaining information by observing conspecifics. In the dog there is some evidence that observing conspecifics can lead to improved performance (Kubinyi et al., 2009). Slabbert and Rasa (1997), for instance, demonstrated that young police dog puppies left with their mother until 3 months old and provided with the opportunity to observe the bitch searching for narcotics, displayed superior performance when learning the same task later by comparison with control pups. In addition, puppies can learn from each other: observing a littermate pulling a small cart on a string facilitates the emergence of the same behavior later (Adler and Adler, 1977). In a more recent study dogs even seem to evaluate the action of a conspecific demonstrator (Range et al., 2007) and, similarly to human infants (Gergely et al., 2002), imitate the demonstrator's action selectively on the basis of whether or not the observed behavior was "rational."

b. Learning from humans   Dogs can use, however, also human behavior as a cue for selecting functionally similar behavior (Kubinyi et al., 2003a; Miller et al., 2009; Topál et al., 2006a) and for obtaining information to solve certain problems. Findings suggest that pet dogs are not particularly good at going around a V-shaped fence (Fig. 2) in order to get to a target (food or toy). In contrast, much improvement in performance was found when dogs were allowed to watch a human demonstrator making the detour (Pongrácz et al., 2001b). Further, dogs were able to rely on this information when they had opposing experience. In one experiment, dogs were allowed to get the food/toy through an opening in the fence at the tip of the "V." If they were prevented from choosing this route by closing the opening, the performance of most dogs fell below that showed by naïve individuals.

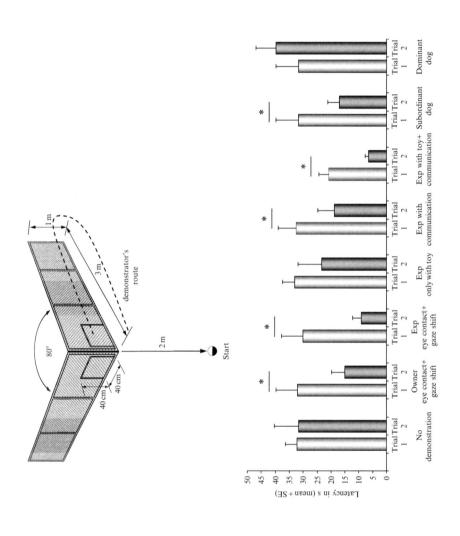

However, observer dogs could overcome this bias and develop the habit of detouring rapidly, which shows that they were able to use the information provided by the humans (Pongrácz et al., 2003a).

Dogs seem to learn differently from humans than from conspecifics (Pongrácz et al., 2008). They easily learn the detouring from another dog but a human walking around the fence can enhance their later performance only if she/he is talking to the dogs during demonstration (Pongrácz et al., 2004). The influence of human communication on the dogs' decisions is even more conspicuous when it is possible for the individual to choose between two exclusive behavioral actions, for example, if there is a conflicting situation to behave either according to earlier human actions or provide a "rational" solution to a problem. In a recent experiment dogs were observed in a two-way choice task, in which human provided information about the location of the reward in different ways (showing the content of either the empty or the baited container) and using different cues of communication (Erdőhegyi et al., 2007). We found that for the dog, the function of human demonstration is probably not transferring knowledge *per se* but transferring those behavior actions that can lead to effective behavioral synchronization (Erdőhegyi et al., 2007).

3. Rule Following

De Waal (1996) and others assume that obedient behavior of dogs and their "desire to please us" is partially based on their social skill at comprehending and following social rules (Bekoff and Allen, 1998). There is some evidence that dogs are inclined to follow social rules of the group in both the short and long term. One simple form of rule following is when the

---

FIG. 2. Dogs are not especially good at making detours. In a series of experiment Pongrácz et al. (2001b, 2004, 2008) studied how quickly the dog learns that it has first to move off from the target in order to reach it at the end of the route. Naïve dogs could develop the habit of detouring by trial-and-error learning only after 4–6 trials. In contrast, dogs improved their performance after watching a detouring human demonstrator. Importantly, human demonstrations were more effective when the detour demonstrations included cues of communication (addressing the dog, eye contact with the dog, gaze shifts between the dog and the target object). Dogs could also utilize detour demonstrations of another dog (group mate) depending on the subject's relative dominance rank with the demonstrator. Subordinate dogs displayed significantly better performance after having observed a dog demonstrator in comparison to dominant dogs. Pairs of columns indicate the latency of making the detour (mean + S.E.) in the first trial (trial 1—naïve subjects) and in the second trial (trial 2—after having observed a demonstration) of different experimental conditions. Drawing of the fence used for the social learning test is also shown. Detours were demonstrated either by the owner, or by an unfamiliar experimenter or by a familiar dog. Significant differences compared to the first trial are indicated with * $p < 0.05$.

individual develops and maintains habitual behavior in a social context in relation to its partner. The function of this form of social influence might be to avoid conflicts in the group and to cooperate in common actions without any deeper insight into the knowledge content of another's mind.

We have also found some indication for this in experimental situations developed for the study of social learning. After observing the demonstration of detouring and having detoured the V-shaped fence with a closed opening several times, dogs showed only a gradual inclination to take the shorter route to the target if the opening became available. Further analysis suggested that dogs noticed the change because they looked more frequently at the opening than they had done earlier (Pongrácz et al., 2003b). Nevertheless, the dogs followed their social tendency and only gradually gave up on this habit and shifted to the use of a more effective behavior to obtain the hidden food by walking through the opening.

In another experiment we tested whether dogs would adopt spontaneously a novel, arbitrary (actually pointless) behavior as a result of interaction with their owner. We asked dog owners to change their route after arriving back from walking the dog (Kubinyi et al., 2003b). Instead of taking the shortest route to their flat, they had to take the dog off leash and make a short detour leading away from the entrance door. They were instructed to ignore the dog during this detour until they arrived back at the door. Over a period of 3–6 months this action was repeated 180 times and the dogs gradually developed a behavior corresponding to their owners' demonstrations: half of the subjects not only escorted the owner but also overtook them and finished the detour earlier than the owner. These results indicate that after a certain amount of repetition, dogs can form expectations about the behavior of the human. This ability to anticipate the action of the other, contributes also to the manifestation of synchronized behavioral interactions between man and dog. At a behavioral level, social anticipation can also be interpreted as a mechanism for reducing conflict in the course of interaction between two parties.

Similarly, we have also explained dogs' behavior in terms of rule following when in an object permanence task (Fig. 3). We found that dogs are able to track the trajectory of an object even if it was concealed in a container (invisible hiding tasks—Watson et al., 2001). After participating in several invisible hiding trials, the object was hidden in full view of the dogs at a new location. Results showed that many subjects, in this case, showed seemingly erroneous behavior. That is, they were more inclined to seek out the hidden object at various locations rather than to go directly to the location of the object which they knew. Repeating a similar type of experiment with children and adults gave similar results, although the proportion of "searchers" in the "game" hiding trial was somewhat smaller in the case of adults

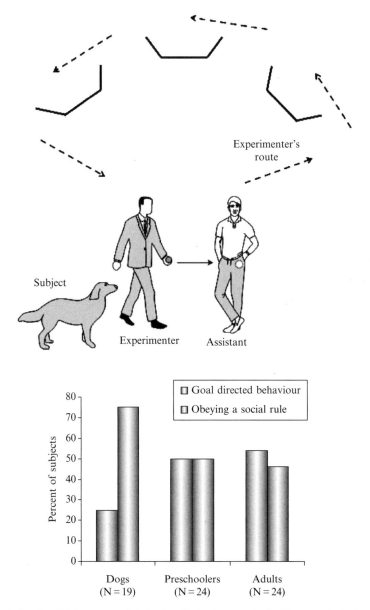

FIG. 3. In object hide-and-search tasks dogs' behavior is controlled by not only their mental representational ability but they can act on the basis of some other search rules. With the participation of a human experimenter the task becomes a sort of social game where the human is doing the hiding and the dog is searching. In a recent study (Topál et al., 2005b), the training phase (hiding the object repeatedly behind one of the identical screens) was followed by a

(Topál et al., 2005b; Fig. 3). On the basis of these observations, we may say that the ability to identify and use social rules that are formed by the interaction with the experimenter during the consecutive object hiding and search tasks may have a significant influence on the performance of both human and dog subjects.

Taken together, it seems that dogs have considerable ability to obtain information of varying complexity by observing their human companion. The accumulation of such social information could play an important role in synchronization of group activities as members of the group can act on the basis of the same knowledge. This could make interactions between companions more easy-going and more efficient.

4. Complementary Cooperation

Goals can often be achieved only by cooperative interactions with others in the group. Evidence suggests that interacting dogs and humans establish a complex behavior pattern when performing joint actions (Kerepesi et al., 2005; Rooney et al., 2001). Dogs are not only sensitive to meta-communicative signals (e.g., the play bow) in order to maintain play but also engage in complex "behavioral projects" in order to continue playing (Mitchell and Thompson, 1991). In another study, detailed observations have revealed complex interwoven behavioral interactions between blind persons and their guide dogs (Naderi et al., 2001). Dog-owner dyads sur-mounted an obstacle course, and determined the ratio of actions initialized by either the dog or the human. Although there was large variation among the dyads on average dogs and human initialized the half of the actions. Moreover, at the individual level we found that the role of the initiator was changed continuously. In most cases neither party initiated more than 2–3 actions in a row, it was most common to relinquish the initialization after one action. Such switching in leadership in addition to the dogs' ability to perform complementing actions to achieve a joint goal closely resembles cooperative activity described in the case of humans (Reynolds, 1993).

"game" trial: the toy was visibly given to the owner (who hides it in a pocket) and the experimenter took the same route without the target ("shammed hiding"). Results show that majority of dogs performed search behavior in the "game" condition. Such "counterproduc-tive" solution to the task was also observed in humans (both children and adults) and this behavior could be interpreted as the result of accepting social rules (Topál et al., 2005b). Figure shows the schematic representation of the experimental arrangement. Columns indicate the proportion of subjects (dogs, preschooler children, and adults) following goal directed behavior ("getting the object") or a social rule ("producing search behavior") when the location of the target object was well known by the subject ("game" condition).

C. CONSTRUCTING COMMUNICATION

When communicating, humans use an infinite number of communicative signals in at least the visual and acoustic modes. In addition, they apply certain signals for initializing and maintaining communication (e.g., eye-contact) and rely on various behavioral cues for recognizing attention. To what extent do dogs demonstrate these features of communication?

1. Initializing Communication with Humans

There are some indications that dogs have a strong propensity to initialize communicative interactions with humans, and for this they rely predominantly on visual signals (looking and gaze alternation) which are functionally similar to those used by humans. This pattern of behavior can be revealed in situations where dogs are exposed to insoluble problems in the presence of humans. Under these circumstances, dogs show many forms of behavior (gazing, gaze alternation, vocalization) that direct the attention of the human onto themselves or the problem to be solved (Miklósi et al., 2000). Comparative experiments have shown that this behavior pattern also emerges more readily in dogs than in hand-reared wolves (Miklósi et al., 2003; Virányi et al., 2008). There are also indications that the preference to look at the human develops very early in dogs in comparison to wolves (Gácsi et al., 2005; Fig. 4), which can in principle provide the basis for the emergence of complex communicative interactions between humans and dogs.

2. Relying on Visual Cues of Human Attention

The preference to look at the human's face might have led to enhanced skills in reading behavioral cues of human attention in dogs. In a series of experiments we have found that dogs are very sensitive to behavioral cues signaling attentiveness. According to work done by Gácsi et al. (2004) dogs readily discriminate face orientation of the human by approaching him mostly from the direction of the face when retrieving an object (see also Bräuer et al., 2004). Dogs display the same performance when they have the choice to beg from persons turning either toward or away from them, and there is suggestive evidence that they also discriminate open versus closed eyes. Dogs use eye-contact and directed talk provided by humans to infer whether they are addressed in a particular situation (Virányi et al., 2004). In the social learning context, we have found that dogs learn detouring much better if the human uses eye contact and verbal signals to get the attention of the dog (Pongrácz et al., 2004). Findings also suggest that dogs are particularly sensitive to behavioral signals of attention in commanding situations (Call et al., 2003; Virányi et al., 2004).

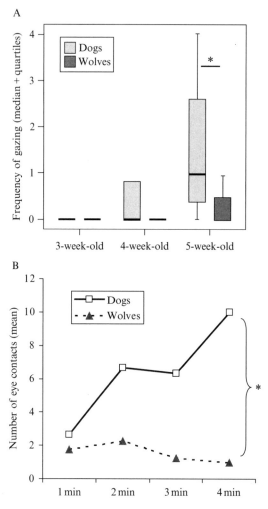

FIG. 4. In the wolf, gazing plays a crucial role in agonistic communication. The use of gazing in intraspecies aggressive interactions in dogs is basically similar to that of described in the wolf (Fox, 1971). However, with respect to nonaggressive communicative interactions dogs differ in their willingness to gaze at the human's face and this difference can be observed in early puppyhood (Gácsi et al., 2005). In contrast to wolf puppies, dogs show a clear preference for establishing eye-contact with humans in a "free approach" test (when puppies were allowed to move freely in the presence of passive "social agents") and in a "reinforced eye-contact" task (when eye-contacts initialized by the puppy was rewarded by the human). (a) the frequency of gazings (number/min) at the human face in 5-week-old hand reared gray wolf and dog puppies in a social preference test (medians + lower and upper interquartile ranges). (b) Mean number of eye contacts of 9-week-old hand reared wolves and dogs with a familiar experimenter during a 4-min-long operant conditioning test. Significant differences are indicated with * $p < 0.05$.

3. Responsiveness to Human Communicative Gestures

Recently, intensive research efforts have revealed that dogs can rely on various human bodily gestures as communicative signals. In these experiments dogs have to find hidden food based on cues provided by a human (for a review, see Miklósi and Soproni, 2006). Dogs can use various forms of pointing (e.g., Hare et al., 1998; Soproni et al., 2002), as well as head turning (Soproni et al., 2001) as indications of the location. The performance of dogs in these experiments can be compared to 1.5–2-year-old children (Lakatos et al., 2009), and young dogs are superior to hand-reared wolves (Miklósi et al., 2003), although the later can also rely on pointing cues after intensive socialization and some training (Virányi et al., 2008; but see also Udell et al., 2008). There is also evidence that dogs can interpret a human pointing gesture even in early puppyhood without any explicit training (Gácsi et al., 2009). Adult dogs are able to rely on pointing types, which lack any discriminative component (Riedel et al., 2008) or require the ability to generalize among contexts (Lakatos et al., 2009; Soproni et al., 2002; Fig. 5). In addition, other experiments have shown that some dogs prefer to rely on the pointing gesture even when they have conflicting visual or olfactory information about the location of the hidden object (Szetei et al., 2003). Recently, it has been shown that dogs are able to rely on a marker used by the experimenter to indicate the correct location of hidden food (Agnetta et al., 2000; Riedel et al., 2006).

4. "Word Learning" Capacities

Even if we have only a limited amount of experimental evidence of "word learning" capacities of dogs, in general owners have the impression that their dog comes to understand the meaning of certain verbal utterances, or at least to act as if they possessed this knowledge (Pongrácz et al., 2001a). More recent research seems to provide evidence that both the acoustic composition of the "word" (Fukuzawa et al., 2005a) and the attentional component (Fukuzawa et al., 2005b) associated with the utterance affect the performance of the dog.

Although it is widely known that dogs are able to make associations between verbal cues (words) and an action (retrieval) or an object (Young, 1991; for a review, see also Mills, 2005), there is some suggestion that dogs can make the association between a novel object and its "name" by observing/ listening to conversing humans. From language learning experiments, we know that children are very sensitive to such situations. For example, 1.5-year-old children will preferentially associate verbal cues to those objects which were in the visual focus of the adult during emitting the utterance (e.g., Baldwin and Baird, 2001). In a similar experimental situation, known as

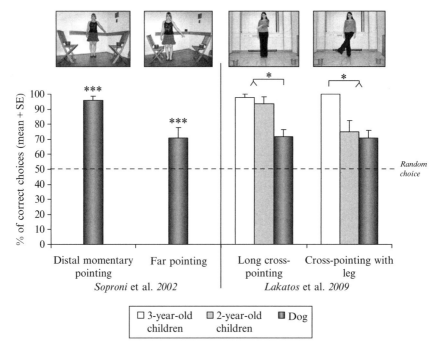

FIG. 5. Comparative investigation of the comprehension of human gestural cues is widely believed to provide useful information on the flexibility of the communicational skills of different animal species (Miklósi and Soproni, 2006). Many assume that distal momentary pointing and other types of directional gestures can be used to measure the subjects' understanding the communicative referential nature of human behavior cues (Hare et al., 2002; Miklósi et al., 1998). Recent evidence suggest that dogs may be able to decode the referential aspect of human directional gestures, and like human children, they show reliably high performance in choice tasks including various types of pointing signals (Lakatos et al., 2009; Soproni et al., 2002). Dogs' and children's performance (percent of correct choices, mean + S.E.) in different types of human pointing tests (based on Lakatos et al., 2009; Soproni et al., 2002). Significant differences compared to random choice are indicated with *** $p < 0.001$, and compared to the performance of other groups are indicated with Φ ($p < 0.05$).

Model–Rival method, Pepperberg (1991) was successful in teaching word-object associations to African gray parrots. Recently, McKinley and Young (2003) presented some evidence that dogs can also learn the name of an object when they have the chance to observe two humans naming the novel object during conversation. Very likely dogs are facilitated in doing this by the behavioral cues of humans indicating attention toward the object, as well as the object being manipulated during the conversation. In an other study, one dog has been shown to base his performance not on human behavioral cues but on previous knowledge about the names of the other familiar objects

(Kaminski et al., 2004). Although there is some disagreement on the interpretation of the underlying cognitive processes (see Bloom, 2004), this dog, knowing the names of about 200 different objects, was able to recognize that a novel utterance indicates the name of the novel object among a set of familiar objects with known names.

5. *"Mindreading" Skills*

Further interesting observations on dog communication with humans suggest that they might be able to complement information that is missing in the human. Nonverbal variants of experiments used to tap into the ability to recognize knowledge or ignorance in others (Gomez, 2004) have been applied to the dog (Topál et al., 2006b; Virányi et al., 2006). In these tasks, dogs could see a human "Hider" placing a toy object or a piece of food in one of the three identical boxes. Dogs could always know the location of the reward; however, they could get it only by the help of another human, a Helper. Experimental conditions were designed to investigate the "requesting" behavior of the dogs (signaling a baited box which is unreachable to them) on the basis of whether human "Helper" participated in object hiding events or not. Results show that in spite of the dogs' restricted gesturing abilities subjects modified their behavior adequately to the knowledge of the Helper. Although one could invoke the ability of dogs to take the other's perspective or recognize knowledge or ignorance in humans, for our purpose it is most important to note that dogs are able to provide humans with information that helps them in obtaining a goal; or, alternatively, dogs can rely on human behavioral cues indicating the lack of certain "knowledge." Cooper et al. (2003) reported corroborating evidence from an experiment utilizing the well-known Guesser–Knower paradigm (Povinelli et al., 1990). In this study, dogs could not see the hiding process, but could see that a human (the "Knower") had perceptual access to the hiding. After the hiding both the "Knower" and another human who could not see the hiding (the "Guesser") appoint one of the hiding places by their behavior and the dog is allowed to choose one of the hiding places (Cooper et al., 2003). Dogs preferred to choose the location indicated by the "Knower," however, this preference manifested only in the first trial and disappeared later, suggesting that the phenomenon is very elusive.

VIII. Conclusions

Increasing evidence suggest that wolf–dog–human behavioral comparisons offer a new and fruitful theoretical framework for comparative studies on the evolutionary emergence of social cognition. In this chapter, we argue for the development of an animal model that not only illustrates a single aspect of human behavior but that is based on a complex level of similarity in a set of functionally shared behavioral features. Our central thesis is that behavioral similarities between the dog and the human represent functional analogies resulting from comparable evolution and development in an environment established and inhabited by humans.

We have argued that three set of skills form the basis for functional behavioral analogies between dogs and humans: (1) the development of social attraction and individualized attachment toward humans and decreased levels of aggression, (2) increased and more flexible means of synchronization (behavioral and emotional synchronization, social learning, and rule following), and (3) complex, prelinguistic forms of communication allowing active information sharing and joint participation in actions. For summary of functionally convergent behavioral features and relevant experimental evidence see Table I.

Note that the wide array social skills allow a very efficient interaction between individuals even in the absence of linguistic abilities. Taking this as an analogy for human sociocognitive evolution, we suggest that early, prehistoric human groups could have engaged in very complex cooperative interactions even if they did not possess the advantages of having a language. From this it follows that the operation of the Dog Behavior Complex has the potential to reflect that early stage of hominid evolution when people facing the need for interaction had to evolve a set of social skills which provided the basis for complex interaction.

The value of this comparative modeling will depend on the degree to which the counterparts of the Human Behavior Complex can be experimentally tested and evaluated in the dog. We think that the theoretical and experimental analysis of Dog Behavior Complex in comparison with the Human Behavior Complex has the potential to provide novel answers to the question of "What makes us human?" future research should extend this approach by making more detailed investigations concerning the convergent aspects of social competence in dogs and humans and the limitations of using the dog as a model species.

IX. SUMMARY

The traditional approach for studying the evolutionary emergence of human social cognition is based on comparisons with apes and monkeys as model species with a homologous relationship to other primates and humans. Recently, however, research interest has focused on other species offering analogous models for the evolution of human social cognitive abilities. Here, we propose that convergent social evolution in dogs can be used to model the early state of human social evolution suggesting that functionally analogous forms of many traits of the Human Behavior Complex are present in dogs.

We argue that the dog as a model species is unique among domesticated species due to its special domestication history including adaptive specialization as well as developmental socialization of dogs in the human environment. Moreover the dog represents a natural experimental model for studying human behavior because (1) socialization to humans is a natural process in dogs, (2) the dog has a living ancestor, the wolf, and (3) comparison with the ancestor is important for convergent modeling.

Having argued the working hypothesis regarding the dog as a model species in studying functionally analogous behaviors of the human complex, we propose the following program of systematic data collection. First, one defines the elements of the Dog Behavior Complex as discrete, functionally separated components and selects a single component for extensive comparisons (Section V.A). Then one investigates intra- and interspecific comparisons of functionally corresponding behaviors between dogs and wolves (Sections V.B and V.C), and one makes direct comparisons of dogs and humans in functionally similar situations (Section V.D). Finally, a comprehensive approach cannot be complete without comparisons of underlying controlling factors at the behavioral, physiological, and genetic levels (Section V.E).

The experimental evidence so far available reveals some apparent, functional similarities between the human and Dog Behavior Complexes not only at the level of main dimensions (sociality, synchronization, and construction) but at the level of the components. Nevertheless, apart from a few exceptions (e.g., attachment) our present knowledge regarding the components of the Dog Behavior Complex, in comparison with the corresponding skills/traits in wolves and humans, is insufficient.

Therefore, the theoretical and practical significance and the predictive value of the dog model in understanding the evolution of human social cognition stands or falls with systematic experimentation subject to the conditions of this paradigm. We believe that further systematic comparisons involving many aspects of the Dog Behavior Complex will allow modeling of interaction between various components of the Human Behavior Complex, in contrast to other models which are mostly restricted only to a single aspect of human social cognitive skills.

Acknowledgments

The research reviewed here was the outcome of a long-term project supported by various organizations and would not have been possible without the help of the many hundreds of dog owners and the active contribution of their dogs. We are also grateful to students taking part in socializing the wolves. We thank the support of the Bolyai Foundation of the Hungarian Academy of Sciences, Hungarian Science Foundation (T049692), the European Union (FP6 NEST 012787), the charity Dogs for Humans and Horatius Ltd. We are grateful for the comments of Csaba Pléh, Daniel Mills, Paul Bloom, Colin Allen, Tim Roper, and two anonymous reviewers on an earlier version of this manuscript. We would like to express our gratitude to Bea Belényi, Borbála Győri, Anita Kurys, Gabriella Lakatos, Richárd Mányik, Csaba Molnár, Dorottya Újfalussy, Dóra Újváry, and Judit Vas.

References

Adler, L.L., Adler, H.E., 1977. Ontogeny of observational learning in the dog (*Canis familiaris*). Dev. Psychobiol. 10, 267–271.
Agnetta, B., Hare, B., Tomasello, M., 2000. Cues to food locations that domestic dogs (*Canis familiaris*) of different ages do and do not use. Anim. Cogn. 3, 107–112.
Ainsworth, M.D.S., 1969. Object relations, dependency and attachment: a theoretical review of the infant-mother relationship. Child Dev. 40, 969–1025.
Albert, A., Bulcroft, K., 1987. Pets and urban life. Anthrozoös 1, 9–25.
Baldwin, D.A., Baird, J.A., 2001. Discerning intentions in dynamic human action. Trends Cogn. Sci. 5, 171–178.
Bekoff, M., 1974. Social play and soliciting by infant canids. Am. Zool. 14, 323–340.
Bekoff, M., Allen, C., 1998. Intentional communication and social play: how and why animals negotiate and agree to play. In: Bekoff, M., Byers, J.A. (Eds.), Animal Play. MIT Press, pp. 97–114.
Bering, J.M., 2004. A critical review of the "enculturation hypothesis": the effects of human rearing on ape social cognition. Anim. Cogn. 7, 201–212.
Bickerton, D., 1990. Species and Language. Chicago University Press.
Bloom, P., 2004. Can a dog learn a word? Science 304, 1605–1606.
Boesch, C., 2007. What Makes Us Human (*Homo sapiens*)? The Challenge of Cognitive Cross-Species Comparison. J. Comp. Psychol. 121, 227–240.
Boesch, C., Marchesi, P., Marchesi, N., Fruth, B., Joulian, F., 1994. Is nut-cracking in wild chimpanzees a cultural behaviour? J. Hum. Evol. 26, 325–338.
Boitani, L., Franscisci, P., Ciucci, P., Andreoli, G., 1995. Population biology and ecology of feral dogs in central Italy. In: Serpell, J. (Ed.), The Domestic Dog: Its Evolution, Behaviour and Interactions with People, Cambridge University Press, Cambridge, pp. 217–244.
Bowlby, J., 1972. Attachment. Penguin Book, Middlesex.
Bradshaw, J.W.S., Cook, S.E., 1996. Patterns of pet cat behaviour at feeding occasions. App. Anim. Behav. Sci. 47, 61–74.
Bradshaw, J.W.S., Horsfield, G.F., Allen, J.A., Robinson, I.H., 1999. Feral cats: their role in the population dynamics of *Felis catus*. Appl. Anim. Behav. Sci. 65, 273–283.
Bräuer, J., Call, J., Tomasello, M., 2004. Visual perspective taking in dogs (*Canis familiaris*) in the presence of barriers. Appl. Anim. Behav. Sci. 88, 299–317.
Brown, R.W., 1973. A First Language: The Early Stages. Harvard University Press.
Byrne, R., 2005. Animal Evolution: foxy Friends. Curr. Biol. 15, 86–87.

Call, J., Bräuer, J., Kaminski, J., Tomasello, M., 2003. Domestic dogs are sensitive to the attentional state of humans. J. Comp. Psychol. 117, 257–263.

Candland, D.K., 1993. Feral Children and Clever Animals. Oxford University Press, New York.

Clutton-Brock, J., 1995. Origins of the dog: domestication and early history. In: Serpell, J. (Ed.), The Domestic Dog. Cambridge University Press, pp. 8–20.

Cooper, J.J., Ashton, C., Bishop, S., West, R., Mills, D.S., Young, R.J., 2003. Clever hounds: social cognition in the domestic dog (Canis familiaris). Appl. Anim. Behav. Sci. 81, 229–244.

Coppinger, R., Coppinger, L., 2001. Dogs: A Starting New Understanding of Canine Origin, Behaviour and Evolution. Scriber Press.

Csányi, V., 1989. Evolutionary Systems and Society: A General Theory. Duke University Press.

Csányi, V., 2000. The 'human behaviour complex' and the compulsion of communication: key factors in human evolution. Semiotica 128, 45–60.

Csányi, V., 2001. An ethological reconstruction of the emergence of culture and language during human evolution. In: Győri, G. (Ed.), Language Evolution. Biological, Linguistic and Philosophical Perspectives. Peter Lang, Frankfurt am Main, pp. 43–53.

Csibra, G., Gergely, G., 2006. Social learning and social cognition: the case for pedagogy. In: Munakata, Y., Johnson, M. (Eds.), Processes of Change in Brain and Cognitive Development. Attention and Performance XXI. Oxford University Press, pp. 249–274.

Daniels, T.J., Bekoff, M., 1989. Feralization: the making of wild domestic animals. Behav. Proc. 19, 79–94.

Elliot, O., Scott, J.P., 1961. The development of emotional distress reactions to separation in puppies. J. Genet. Psychol. 99, 3–22.

Emery, N.J., Clayton, N.S., 2001. Effects of experience and social context on prospective caching strategies by scrub jays. Nature 414, 443–446.

Engel, J., Lamprecht, J., 1997. Doing what everybody does? A procedure for investigating behavioural synchronization. J. Theor. Biol. 185, 255–262.

Erdőhegyi, Á., Topál, J., Virányi, Zs., Miklósi, Á., 2007. Dogs use inferential reasoning in a two-way choice task—only if they cannot choose on the basis of human-given cues. Anim. Behav. 74, 725–737.

Feddersen-Petersen, D., 1986. Observations on social play in some species of Canidae. Zoologischer Anzeiger 217, 130–144.

Feddersen-Petersen, D., 2000. Vocalization of European wolf (Canis lupus lupus) and various dog breeds (Canis lupus f. fam.). Archieves für Tierzüchtung (Dummerstorf) 43, 387–397.

Fentress, J.C., 1967. Observations on the behavioural development of a hand-reared male timber wolf. Am. Zool. 7, 339–351.

Fisher, A.E., 1955. The effects of differential early treatment on the social and exploratory behaviour of puppies. Doctoral dissertation, Pennsylvania. State University.

Flom, R., Deák, G.O., Phill, C.G., Pick, A.D., 2004. Nine-month-olds shared visual attention as a function of gesture and object location. Infant Behav. Dev. 27, 181–194.

Fox, M.W., 1971. Behaviour of Wolves, Dogs and Related Canids. Jonathan Cape, London.

Fox, M.W., 1975. Pet-owner relations. In: Anderson, R.S. (Ed.), Pet Animals and Society. Tindall, pp. 37–52.

Frank, H., 1980. Evolution of Canine Information processing under conditions of natural and artificial selection. Zeitschrift für Tierpsychologie 59, 389–399.

Frank, H., Frank, M.G., 1982. On the effects of domestication on canine social development and behaviour. Appl. Anim. Ethol. 8, 507–525.

Friedmann, E., 1995. The role of pets in enhancing human well-being: physiological effects. In: Robinson, I. (Ed.), The Waltham Book of Human–Animal Interaction. Pergamon Press, pp. 33–52.

Fukuzawa, M., Mills, D.S., Cooper, J.J., 2005a. The effect of human command phonetic characteristics on auditory cognition in dogs (Canis familiaris). J. Comp. Psychol. 119, 117–120.

Fukuzawa, M., Mills, D.S., Cooper, J.J., 2005b. More than just a word: non-semantic command variables affecting obedience in the domestic dog (Canis familiaris). Appl. Anim. Behav. Sci. 91, 129–141.

Gácsi, M., Topál, J., Miklósi, Á., Dóka, A., Csányi, V., 2001. Attachment behaviour of adult dogs (Canis familiaris) living at rescue centres: forming new bonds. J. Comp. Psychol. 115, 423–431.

Gácsi, M., Miklósi, Á., Varga, O., Topál, J., Csányi, V., 2004. Are readers of our face readers of our minds? Dogs (Canis familiaris) show situation- dependent recognition of human's attention. Anim. Cogn. 7, 144–153.

Gácsi, M., Győri, B., Miklósi, Á., Virányi, Z.s., Kubinyi, E., Topál, J., Csányi, V., 2005. Species-specific differences and similarities in the behaviour of hand raised dog and wolf puppies in social situations with humans. Dev. Psychobiol. 47, 111–122.

Gácsi, M., Kara, E., Belényi, B., Topál, J., Miklósi, Á., 2009. The effect of development and individual differences in pointing comprehension of dogs. Anim. Cogn. 12, 471–479.

Gácsi, M., 2003. Dog-Human Attachment. Doctoral dissertation, Department of Ethology, Eötvös University (in Hungarian).

Gergely, G.y., Egyed, K., Király, I., 2007. On pedagogy. Dev. Sci. 10, 139–146.

Gergely, G.y., Bekkering, H., Király, I., 2002. Rational imitation in preverbal infants. Nature 415, 755.

Gomez, J.C., 2004. Apes, Monkeys, Children and the Growth of Mind. Harward University Press, Cambridge MA.

Goodwin, D., Bradshaw, J.W.S., Wickens, S.M., 1997. Paedomorphosis affects visual signals of domestic dogs. Anim. Behav. 53, 297–304.

Gould, S.J., Vbra, E.S., 1982. Exaptation—a missing term in the science of form. Paleobiology 8, 4–15.

Hare, B., 2001. Can competitive paradigms increase the validity of experiments on primate social cognition? Anim. Cogn. 4, 269–280.

Hare, B., Tomasello, M., 2005. One way social intelligence can evolve: the case of domestic dogs. Trends Cogn. Sci. 9, 439–444.

Hare, B., Call, J., Tomasello, M., 1998. Communication of food location between human and dog (Canis familiaris). Evol. Commun. 2, 137–159.

Hare, B., Call, J., Agnetta, B., Tomasello, M., 2000. Chimpanzees know what con-specifics do and do not see. Anim. Behav. 59, 771–785.

Hare, B., Brown, M., Williamson, C., Tomasello, M., 2002. The domestication of cognition in dogs. Science 298, 1634–1636.

Hare, B., Plyusina, I., Ignacio, N., Schepina, O., Stepika, A., Wrangham, R., Trut, L., 2005. Social cognitive evolution in captive foxes is a correlated by-product of experimental domestication. Curr. Biol. 16, 226–230.

Hart, L.A., 1995. Dogs and companions: review of the relationship. In: Serpell, J. (Ed.), The Domestic Dog. Cambridge University Press, pp. 162–178.

Hatfield, E., Cacioppo, J.T., Rapson, R.L., 1993. Emotional contagion. Curr. Dir. Psychol. Sci. 2, 96–99.

Héjjas, K., Vas, J., Topál, J., Rónai, Zs., Székely, A., Kubinyi, E., et al., 2007a. Association of polymorphism in the dopamine D4 receptor gene and the "activity-impulsivity" endophenotype in dogs. Anim. Genet. 38, 629–633.

Héjjas, K., Vas, J., Kubinyi, E., Sasvári-Székely, M., Miklósi, Á., Rónai, Zs., 2007b. Novel repeat polymorphisms of the dopaminergic neurotransmitter genes among dogs and wolves. Mamm. Genome 18, 871–879.

Héjjas, K., Kubinyi, E., Rónai, Zs., Székely, A., Vas, J., Miklósi, Á., Sasvári-Székely, M., Kereszturi, É., 2009. Molecular and behavioral analysis of the intron 2 repeat polymorphism in canine dopamine D4 receptor gene. Genes Brain Behav. 8, 330–336.

Herman, L.M., 2002. Vocal, social, self-imitation by bottlenosed dolphins. In: Dautenhahn, K., Nahaniv, C.L. (Eds.), Imitation in Animals and Artifact. MIT Press, pp. 63–72.

Hermann, E., Call, J., Hernández-Llorenda, M.V., Hare, B., Tomasello, M., 2007. Humans have evolved specialized skills of social cognition: the cultural intelligence hypothesis. Science 317, 1360–1366.

Hirsch-Pasek, K., Treiman, R., 1981. Doggerel: motherese in a new context. J. Child Lang. 9, 229–237.

Horner, V., Whiten, A., 2005. Causal knowledge and imitation/emulation switching in chimpanzees (Pan troglodytes) and children (Homo sapiens). Anim. Cogn. 8, 164–181.

Humphrey, N.K., 1976. The social function of intellect. In: Bateson, P.P.G., Hinde, R.A. (Eds.), Growing Points in Ethology. Cambridge University Press, Cambridge, pp. 303–317.

Inoue-Murayama, M., Matsuura, N., Murayama, Y., Tsubota, T., Iwasaki, T., Kitagawa, H., Ito, S., 2002. Sequence Comparison of the Dopamine Receptor D4 Exon III Repetitive Region in Several Species of the Order Carnivora. J. Vet. Med. Sci. 64, 747–749.

Insel, T.R., Young, L.J., 2000. Neuropeptides and the evolution of social behaviour. Curr. Opin. Neurobiol. 10, 788–789.

James, N.A., MacDonald, C., 2000. Service dogs for disabled children: effect on level of independence and quality of life. Top. Spinal Cord. Rehabil. 6, 96–104.

Jones, A.C., Gosling, S.D., 2005. Temperament and personality in dogs (Canis familiaris): a review and evaluation of past research. Appl. Anim. Behav. Sci. 95, 1–53.

Kaminski, J., 2009. Neurobiology of Umwelt: How Living Beings Perceive the World Springer Verlag, Berlin, pp. 103–107.

Kaminski, J., Call, J., Fischer, J., 2004. Word learning in a domestic dog: evidence for "fast mapping". Science 304, 1682–1683.

Kerepesi, A., Johnsson, G.K., Miklósi, Á., Topál, J., Csányi, V., Magnusson, M.S., 2005. Direction of temporal patterns in dog–human interaction. Behav. Proc. 70, 69–79.

Kubinyi, E., Topál, J., Miklósi, Á., Csányi, V., 2003a. Dogs learn from their owner via observation in a manipulation task. J. Comp. Psychol. 117, 156–165.

Kubinyi, E., Miklósi, Á., Topál, J., Csányi, V., 2003b. Social mimetic behaviour and social anticipation in dogs: preliminary results. Anim. Cogn. 6, 57–63.

Kubinyi, E., Virányi, Zs., Miklósi, Á., 2007. Comparative social cognition: from wolf and dog to humans. Comp. Cogn. Behav. Rev. 2, 26–46.

Kubinyi, E., Pongrácz, P., Miklósi, Á., 2009. Dog as a model for studying con- and heterospecific social learning. J. Vet. Behav. 4, 31–41.

Lakatos, K., Tóth, I., Nemoda, Z., Ney, K., Sasváry-Székely, M., Gervai, J., 2000. Dopamine D4 receptor (DRD4) gene polymorphism is associated with attachment disorganization in infants. Mol. Psychiatr. 5, 633–637.

Lakatos, G., Soproni, K., Dóka, A., Miklósi, Á., 2009. A comparative approach of how dogs and human infants are able to utilize various forms of pointing gestures. DOI: 10.1007/s 10071-009-0221-4.

LeBoeuf, B.J., 1967. Interindividual association in dogs. Behaviour 29, 268–295.

LeVine, R.A., Campbell, D.T., 1973. Etnocentrism: Theories of Conflict, Ethnic Attitudes, and Group Behaviour. Wiley.

Lindblad-Toh, K., Wade, C.M., Mikkelsen, T.S., Karlsson, E.K., Jaffe, D.B., Kamal, M., et al., 2005. Genom sequence, comparative analysis and haplotype structure of the domestic dog. Nature 438, 803–819.

Marino, L., 2002. Convergence of complex cognitive abilities in cetaceans and primates. Brain Behav. Evol. 59, 21–32.

Maros, K., Dóka, A., Miklósi, Á., 2008. Behavioural correlation of heart rate changes in family dogs. Appl. Anim. Behav. Sci. 109, 329–341.

Marston, L.C., Bennett, P.C., Coleman, G.J., 2005. Factors affecting the formation of a canine-human bond. IWDBA Conf. Proc. 132–138.

Matas, L., Arend, R.A., Sroufe, L.A., 1978. Continuity of adaptation in second year: the relationship between quality of attachment and later competence. Child Dev. 49, 547–556.

McKinley, S., Young, R.J., 2003. The efficacy of the model–rival method when compared with operant conditioning for training domestic dogs to perform a retrieval–selection task. Appl. Anim. Behav. Sci. 81, 357–365.

Mech, L.D., 1970. The wolf: The Ecology and Behaviour of an Endangered Species. Natural History Press.

Mech, L.D., Boitani, L., 2003. Wolf social ecology. In: Mech, D.L., Boitani, L. (Eds.), Wolves: Behaviour, Ecology and Conservation. University Chicao Press, Chicago, pp. 1–34.

Melis, A.P., Hare, B., Tomasello, M., 2006. Engineering cooperation in chimpanzees: tolerance constraints on cooperation. Anim. Behav. 72, 275–286.

Milgram, N.W., Head, E., Muggenburg, B., Holowachuk, D., Murphey, H., Estrada, J., et al., 2002. Landmark discrimination learning in the dog: effects of age, an antioxidant fortified food, and cognitive strategy. Neurosci. Biobehav. Rev. 26, 679–695.

Miklósi, Á., 2007. Dog Behaviour, Evolution, and Cognition. Oxford University Press.

Miklósi, Á., Soproni, K., 2006. Comprehension of the human pointing gesture in animals: a comparative approach. Anim. Cogn. 9, 81–94.

Miklósi, Á., Polgárdi, R., Topál, J., Csányi, V., 2000. Intentional behaviour in dog–human communication: an experimental analysis of 'showing' behaviour in the dog. Anim. Cogn. 3, 159–166.

Miklósi, Á., Kubinyi, E., Topál, J., Gácsi, M., Virányi, Zs., Csányi, V., 2003. A simple reason for a big difference: wolves do not look back at humans but dogs do. Curr. Biol. 13, 763–767.

Miklósi, Á., Topál, J., Csányi, V., 2004. Comparative social cognition: what can dogs teach us? Anim. Behav. 67, 995–1004.

Miklósi, Á., Topál, J., Csányi, V., 2007. Big thoughts in small brains? Dogs as model for understanding human social cognition. NeuroReport 18, 467–471.

Miller, H.C., Rayburn-Reeves, R., Zentall, T.R., 2009. Imitation, emulation by dogs using a bidirectional control procedure. Behav. Proc. 80, 109–114.

Mills, D.S., 2005. What's in a word? A review of the attributes of a command affecting the performance of pet dogs. Anthrozoös 18, 208–221.

Mitchell, R.W., 2001. Americans' talk to dogs: similarities and differences with talk to infants. Res. Lang. Soc. Interac. 34, 183–210.

Mitchell, R.W., Thompson, N.S., 1991. Projects routines and enticements in dog–human play. In: Bateson, P., Klopfer, P. (Eds.), Perspectives in Ethology. Plenum Press, pp. 189–216.

Naderi, S.z., Miklósi, Á., Dóka, A., Csányi, V., 2001. Cooperative interactions between blind persons and their dog. Appl. Anim. Behav. Sci. 74, 59–80.

Nagasawa, M., Takefumi, K., Tatshusi, O., Mitsuaki, O., 2009. Dog's gaze at its owner increases owner's urinary oxitocyn during social interaction. Horm. Behav. 55, 434–441.

Oakes, P., Haslam, S.A., Turner, J.C., 1998. The role of prototypicality in group influence and cohesion: contextual variation in the graded structure of social categories. In: Worchel, S., Moraleas, J.F., Párez, D., Deschamps, J.C. (Eds.), Social Identity: International Perspectives, Sage Publ. Ltd, pp. 75–92.

Odendaal, J.S., Meintjes, R.A., 2003. Neurophysiological correlates of affiliative behaviour between humans and dogs. Vet. J. 165, 296–301.

Odendaal, J.S., 2000. Animal assisted therapy - magic or medicine? J. Psychosom. Res. 49, 275–294.

Overall, K.L., 2000. Natural animal model of human psychiatric conditions: assessment of mechanism and validity. Prog. Neuropsychopharmacol. Biol. Psychiatry 24, 727–776.

Palestrini, C., Prato-Provide, E., Spiezio, C., Verga, M., 2005. Heart rate and behavioural responses of dogs in the Ainsworth's strange situation: a pilot study. Appl. Anim. Behav. Sci. 94, 75–88.

Palmer, R., Custance, D., 2008. A counterbalanced version of Ainsworth's Strange Situation Procedure reveals secure-base effects in dog human relationships. Appl. Anim. Behav. Sci. 109, 306–319.

Parker, H.G., Kim, L.V., Sutter, N.B., Carlson, S., Lorentzen, T.D., Malek, T.B., et al., 2004. Genetic Structure of the Purebred Domestic Dog. Science 304, 1160–1164.

Parthasarathy, V., Crowell-Davis, S.L., 2006. Relationship between attachment to owners and separation anxiety in pet dogs (Canis lupus familiaris). J. Vet. Behav. 1, 109–120.

Paxton, D.W., 2000. A case for a naturalistic perspective. Anthrozoös 13, 5–8.

Pepperberg, I.M., 1987. Evidence for conceptual quantitative ability in the African Grey parrot: labeling of cardinal sets. Ethology 75, 37–61.

Pepperberg, I.M., 1991. Learning to communicate: the effects of social interaction. In: Bateson, P.J.B., Klopfer, P.H. (Eds.), Perspectives in Ethology. Plenum Press, pp. 119–164.

Pepperberg, I.M., 1992. Social interaction as a condition for learning in avian species: a synthesis of the disciplines of ethology and psychology. In: Davis, H., Balfour, D. (Eds.), The Inevitable Bond. Cambridge University Press, pp. 178–205.

Pepperberg, I.M., McLaughlin, M.A., 1996. Effect of avian–human joint attention on allospecific vocal learning by grey parrots (Psittacus erithacus). J. Comp. Psychol. 110, 286–297.

Pettijohn, T.F., Wont, T.W., Ebert, P.D., Scott, J.P., 1977. Alleviation of separation distress in 3 breeds of young dogs. Dev. Psychobiol. 10, 373–381.

Pongrácz, P., Miklósi, Á., Csányi, V., 2001a. Owners' beliefs on the ability of their pet dogs to understand human verbal communication: a case of social understanding. Curr. Psychol. Cogn. 20, 87–107.

Pongrácz, P., Miklósi, Á., Kubinyi, E., Gurobi, K., Topál, J., Csányi, V., 2001b. Social learning in dogs: the effect of a human demonstrator on the performance of dogs in a detour task. Anim. Behav. 62, 1109–1117.

Pongrácz, P., Miklósi, Á., Kubinyi, E., Topál, J., Csányi, V., 2003a. Interaction between individual experience and social learning in dogs. Anim. Behav. 65, 595–603.

Pongrácz, P., Miklósi, Á., Timár-Geng, K., Csányi, V., 2003b. Preference for copying unambiguous demonstrations in dogs (Canis familiaris). J. Comp. Psychol. 117, 337–343.

Pongrácz, P., Miklósi, Á., Timár-Geng, K., Csányi, V., 2004. Verbal attention getting as a key factor in social learning between dog (Canis familiaris) and human. J. Comp. Psychol. 118, 375–383.

Pongrácz, P., Vida, V., Bánhegyi, P., Miklósi, Á., 2008. How does dominance rank status affect individual and social learning performance in the dog (Canis familiaris)? Anim. Cogn. 11, 75–82.

Poresky, R.H., Hendrix, C., Mosier, J.E., 1987. The companion animal bonding scale - internal reliability and construct validity. Psychol. Rep. 60, 743–746.

Povinelli, D.J., Nelson, K.E., Boysen, S.T., 1990. Inferences about guessing and knowing by chimpanzees (Pan troglodytes). J. Comp. Psychol. 104, 203–210.

Povinelli, D.J., Bierschwale, D.T., Cech, C.G., 1999. Comprehension of seeing as a referential act in young children, but not juvenile chimpanzees. Br. J. Dev. Psychol. 17, 37–60.

Prato-Previde, E., Custance, D.M., Spiezio, C., Sabatini, F., 2003. Is the dog-human relationship an attachment bond? An observational study using Ainsworth's strange situation. Behaviour 140, 225–254.

Prato-Previde, E., Fallani, G., Valsecchi, P., 2006. Gender differences in owners interacting with pet dogs: an observational study. Ethology 112, 64–73.

Price, E.O., 1999. Behavioural development in animals undergoing domestication. Appl. Anim. Behav. Sci. 65, 245–271.

Rabb, G.B., Woolpy, J.H., Ginsburg, B.E., 1967. Social relationships in a group of captive wolves. Am. Zool. 7, 305–311.

Rajecki, D.W., Lamb, M.E., Obmascher, P., 1978. Toward a general theory of infantile attachment: a comparative review of aspects of the social bond. Behav. Brain Sci. 3, 417–464.

Range, F., Horn, L., Virányi, Zs., Huber, L., 2007. Selective imitation in domestic dogs. Curr. Biol. 17, 868–872.

Range, F., Virányi, Zs., Huber, L., 2009. The absence of reward induces inequity aversion in dogs. Proc. Natl. Acad. Sci. USA 106, 340–345.

Rasmussen, J.L., Rajecki, D.W., 1995. Differences and similarities in humans' perceptions of the thinking and feeling of a dog and a boy. Soc. Anim. 3, 117–137.

Reynolds, P.C., 1993. The complementation theory of language and tool use. In: Gibson, K.R., Ingold, T. (Eds.),. Tool Use, Language and Cognition in Human Evolution. Cambridge University Press.

Riedel, J., Buttelmann, D., Call, J., Tomasello, M., 2006. Domestic dogs (Canis familiaris) use a physical marker to locate hidden food. Anim. Cogn. 9, 27–35.

Riedel, J., Suchmann, K., Kaminski, J., Call, J., Tomasello, M., 2008. Anim. Behav. 75, 1003–1014.

Rooney, N.J., Bradshaw, J.W.S., Robinson, I.H., 2001. Do dogs respond to play signals given by humans? Anim. Behav. 61, 715–722.

Ross, S., Scott, J.P., Cherner, M., Denenberg, V.H., 1960. Effects of restraint and isolation on yelping in puppies. Anim. Behav. 8, 1–5.

Rossi, A.P., Ades, C., 2008. A dog at the keyboard: using arbitrary signs to communicate requests. Anim. Cogn. 11, 329–338.

Savolainen, P., Zhang, Y., Ling, J., Lundeberg, J., Leitner, T., 2002. Genetic evidence for an East Asian origin of domestic dogs. Science 298, 610–613.

Schleidt, W.M., Shalter, M.D., 2003. Co-evolution of humans and canids. Evol. Cogn. 9, 57–72.

Schwab, C., Huber, L., 2006. Obey or not obey? Dogs (Canis familiaris) behave differently in response to attentional states of their owners. J. Comp. Psychol. 120, 169–175.

Scott, J.P., 1992. The phenomenon of attachment in human–nonhuman relationships. In: Davis, H., Balfour, D. (Eds.), The Inevitable Bond. Cambridge University Press, Cambridge, MA, pp. 72–92.

Scott, J.P., Fuller, J.L., 1965. Genetics and the Social Behaviour of the Dog. University of Chicago Press.

Serpell, J., 1996. Evidence for association between pet behaviour and owner attachment levels. Appl. Anim. Behav. Sci. 47, 49–60.

Slabbert, J.M., Rasa, O.A.E., 1997. Observational learning of an acquired maternal behaviour pattern by working dog pups: an alternative training method? Appl. Anim. Behav. Sci. 53, 309–316.

Soproni, K., Miklósi, Á., Topál, J., Csányi, V., 2001. Comprehension of human communicative signs in pet dogs. J. Comp. Psychol. 115, 122–126.

Soproni, K., Miklósi, Á., Topál, J., Csányi, V., 2002. Dogs' (Canis familiaris) responsiveness to human pointing gestures. J. Comp. Psychol. 116, 27–34.

Spangler, G., Grossmann, K.E., 1993. Biobehavioural Organization in Securely and Insecurely Attached Infants. Child Dev. 64, 1439–1450.

Stanley, W.C., Elliot, O., 1962. Differential human handling as reinforcing events and as treatments influencing later social behaviour in basenji puppies. Psychol. Rep. 10, 775–788.

Sutter, N.B., Zhu, L., Padhukasahasram, B., Karlins, E., Davis, S., Jones, P.G., et al., 2007. A single IGF1 allele is a major determinant of small size in dogs. Science 316, 112–115.

Szetei, V., Miklósi, Á., Topál, J., Csányi, V., 2003. When dogs seem to loose their nose: an investigation on the use of visual and olfactory cues in communicative context between dog and owner. Appl. Anim. Behav. Sci. 83, 141–152.

Timberlake, W., 1993. Animal behaviour: a continuing synthesis. Annu. Rev. Psychol. 44, 675–708.

Tinbergen, N., 1963. On aims and methods of ethology. Zeitschrift für Tierpsychologie 20, 410–433.

Tomasello, M., Call, J., 1997. Primate Cognition. Oxford University Press, Oxford.

Tomasello, M., Kruger, A.E., Ratner, H., 1993. Cultural Learning. Behav. Brain Sci. 16, 495–552.

Tomasello, M., Call, J., Hare, B., 2003. Chimpanzees versus humans: it's not that simple. Trends Cogn. Sci. 7, 239–240.

Tomasello, M., Carpenter, M., Call, J., Behne, T., Moll, H., 2005. Understanding and sharing intentions: the origins of cultural cognition. Behav. Brain Sci. 28, 675–690.

Topál, J., Miklósi, Á., Csányi, V., 1997. Dog–human relationship affects problem solving behaviour in the dog. Anthrozoös 10, 214–224.

Topál, J., Miklósi, Á., Csányi, V., Dóka, A., 1998. Attachment behaviour in dogs (Canis familiaris): a new application of Ainsworth's (1969) strange situation test. J. Comp. Psychol. 112, 219–229.

Topál, J., Gácsi, M., Miklósi, Á., Virányi, Zs., Kubinyi, E., Csányi, V., 2005a. The effect of domestication and socialization on attachment to human: a comparative study on hand reared wolves and differently socialized dog puppies. Anim. Behav. 70, 1367–1375.

Topál, J., Kubinyi, E., Gácsi, M., Miklósi, Á., 2005b. Obeying social rules: a comparative study on dogs and humans. J. Comp. Evol. Psychol. 3, 213–239.

Topál, J., Byrne, R.W., Miklósi, Á., Csányi, V., 2006a. Reproducing human actions and action sequences: "Do as I Do!" in a dog. Anim. Cogn. 9, 355–367.

Topál, J., Erdőhegyi, Á., Mányik, R., Miklósi, Á., 2006b. Mindreading in a dog: an adaptation of a primate 'mental attribution' study. Int. J. Psychol. 6, 365–379.

Topál, J., Gergely, G.y., Miklósi, Á., Erdőhegyi, Á., Csibra, G., 2008. Infants perseverative search errors are induced by pragmatic misinterpretation. Science 321, 1831–1834.

Tuber, D.S., Henessy, M.B., Sanders, S., Miller, J.A., 1996. Behavioural and glucocorticoid responses of adult domestic dogs (Canis familiaris) to companionship and social separation. J. Comp. Psychol. 110, 103–108.

Udell, M.A.R., Dorey, N.R., Wynne, C.D.L., 2008. Wolves outperform dogs in following human social cues. Anim. Behav. 76, 1767–1773.

Vas, J., Topál, J., Péch, É., Miklósi, Á., 2007. Measuring attention deficit and activity in dogs: a new application and validation of a human ADHD questionnaire. Appl. Anim. Behav. Sci. 103, 105–117.

Vas, J., Topál, J., Gácsi, M., Miklósi, Á., Csányi, V., 2005. A friend or an enemy? Dogs' reaction to an unfamiliar person showing behavioural cues of threat and friendliness at different times. Appl. Anim. Behav. Sci. 94, 99–115.

Virányi, Zs., Topál, J., Gácsi, M., Miklósi, Á., Csányi, V., 2004. Dogs respond appropriately to cues of human's attentional focus. Behav. Proc. 66, 161–172.

Virányi, Zs., Topál, J., Miklósi, Á., Csányi, V., 2006. A nonverbal test of knowledge attribution: a comparative study on dogs and human infants. Anim. Cogn. 9, 13–26.

Virányi, Zs., Gácsi, M., Kubinyi, E., Topál, J., Belényi, B., Ujfalussy, D., Miklósi, Á., 2008. Comprehension of the human pointing gesture in young socialized wolves and dogs. Anim. Cogn. 11, 373–388.

de Waal, F.B.M., 1996. Good Natured: The Origins of Right and Wrong in Humans and Other animals. Harvard University Press.

Warneken, F., Tomasello, M., 2007. Helping and cooperation at 14 months of age. Infancy 11, 271–294.

Watson, J.S., Gergely, G.y., Topál, J., Gácsi, M., Sárközi, Z.s., Csányi, V., 2001. Distinguishing logic versus association in the solution of an invisible displacement task by children and dogs: using negation of disjunction. J. Comp. Psychol. 115, 219–226.

Wells, D.L., 2004. The facilitation of social interactions by domestic dogs. Anthrozoös 17, 340–352.

Wickler, W., 1976. The ethological analysis of attachment. Sociometric, motivational and sociophysiological aspects. Zeitschrift für Tierpsychologie 42, 12–28.

Wilson, C.C., 1991. The pet as an anxiolytic intervention. J. Nerv. Ment. Dis. 179, 482–489.

Young, C.A., 1991. Verbal commands as discriminative stimuli in domestic dogs (*Canis familiaris*). Appl. Anim. Behav. Sci. 32, 75–89.

Zimen, E., 1987. Ontogeny of approach and flight behaviour towards humans in wolves, poodles and wolf-poodle hybrids. In: Frank, H. (Ed.), Man and Wolf. W. J. Publishers, Dordrecht, pp. 275–292.

Strategies for Social Learning: Testing Predictions from Formal Theory

BENNETT G. GALEF

DEPARTMENT OF PSYCHOLOGY, NEUROSCIENCE AND BEHAVIOUR,
McMASTER UNIVERSITY, HAMILTON, ONTARIO, CANADA L8S 4K1

I. INTRODUCTION

Although the past two decades have seen a significant increase in both theoretical analyses and experimental studies of social learning in animals, there has been relatively little productive interchange between theoreticians and empirical investigators; formal models have had relatively little impact on the experiments undertaken by empiricists, and experimental data have played little role in the construction of models. As Laland (2004, p. 12) has suggested, "There is a need for empirical research explicitly evaluating the strategies proposed by theoretical models."

Animals can acquire adaptive information either directly, as a result of their own personal experience of the consequences of engaging in alternative behaviors, or indirectly, using various aspects of the behavior of others to guide development of their own behavioral repertoires. Personal sampling results in acquisition of accurate, current information about the environment. However, the errors that are an inescapable part of individual, trial-and-error learning can be costly, and personal exploration of the environment not only requires time and energy but also increases exposure to both predation and other environmental threats.

Social learning has the potential to reduce costs of individual learning. However, in environments that change over time, social learning is likely to be less reliable than individual learning because, in changing environments, social information can be outdated. Similarly, in environments that vary spatially, there is a risk that potential models are engaged in behavior more suited to environmental conditions other than those facing a potential social learner. Relative reliance on social and individual learning can thus be

117

0065-3454/09 $35.00
DOI: 10.1016/S0065-3454(09)39004-X

viewed as involving a tradeoff between accuracy and cost (e.g., Boyd and Richerson, 1985, 1988; Enquist et al., 2007; Giraldeau et al., 2002; Kendal et al., 2005; Laland, 2004; Rogers, 1988).

Although, intuitively, it might seem that an individual would always increase its fitness by avoiding the potential costs of individual learning, formal, mathematical analyses of the tradeoffs between relatively inexpensive, but potentially inaccurate, social learning and relatively expensive, but accurate, individual learning indicate that both the circumstances under which an individual learns and the characteristics of those that it learns from can affect the relative fitness value of engaging in social as compared with individual learning (Boyd and Richerson, 1985, 1988; Enquist et al., 2007; Giraldeau et al., 2002; Kendal et al., 2005; Laland, 2004; Rogers, 1988).

Table I, modified from Laland (2004), provides a list, based on an extensive theoretical literature (reviewed in Laland, 2004), of predictions from formal theory as to when animals should increase their reliance on social cues ("when strategies") and the characteristics of individuals whose behavior should provide the most valuable information ("who strategies"). These "when strategies" and "who strategies," are, in essence, information-gathering tactics that formal models indicate should have been favored by natural selection.

TABLE I

SUMMARY OF PREDICTIONS FROM FORMAL MODELS OF SOCIAL LEARNING STRATEGIES (ADAPTED FROM LALAND, 2004)

"When" strategies of social learning

Copy when established behavior is unproductive
Copy when asocial learning is costly
Copy when uncertain
Copy when dissatisfied
Copy when the environment is relatively stable[a]

"Who" strategies of social learning
Copy the majority
Copy successful individuals
Copy good social learners
Copy kin
Copy familiar individuals
Copy older individuals

[a]Not considered in Laland (2004).

A. TESTS OF PREDICTIONS FROM THEORY

Both Galef (2006) and Kendal et al. (2005) have recently provided general reviews of findings in the literature that largely by happenstance, provide evidence relevant to predictions from formal models, and I shall not repeat that exercise here. Rather, I shall review a series of experiments conducted over the past several years in which my coworkers and I have used social learning of food preferences by Norway rats, *Rattus norvegicus*, as an experimental system in which to investigate predictions from theoretical models as to when animals should increase their reliance on social information relative to individual learning and whom they should select as models. Below, I summarize and discuss the results of both of these studies and of other animal studies explicitly testing predictions from formal models of social learning.

B. THE EXPERIMENTAL SYSTEM: NORWAY RATS'
     SOCIAL LEARNING ABOUT FOODS

Studies of the role of social learning in the development of feeding repertoires of Norway rats show that rats' food choices are open to many kinds of socially induced bias (for review, see Galef, 1996). Possibly the most potent of the many social-learning processes involved in the development of rats' food choices is a robust enhancement of the preference of a naïve rat ("an observer") for a food following interaction with a "demonstrator" rat that has recently eaten that food (Galef and Wigmore, 1983). The breath of a demonstrator rat carries odor cues that enable other rats to identify the foods that it has recently eaten. After such diet-identifying cues are experienced by an observer rat together with contextual cues, metabolic products that are a normal part of rats' breath, an observer rat exhibits a long-lasting, enhancement of its preference for foods that its demonstrator ate (Galef and Stein, 1985; Galef et al., 1985, 1988).

Rats' social transmission of food choice is unlikely to be a laboratory artifact. Free-living, wild Norway rats are central-place foragers that should have ample opportunity to extract information from colony mates returning to their shared burrow between foraging bouts. Indeed, field observations indicate that the food choices of wild rats are strongly influenced by the food choices that others of their social group are making. For example, Steiniger (1950), an applied ecologist who investigated methods to increase the efficiency of poison baits used in rodent control, observed that if the same poison bait were used in an area for an extended period of time, despite initial success, later acceptance of the bait was extremely poor. Naïve young that were born to colony members that had survived their initial ingestion of the poison bait and had learned to avoid eating it, ate only foods that adults of their colony were eating and would not even taste the poison bait for themselves so long as knowledgeable adults were present in their colony. The young rats appeared to be learning from their elders either what foods to eat or what foods to avoid eating (Galef, 1985).

Our laboratory procedure for exploring such social transmission of information concerning foods in Norway rats consists of three stages (Galef, 2002) that provide a laboratory analogue of interactions that might occur in a rat burrow between a returning, successful forager and a burrow mate. We first (stage 1) feed a demonstrator rat one of two roughly equally palatable, distinctively flavored foods, diets A and B. We then (stage 2) place the recently fed demonstrator rat in the home cage of an observer rat and allow the observer and demonstrator to interact freely before (stage 3) removing the demonstrator and offering the observer a choice between diets A and B, one of which is the diet that its demonstrator ate.

We invariably find that during stage 3, observer rats show an enhanced preference for whatever diet their demonstrator ate during step 2 (for review, see Galef, 1996). Mammals ranging from short-tailed fruit bats (*Carollia perspicillata*; Ratcliffe and ter Hofstede, 2005) to spotted hyenas (*Crocuta crocuta*; Yoerg, 1991) have been shown, similarly, to learn from conspecifics what foods to eat, though the behavioral processes supporting such social learning have been investigated more thoroughly in Norway rats than in other species.

II. Testing Formal Models of Social Learning

A. When Strategies

Theory suggests five circumstances in which animals faced with a decision should increase in their reliance on socially acquired information (Table I; see Laland, 2004 for review): (1) when individual learning is unproductive, (2) when individual learning is costly, (3) when uncertain, (4) when the environment is relatively stable, and (5) when dissatisfied. Below, I describe experiments in which Norway rats' social learning about foods was used as an empirical system in which to examine each of these five predictions.

1. Copy When Individual Learning Is Unproductive

Boyd and Richerson (1988, p. 44) suggested some years ago, in discussing unproductive behavior, that "... for a particular species, there will be some aspects of diet about which it will be difficult for individuals to learn what is best, but there will be other aspects about which it will be easy for individuals to learn. The models predict that the former will be acquired disproportionately by social learning and the latter disproportionately by individual learning."

Like other mammals examined to date, Norway rats find it easy to detect some nutrients in potential foods and difficult to detect others. For example, the first time that a rat experiences a sodium deficiency and is offered a cafeteria of foods only one of which contains a sodium salt, the rat will prefer to ingest the food that is rich in sodium and will do so within minutes of first sampling it (Epstein and Stellar, 1955; Friedman, 2000; for review, see Stricker, 2000). In contrast, protein-deficient rats find it difficult to learn which of several foods presented to them contains protein (for review, see Friedman, 2000; Galef, 2000). Depending on details of the experimental situation, it can take from days to weeks for a rat to learn to focus its intake on a single protein-rich food presented in a cafeteria together with several protein-poor foods (Galef, 1991).

Our procedure for testing Boyd and Richerson's (1988) prediction was straightforward (Galef and Whiskin, 2008b). First, we induced either a sodium deficiency or a protein deficiency in rats by feeding them either sodium-deficient or protein-deficient diet for seven consecutive days. We then used these deficient animals as observers in our three-stage procedure for social induction of food preference. We offered observers that had interacted in stage 2 with a demonstrator rat that had eaten either cinnamon-flavored or cocoa-flavored food in stage 1, a choice in stage 3 between cinnamon- and cocoa- flavored foods rich in both protein and sodium.

If, as Boyd and Richerson's (1988) model predicts, animals that, individually, are unable to make productive decisions as to what to eat rely more heavily on socially acquired information than animals able to make productive food choices, then protein-deficient rats should show greater social influence on their food choices than sodium-deficient rats. In fact, whether severely or moderately deprived, protein-deprived observer rats relied more heavily on socially acquired information than did sodium-deprived observer rats (Fig. 1), confirming Boyd and Richerson's (1988) prediction.

2. Copy When Dissatisfied

Laland (2004) categorized copy-if-dissatisfied as a "who strategy" reflecting its origins in Schlag's (1998) prediction that animals should tend to copy individuals more successful than themselves. In particular, Schlag (1998) proposed that an individual should adjust its probability of copying to make that probability proportional to the difference in success between itself and an individual that it might copy. Laland (2004) labeled this a "copy-if-

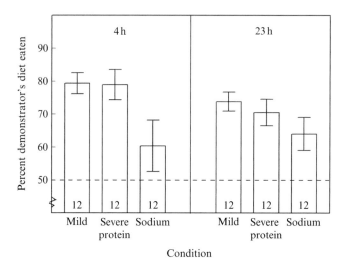

Fɪɢ. 1. Mean ± S.E. percentage demonstrators' diet eaten by protein-deficient and sodium-deficient observers during 4 h (left panel) and 23 h (right panel) of testing Number in histograms = N/group (from Galef and Whiskin, 2008b reprinted with permission of Elsevier).

better" strategy and preferred an alternative model that Schlag (1998) had called "proportional reservation" and Laland (2004) subsequently labeled "copy-if-dissatisfied."

In copy-if-dissatisfied, the reward that an individual receives for its current behavior is positively related to its current level of satisfaction, and the probability that it will copy others is inversely related to its current level of satisfaction. Schlag (1998) had shown that, at evolutionary equilibrium, copy-if-better and copy-if-dissatisfied have equivalent fitness consequences. However, because copy-if-dissatisfied requires evaluation only of one's own success, not of the relative success of oneself and of others, copy-if-dissatisfied seems more likely than copy-if-better to have evolved (Laland, 2004). Consequently, we investigated the possibility that rats would be more likely to "copy if dissatisfied," which is a "when strategy."

a. Copy when sick We proceeded on the premise that, relative to a healthy animal, a sick animal, for example, one deprived of a needed nutrient or injected with a toxin, would have a reduced level of satisfaction. Sick animals would, therefore, be predicted on both Laland (2004) and Schlag's (1998) models to be more likely to copy the food choices of others than healthy animals.

Results of previous experiments in our laboratory that were not explicitly designed to examine effects of dissatisfaction on reliance on socially acquired information were consistent with the prediction that dissatisfied animals would be more reliant than healthy animals on socially acquired information. For example, when Galef et al. (1991) compared the effectiveness of demonstrator rats in influencing the food choices of protein-replete and protein-deprived observers, we found protein-deprived observers significantly more susceptible to social influence than protein-replete observers.

In explicit tests of the hypothesis that dissatisfied rats are more susceptible to social influence than satisfied rats, we made observer rats dissatisfied in three different ways and then compared the susceptibility to social influence on food preference of dissatisfied observers and relevant controls.

b.   Diluted diets   We maintained rats randomly assigned to the dissatisfied condition for 7 days on powdered rat chow diluted 15% by weight with cellulose, a nonnutritive filler (Galef et al., 2008). When given a choice between the calorically dilute diet and undiluted chow, rats will eat eight times as much undiluted as diluted food, indicating that they find the diluted food distasteful. None the less, subjects given access only to calorically dilute chow increase their intake to compensate for dilution and gained weight normally.

Despite being able to maintain their body weights and presumably remain healthy, observer rats fed only diluted diet had to eat a relatively unpalatable food and experienced greater food-handling costs than rats maintained on undiluted diet. Thus, rats maintained on diluted diet should have been healthy, but, we hoped, somewhat dissatisfied. Indeed, as Laland's (2004) and Schlag's (1998) model would predict, rats maintained on calorically diluted rat chow exhibited greater social influence on their food choices than did more-satisfied rats maintained on unadulterated chow (Fig. 2).

c.   Unpalatable diets   We also maintained observer rats for 7 days on a diet made relatively unpalatable by the addition of cayenne pepper (a substance rats find aversive) and found that these observer rats, when subsequently allowed to interact with a demonstrator rat fed either cinnamon- or cocoa-flavored diet and then offered a choice between those two diets showed significantly greater social influence on their food choices than did rats maintained for 7 days on a relatively palatable base diet (Galef and Whiskin, unpublished data; Fig. 3).

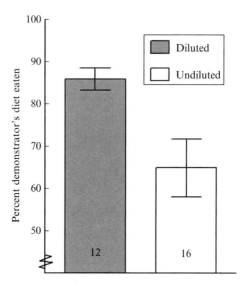

FIG. 2. Mean ± S.E. percentage demonstrator's diet eaten by observers fed either diluted or undiluted rat chow for 1 week before interacting with a demonstrator. Number in histograms = N/group (from Galef et al., 2008, reprinted with permission of Elsevier).

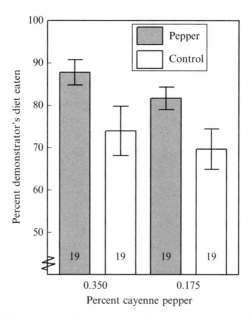

FIG. 3. Mean ± S.E. percentage demonstrator's diet eaten by observers fed either cayenne-pepper flavored rat chow (pepper groups) or unflavored rat chow (control) for 1 week before interacting with a demonstrator. Number in histograms = N/group (Galef and Whiskin, unpublished data).

d. Uncomfortable living conditions   We also attempted to make rats dissatisfied by maintaining them for 7 days in uncomfortable circumstances (Galef et al., 2008). We housed rats assigned to the uncomfortable condition in a cage with a wire-mesh floor, placed the cage in a constantly illuminated room and heated the room to an uncomfortably warm (for rats) 30 °C. Observer rats made uncomfortable, like those maintained on diluted or unpalatable diets, were significantly more reliant on socially-acquired information than observer rats maintained under standard laboratory conditions (Fig. 4). Thus, the results of three experiments, two previously published in peer-reviewed journals and one not, were consistent in supporting the prediction that dissatisfied animals would be more susceptible than satisfied animals to social influence on their food choices.

3. Copy When Uncertain

Boyd and Richerson's (1985, 1988) population genetics-based models consider the fitness consequences of reliance on individual and social learning as a function of the degree of environmental variability. Starting with the assumption that individuals must determine the current state of the environment before they can engage in behavior appropriate to that

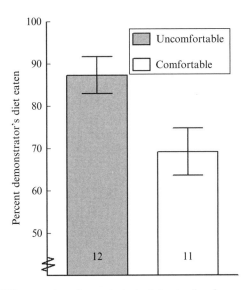

Fig. 4. Mean ± S.E. percentage demonstrator's diet eaten by observers maintained under either comfortable or uncomfortable conditions for 1 week before interacting with a demonstrator. Number in histograms = *N*/group (from Galef et al., 2008, reprinted with permission of Elsevier).

environment, the models predict that individuals uncertain as to which of two environments they are in should be more reliant on socially acquired information than individuals that are sure of the current state of the world. Laland (2004) labeled this bias toward reliance on social learning a "copy when uncertain" strategy, and. we have carried out two experiments, one that has undergone peer review, and one that has not, examining effects of uncertainty on reliance on socially acquired information (Galef and Whiskin, unpublished data; Galef et al., 2008).

a.   Uncertainty as to the cause of illness   We first undertook manipulations to make Norway rats either certain or uncertain about the causal relationship between ingesting an unfamiliar flavor and experiencing gastrointestinal upset. All subjects were equally ill; they differed only in the certainty with which they could attribute their illness to specific foods that they had ingested. We then examined the susceptibility of these "certain" and "uncertain" rats to socially induced food preferences (Galef et al., 2008).

To produce observer rats certain as to the cause of their illness, we fed them a food with a single unfamiliar flavor (cinnamon) and then injected them with a toxin (lithium chloride). To cause uncertainty in observer rats, we fed them a food containing two unfamiliar flavors (cinnamon and cocoa) and then injected them with lithium chloride. Rats assigned to the former group were certain as to the cause of their illness. Whereas those assigned to the latter condition could not know whether cinnamon, cocoa, or the combination of cinnamon and cocoa was related to their discomfort. After poisoning, we allowed subjects assigned to both conditions to interact with demonstrator rats that had just eaten either anise- or marjoram-flavored food and then gave all observers access to weighed samples of anise- and marjoram-flavored food for 23 h.

If uncertainty increases reliance on socially acquired information, then during the 23-h choice between anise- and marjoram-flavored foods, uncertain subjects should have eaten more of the diet that their respective demonstrators had eaten than subjects certain as to the cause of their illness. Consistent with Boyd and Richerson's (1985, 1988) models, uncertain rats showed a significantly greater preference for their respective demonstrators' diets than did certain rats (Fig. 4 in Galef et al., 2008).

b.   Uncertainty as to the safety of unfamiliar foods   A rat presented with unfamiliar potential foods should be less certain as to whether those foods are safe to eat than a rat presented with foods it has previously eaten without ill effect. If so, a rat choosing between unfamiliar foods should be more uncertain, and therefore more reliant on socially acquired information than a rat choosing between foods that it previously ate and found safe.

We fed one group of observer rats both cinnamon-flavored chow and cocoa-flavored chow for 24 h while we fed another group of observer rats unflavored chow. We then allowed each member of both groups to interact with a demonstrator rat fed either cinnamon- or cocoa-flavored diet before offering each observer a choice between cinnamon- and cocoa-flavored diets.

As predicted from the hypothesis that uncertainty increases reliance on social learning, demonstrators had significantly greater influence on the food choices of rats choosing between unfamiliar than familiar foods (Galef and Whiskin, unpublished data; Fig. 5). Consistent with this unpublished finding, Forkman (1991) and Visalberghi and Fragaszy (1995) have reported, respectively, that Mongolian gerbils (*Meriones unguiculatus*) and capuchin monkeys (*Cebus apella*) increased their consumption of food in the presence of feeding conspecifics when the food was unfamiliar, but not when it was familiar.

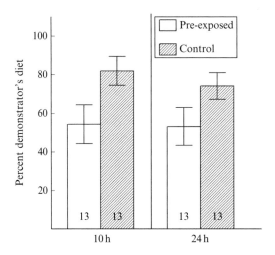

FIG. 5. Mean ± S.E. percentage demonstrator's diet eaten after 10 and 24 h by observer rats offered a choice between cinnamon- and cocoa-flavored diet following maintenance for 7 days with *ad libitum* access to either both cinnamon- and cocoa- flavored rat diet or to unflavored rat chow. Number in histograms = *N*/group (Galef and Whiskin, unpublished data).

4. Copy When Individual Learning is Costly

Sampling unfamiliar, potentially toxic substances has greater potential cost than ingesting familiar foods known to be safe. Consequently, the finding that rats choosing between two foods are less reliant on socially acquired information when those foods are familiar than when they are unfamiliar (Galef and Whiskin, unpublished data) is consistent not only with the prediction that uncertain rats should be more reliant on social information than certain rats, but also with the prediction from formal models that animals should increase reliance on socially acquired information as the potential cost of individual learning increases (Boyd and Richerson,1985; Feldman et al., 1996; Kendal et al., 2005). For example, as the risk of predation rises so does the cost of individual assessment of alternatives (e.g., Lima and Dill, 1990; Sih, 1994), and theory therefore predicts that dependence on socially acquired information should increase when cues are present that indicate enhanced risk of predation.

Cues indicating enhanced predation risk can be either direct (if a predator or cues directly associated with the presence of a predator are detected, e.g., Powell and Banks, 2004) or indirect (if environmental cues indicate that an attacking predator would be likely to be successful), for example, when a potential prey animal is far from shelter (e.g., Orrock et al., 2004). We examined effects of both direct and indirect cues of predation risk on rats' social learning of food preferences.

a.   Direct cues of predation risk   Assessing the relative nutritive value of alternative potential foods, requires that an individual sample them repeatedly (Beck et al., 1988; Rozin, 1969; Rozin and Schulkin, 1990), and such sampling can necessitate spending time at a distance from cover and therefore at heightened risk of predation. Consequently, cues of enhanced predation risk in an environment should decrease individual assessment of alternative foods and increase reliance on social information.

To examine effects of direct risk of predation on reliance on socially acquired information, we first exposed observer rats to conspecific demonstrators that had eaten either cinnamon- or cocoa-flavored diet. We then placed each observer rat in a large floor enclosure and offered it a choice, for 24 h, between cinnamon- and cocoa-flavored diets. We exposed observers assigned to experimental conditions to one of three types of direct cues of predation risk: (1) a pair of domestic cats, *Felis catus*, roaming free in a room containing a caged (and therefore safe) rat, or (2) a pair of cats caged some distance from the rat's cage either throughout the 24-h test period, or (3) for the first 4 h of the 24-h test period (Galef and Whiskin, 2006).

We treated control subjects assigned to each of these three conditions just as we treated experimental subjects, except that we did not expose control subjects to any cues of predation.

Although observer rats showed clear indications of a response to the physical presence of cats, eating substantially less during 24 h than observers not exposed to cats, we found no indication that observers assigned to experimental conditions relied more heavily than observers assigned to control conditions on information provided by demonstrators (Galef and Whiskin, 2006; Fig. 6). To the contrary, the effect of the presence of cats was, if anything, to reduce attention to social information, possibly by reducing the "choosiness" of observers when exposed to direct cues of enhanced risk of predation (e.g., Briggs et al.,1996; Crowley et al., 1991; Real, 1990). Although none of the differences between groups in Fig. 6 was statistically reliable, contrary to prediction from theory, observer rats assigned to the control group in each of the three conditions ate more, not less, of the diet that their demonstrator had eaten than observer rats feeding in the presence of predators.

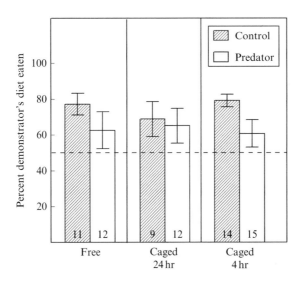

FIG. 6. Mean ± S.E. percentage demonstrator's diet eaten during testing when observers were tested in the presence or absence of a predator. Dashed line = expected percentage demonstrator's diet eaten by observers if observers' food choices were not influenced by prior interaction with demonstrators. Number in histograms = N/group (from Galef and Whiskin, 2006, reprinted with permission of Elsevier).

When we subsequently exposed observer rats to cat odor during testing by placing a piece of cloth rubbed on a cat near the food bowls available to observer rats, presumably providing weak direct cues of predation risk relative to the actual presence of cats, observer rats preferred the diet their respective demonstrators had eaten, but still showed no greater reliance on socially acquired information than rats choosing between foods in the absence of cat odor (Galef and Yarkovsky, 2009; Fig. 7).

b.   Indirect cues of predation risk   The farther an animal ventures from cover when foraging and the more exposed a feeding site, the greater its risk of predation. Consequently, if indirect cues of predation risk increase reliance on socially acquired information, then animals feeding far from a harborage site or in the open should be more reliant on socially acquired information than animals either foraging near a harborage site or eating whilst under cover.

We first gave all observer rats an opportunity to interact with demonstrator rats fed either cinnamon- or cocoa-flavored diet, then in a 2 × 2 design, varied the distance from harborage site to feeding site (near or far) and the presence or absence of cover at the feeding site where cinnamon- and

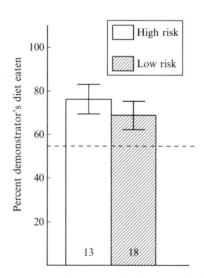

FIG. 7. Mean ± S.E. percentage demonstrator's diet eaten during testing by observers assigned to high-risk and low-risk conditions. Dashed line = expected percentage demonstrator's diet eaten by observers' if observers' food choices were not influenced by prior interaction with demonstrators. Number in histograms = *N*/group (from Galef and Yarkovsky, 2009, reprinted with permission of Elsevier).

cocoa-flavored foods were available. We found no effect of either distance to a harborage site or presence of cover at a feeding site on observer rats' reliance on socially acquired information. Unfortunately, we also found no effect of indirect cues of predation on the amount that observer rats ate during testing, suggesting that their foraging behavior may have been unaffected by the indirect cues of predation that we were using (Galef and Whiskin, 2006).

In a subsequent study, we attempted to magnify the effects of indirect cues of predation on foraging by comparing the behavior of observer rats that could both move from harborage site to feeding site and feed whilst under cover with that of observer rats that had both to travel a meter to food and to eat in the open. In this experiment, although observers moving and feeding under cover ate significantly more (9.4 ± 1.1 g) than observers moving and feeding in the open (6.0 ± 65 g), we still found no effect of indirect cues of predation risk observers' reliance on socially acquired information (Galef and Yarkovsky, 2009; Fig. 8).

Studies of foraging behavior in guppies (*Poecelia reticulate*) and stickle-backs (*Gasterosteus aculeatus* and *Pungitius pungitius*) have been more successful than our studies with Norway rats in providing evidence of

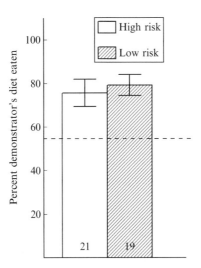

FIG. 8. Mean ± S.E. percentage demonstrator's diet eaten during testing by observers assigned to high-risk and low-risk conditions. Dashed line = expected percentage demonstrator's diet eaten by observers if observers' food choices were not influenced by prior interaction with demonstrators. Number in histograms = N/group (from Galef and Yarkovsky, 2009, reprinted with permission of Elsevier).

increased reliance on socially acquired information in the face of indirect
cues of predation risk. For example, Kendal et al. (2004) report that guppies
rely more heavily on social information in choosing a foraging site when the
choice involves leaving the protection of contact with a shoal than when it
does not, and Coolen et al. (2003) found that three-spined sticklebacks, that
are at greater risk of predation than nine-spined sticklebacks, are also more
susceptible to social influence when selecting a feeding site. However,
studies of effects of direct cues of predation risk on social influences on
mate choice in guppies, like studies of direct cues of predation risk on food
choice in rats, have failed to provide evidence of enhanced reliance on
social information in the presence of predators (Briggs et al., 1996)

c. Increased risk of ingesting toxins   Although tests of predictions from
formal models concerning effects of increased cost of individual learning on
reliance on social learning have generally looked at effects of threats of
predation on reliance on social learning, factors other than predation
risk that also increase the cost of individual assessment should similarly
increase reliance on social learning (e.g., Dewar, 2004). In particular,
observer rats with experiences suggesting that sampling unfamiliar foods
can lead to illness might be expected to increase their reliance on socially
acquired information when subsequently choosing between additional
unfamiliar foods.

We fed observer rats assigned to experimental conditions either one, two,
or four different unfamiliar foods and injected them with a mild toxin after
they ate each, whereas we injected rats assigned to corresponding
control conditions with saline solution after they ate each of one, two or
four unfamiliar foods. We then allowed all observer rats to interact with
demonstrator rats that had been fed one of two additional diets that were
unfamiliar to the observers before allowing observers to choose between
those two diets. Experience with toxic foods had no effect on observers' use
of socially acquired information (Galef and Whiskin, 2006; Galef and
Yarkovsky, 2009).

5. Copy When the Environment Is Relatively Stable

A number of models (e.g., Aoki and Feldman, 1987; Boyd and Richerson,
1988; Laland et al., 1996; Rogers, 1988) predict that social learning is more
likely to be adaptive when environments are relatively stable than when
environments are highly unpredictable because in rapidly changing environments, the behavior of a potential model is likely to reflect past rather
than current conditions. Consequently, copying the behavior of others in
rapidly changing environments may prove maladaptive.

We maintained observer rats that we had assigned to an experimental group for 12 days under rapidly changing conditions (each day, we fed each observer a different food at a different time of day for a different length of time, and moved each observer from one cage to another). We left observer rats assigned to a control group in the same cage for 12 days (but removed each observer from and returned it to its cage daily) and fed each of the observers on one of the 27 feeding regimes to which we exposed each observer assigned to the experimental condition (Galef and Whiskin, 2004).

After 12 days of exposure to either relatively stable or highly variable environments, each observer rat interacted with a demonstrator rat fed a diet unfamiliar to its observer and the observer then chose between that diet and a second unfamiliar diet. As predicted, although both groups of observer rats showed significantly enhanced preferences for their respective demonstrators' diets, interaction with demonstrator rats had a significantly greater effect on the food choices of observer rats assigned to the to the stable than to the highly variable condition (Fig. 9).

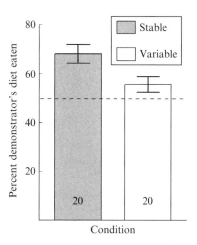

FIG. 9. Mean ± S.E. percentage demonstrator's diet eaten during testing by observers assigned to stable and variable conditions. Dashed line = expected percent demonstrator's diet eaten by observers if observers' food choices were not influenced by prior interaction with demonstrators. Number in histograms = N/group (from Galef and Whiskin, 2004, reprinted with permission of Elsevier).

B. Who Strategies

Formal models make predictions concerning not only the conditions that should lead to enhanced reliance on social information, but also as to the characteristics of individuals whose behavior would be most advantageous to copy. Like the "when strategies" discussed in the preceding section, these "who strategies" are open to empirical investigation.

1. Copy Older Individuals

Survival to adulthood depends on adequate response to myriad environmental challenges. Consequently, behaviors engaged in by adults are likely to be well adapted to the demands of the locales in which those adults live. Juveniles are more likely than adults to be in the error phase of trial-and-error learning, and a naïve, young individual might, therefore, be expected to have a greater probability of acquiring adaptive behavior if it copied the behavior of an adult rather than that of a fellow juvenile.

In our first exploration of possible effects of demonstrator age on observers' social learning (Galef et al., 1984), we used a 2 × 2 design to examine the consequences of interaction of both old and young observer rats with both old and young demonstrators. The results indicated that both young and old observers learned from both old and young demonstrators, and that there was little difference in the magnitude of social learning as a consequence of the relative ages of demonstrators and observers (Galef et al., 1984).

More recently (Galef and Whiskin, 2004), we both repeated a portion of Galef et al.'s (1984) experiments and directly compared the relative influence of old and young demonstrators, one fed cinnamon-flavored diet and the other cocoa-flavored diet when those demonstrators were presented sequentially to the same observer. The results were in complete accord with those of Galef et al. (1984). Adult and juvenile demonstrators had equivalent effects on their observers and direct comparison of the effectiveness of older and younger demonstrators revealed no reliable difference. If anything, juvenile demonstrators had greater effect than adult demonstrators on their observers' diet choices.

Failure to find greater effectiveness of older demonstrators is not unique to social learning about food in rats. For example, Lachlan et al. (1998) report that small guppies prefer to shoal with others their own size rather than with larger guppies, and shoaling is known to play a major role in selection of a feeding site (Laland and Williams, 1997). On the other hand, Gerrish and Alberts (1995) found that weanling Norway rats prefer a feeding site where an adult is eating to one where a juvenile is feeding, and Dugatkin and Godin (1993) report that mate choices of small female guppies are affected by observing the choices of larger (and presumably older) females, whereas the mate choices of large female guppies are not affected by observing those of smaller individuals. Clearly, much remains to be learned about when and how demonstrator age affects demonstrator effectiveness.

2. Copy Kin or Familiar Individuals

Theoretically, copying familiar individuals or kin should have greater fitness benefits than copying unfamiliar or unrelated potential models because: (1) social learning is useful only when models and copiers are exposed to similar environments and experience similar outcomes as a result of engaging in similar behaviors and (2) an individual is more likely to share environments and behavioral outcomes with kin or familiar individuals than with nonkin or strangers (Boyd and Richerson, 1985, 1988).

In many species, young spend more time interacting with parents, siblings, or other kin than with unrelated conspecifics, and should therefore have greater opportunity to acquire information from relatives than from nonkin (Coussi-Korbel and Fragaszy, 1995) Consequently, any observed differences in the frequencies with which juveniles living in natural circumstances behave like relatives than like nonrelatives cannot be used to infer that young treat information acquired from related individuals differently than they treat information acquired from others. A "strategy" of copying kin or familiar individuals requires such differential treatment of information acquired from familiar/kin and unfamiliar/nonkin, and is probably demonstrable only under controlled conditions.

In our first exploration of effects of familiarity and kinship on social learning about foods in Norway rats (Galef et al., 1984), we found that familiar and unfamiliar nonkin were equally effective in influencing the food choices of their observers. Consequently, we were surprised when Valsecchi et al. (1996) found, in studies of social influence on the food choices of Mongolian gerbils (*M. unguiculatus*), that only demonstrators that were both genetically related to and familiar with observers exerted any influence on their observers' food choices.

Subsequent work by Choleris et al. (1998) revealed that treatment of gerbils with benzodiazepine chloride, an anxiolitic agent, resulted in familiar kin and unfamiliar nonkin being equally effective in altering their observers' food preferences. This result suggests that at least part of the difference between Mongolian gerbils and Norway rats in the role of kinship and familiarity in affecting social influence on food choice might be due to differences in the probability of anxiety-induced behaviors when rats or gerbils first meet conspecifics.

The unfamiliar/unrelated, young female rats that have acted as demonstrators and observers in essentially all studies of social learning about food in *R. norvegicus* rarely fight when they meet for the first time, whereas unrelated/unfamiliar adult *M. unguiculatus*, frequently interact aggressively during a first encounter. If, as seems likely, aggressive interaction interferes with extraction of information from conspecifics concerning foods that they have recently eaten and anxiolitic agents reduce the probability of such aggression when unfamiliar gerbils first encounter one another, then the observed difference in the effects of familiarity and relatedness on social learning about foods in gerbils and rats might be expected.

In a pair of recent studies employing 2 × 2 designs, we examined the impact on an observer rats' preferences between two foods, one fed to each of two demonstrators, one familiar and the other unfamiliar to the observer, when we presented the two demonstrators simultaneously to an observer. We found, somewhat surprisingly, that observers in each of two experiments tended to eat more of a diet after interacting with an unfamiliar than with a familiar demonstrator fed that diet (Galef and Whiskin, 2008a; Fig. 10).

To test the hypothesis that the greater effectiveness of unfamiliar demonstrators might reflect a tendency on the part of rats to spend more time interacting with unfamiliar than with familiar conspecifics, we looked at the

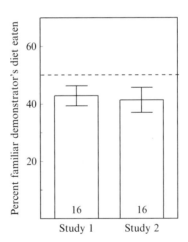

FIG. 10. Mean ± S.E. percentage demonstrator's diet eaten during testing by observers interacting with familiar and unfamiliar demonstrators. Dashed line = expected percent demonstrator's diet eaten by observers if observers' food choices were not influenced by prior interaction with demonstrators. Numbers in histograms = N/group (from Galef and Whiskin, 2008a,b, reprinted with permission of Elsevier).

behavior of naïve observer rats placed in a large cage with demonstrator rats fed different foods restrained behind screen barriers (Galef and Whiskin, 2008a). Consistent with the hypothesis that observers spend longer interacting with unfamiliar than familiar demonstrators, observers spent more time at the end of the cage closer to unfamiliar than to familiar individuals (Fig. 11).

Saggerson and Honey (2006) have reported possibly similar results in two experiments in which rats observed members of a familiar or unfamiliar strain pull on a chain to receive a food reward. The subjects behaved similarly to a demonstrator rat of an unfamiliar strain but not to a demonstrator rat of their own familiar strain. Saggerson and Honey (2006) attributed this difference in social learning following observation of relatively familiar and unfamiliar demonstrators to latent inhibition (i.e., reduced attention to familiar stimuli).

The finding that rats spend more time in the vicinity of unfamiliar than of familiar conspecifics (Galef and Whiskin, 2008a) suggests that the greater effect of unfamiliar than familiar demonstrators on observers' food choices is the result of greater amounts of information passing from unfamiliar than familiar demonstrators to observers. However, we have no direct evidence that the duration of interactions between an observer rat and its rat demonstrator affects the magnitude of the effect of demonstrators on their

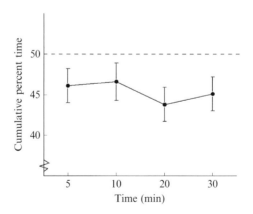

FIG. 11. Mean ± S.E. percentage of 30-min test that observers spent within 10 cm of the familiar demonstrator when choosing between familiar and unfamiliar demonstrators. Dashed line = expected percentage of time observer spent within 10 cm of a familiar demonstrator if familiarity with a demonstrator had no effect on observers' behavior (from Galef and Whiskin, 2008a, reprinted with permission of Elsevier).

observers' food choices. Unfortunately, it is not possible to either control or measure the amount of relevant information passing from interacting rat demonstrators to their rat observers.

As discussed in greater detail in Section I.B., analysis of the processes underlying influence of demonstrator rats on their observers' food preferences has shown that the critical stimulus passing from a demonstrator rat to its observer is a combination of a food odor and chemical cues that are a part of normal rat breath (Galef et al., 1988). We discovered some years ago (Galef, unpublished data; Lupfer-Johnson, personal communication, 2008) that if a human demonstrator eats cinnamon- or cocoa-flavored rat diet and then breathes on a rat, the rat subsequently shows an enhanced preference for the diet that its human demonstrator ate. Of course, a human demonstrator can be instructed to breathe on an observer rat a fixed number of times and can therefore vary systematically the amount of social information provided to an observer rat. Consequently, we could use human demonstrators to examine experimentally any effects of amount of information passing from a demonstrator to an observer on observers' subsequent food choices.

We have compared the magnitude of the effect on observer rats' choices between cinnamon- and cocoa-flavored rat chow of exposure to 1, 2, 10, 20, or 40 breaths from a human demonstrator that had just eaten 10 g of either cinnamon- or cocoa-flavored rat chow. We found a significant ($P < 0.02$) positive linear relationship between the number of human breathes an observer rat experienced and its reliance on such "social" information when subsequently choosing between cinnamon- and cocoa-flavored diet. (Galef and Tong, unpublished data; Fig. 12).

An interesting instance of variation in tendency to associate with familiar individuals social behavior has been provided by Frommen et al. (2007) who recently reported that three-spined stickleback prefer to shoal with familiar fish when sated but with unfamiliar fish when hungry, a finding that Frommen et al. (2007) attributed to avoidance of competition with kin. Shoaling in stickleback is known to affect choice of foraging site (Laland and Williams, 1997), so it might be predicted that stickleback would learn socially from familiar individuals when sated but from unfamiliar fish when hungry.

Taken together, results of explorations of the effects of familiarity/relatedness on the effectiveness of demonstrators suggest a rather complex picture. Apparently, there are circumstances in which familiar/related demonstrators have greater influence than unfamiliar/unrelated demonstrators, and other conditions where the reverse is true.

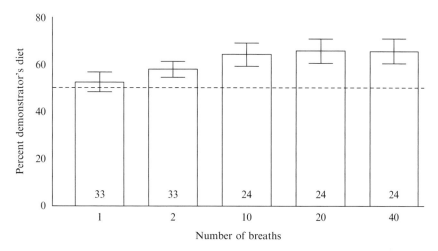

FIG. 12. Mean ± S.E. percentage demonstrator's diet eaten during testing by observer rats offered a choice between cinnamon- and cocoa-flavored diet after interacting with a human demonstrator that had eaten either cinnamon- or cocoa-flavored rat chow and breathed on each observer rat either 1, 2, 10, 20, or 40 times. Horizontal line = expected percent demonstrator's diet eaten by observers if observers' food choices were not influenced by prior interaction with a human demonstrator. Numbers in histograms = N/group (Galef and Tong, unpublished data).

3. Copy Successful Individuals

Successful foragers that are eating a nutritionally balanced diet and avoiding ingesting deleterious quantities of naturally occurring toxins will be healthier than those failing to secure a balanced diet or ingesting naturally occurring toxins. In particular, successful foragers should be less likely than unsuccessful foragers to be suffering observable gastrointestinal distress.

Numerous investigations both in our laboratory and elsewhere have explored the possibility that healthy demonstrators are more effective than ill demonstrators in altering their observers' food choices. Some laboratories (Galef et al., 1983, 1990; Grover et al., 1988) have been unable to provide evidence of a superiority of successful to unsuccessful demonstrators; others, for example, Hishamura (1998, 2000) and Kuan and Colwill (1997) may have had better luck. However, Hishamura (2000, p. 185) injected his ill demonstrators with an extremely hypertonic LiCl solution (0.7 M) that severely disrupted their behavior. "The injected demonstrator rats struggled wildly immediately after injection. After a few seconds they became quiet, and crouched for a few hours." Perhaps such debilitated demonstrators were unwilling to engage in social interaction with potential observers and consequently failed to affect their observers' food choices. An attempt in our laboratory to replicate Kuan and Colwill (1997) provided marginal evidence of a superiority of poisoned to unpoisoned demonstrators in altering their observers' food choices, a result opposite that reported by Kuan and Colwill (Galef and Whiskin, 2000).

Hill and Ryan (2006) report that female sailfin mollies (*Poecilia latipinna*), a species in which males mate with both conspecific and heterospecific females but prefer conspecific to heterospecific females as partners (1) increase their affiliation with nonpreferred conspecific males seen consorting with conspecific females, but (2) decrease their tendency to affiliate with nonpreferred males seen consorting with heterospecific females. Hill and Ryan (2006) interpreted this finding as providing evidence that females copy the mate choices of high, but not of low quality females, although alternative interpretations of the observed result are surely possible. For example, if male sailfin mollies compete for access to conspecific females, observation of a male molly with a conspecific female would provide an observing female molly with information as to the male's quality, and she might be expected to increase her preference only for males that appeared to have been successful in competition for access to preferred females. Consequently, whether focal female mollies should be thought of as copying the mate choices of successful but not of unsuccessful female models is not clear.

4. Copy the Majority

Chou and Richerson (1992) used social transmission of food choice to look for evidence that the relative number of demonstrators eating each of two diets would influence the subsequent preference of a naïve observer rat choosing between those diets. In each of four experiments, Chou and Richerson (1992) found that the greater the proportion of five demonstrator rats with which a single observer rat interacted that had eaten a diet, the greater that observer's preference for that diet in a subsequent choice test. Galef and Whiskin (1995) have repeated that result.

In related experiments, Beck and Galef (1989) showed that three demonstrator rats were significantly more effective than one in causing young rats to ingest a relatively unpalatable diet containing protein when that diet was presented together with three more-palatable, protein-poor diets, and Galef (1986) found that interaction with two demonstrators that had eaten a diet to which observers had previously learned a poison-induced aversion were more effective in reversing that aversion than was interaction with a single demonstrator that had eaten the averted diet. Studies by Lachlan et al. (1998) and Laland and Williams (1998) in guppies and by Lefebvre and Giraldeau (2002) in pigeons (*Columba livia*) provide additional evidence that the probability that a naïve animal will adopt a pattern of behavior increases as the proportion or number of demonstrators exhibiting that behavior increases. However, it has been argued that a linear association between the proportion of demonstrators exhibiting a behavior and the probability that an observer will adopt that behavior does not provide convincing evidence of a strategy of copying majorities (Laland, 2004).

All else being equal, a naïve individual should be exposed more frequently to information provided by a majority than by a minority of demonstrators, and as indicated in earlier discussion of copying familiar and unfamiliar demonstrators, (Section II. B. 2) may simply respond to the relative amount of information received regarding available alternatives. Indeed, the relatively linear response of observers to the ratio of demonstrators that have eaten each of two foods reported by Chou and Richerson (1992) and Galef and Whiskin (1995) is consistent with the view that the greater the amount of information an observer rat receives from conspecifics regarding a food, the greater the social enhancement of its preference for that food. Only if observers were to show a disproportionate tendency to copy a majority of demonstrators would there be evidence of a strategy of copying majorities (Laland, 2004).

5. Copy Good Social Learners

Whether copying good imitators is an effective strategy is a matter of debate. Some theoreticians follow Blackmore (1999) in suggesting that an enhanced ability to acquire cultural memes should prove adaptive (e.g., Higgs, 2000), while others maintain the opposite, (e.g., Kendal, 2003). Empirical work on the issue is limited, although results of a few studies suggest that at least some birds can identify good social learners and are therefore consistent with the hypothesis that good social learners might be preferred models. For example, Nowicki et al. (2002) report that female song sparrows (*Melospiza melodia*) prefer the songs of males that copy accurately, and suggest that ability to copy songs is a reliable index of a male's quality, while Hile et al. (2005) have proposed that, early in courtship, female budgerigars (*Melopsittacus undulatus*) prefer males that learn rapidly to mimic their vocalizations.

Although it remains unclear just how rats, unlike birds, might identify individuals that were better social learners than others, we have recently completed a study in which, in each of three replicates, we allowed 18 naïve observer rats to interact with demonstrator rats fed a cinnamon-flavored diet, and then selected the six that, when subsequently offered a choice between cinnamon and cocoa-flavored diets for 24 h, showed greatest and least preference for cinnamon-flavored diet. The social learning exhibited

by the six "best" and six "worst" social learners differed dramatically, with
the best social learners eating an average of 94.0 ± 2.7% and the worst
social learners eating only 36.3 ± 2.0% cinnamon-flavored diet. We then
used these 12 observer rats as demonstrators for 12 new observer rats
(Galef and Whiskin, unpublished data) that first interacted with a demonstrator fed cinnamon-flavored diet and then chose for 23 h between
cinnamon- and cocoa-flavored diets.

Although there was a tendency for observers to eat more cinnamon-
flavored diet after interacting with a best than with a worst social learner
as demonstrator, the effect was not significant (Fig. 13). Further, when we
repeated the experiment with an additional group of 12 observers each of
which interacted simultaneously with two demonstrators, one chosen from
among six "best" social learners and the other from among six "worst"
social learners and one fed cinnamon-flavored diet and the other cocoa-
flavored diet (counterbalanced across the quality of demonstrators' prior
social learning), we found no effect of demonstrators' previous performance as social learners on their observers' preferences (Fig. 13).

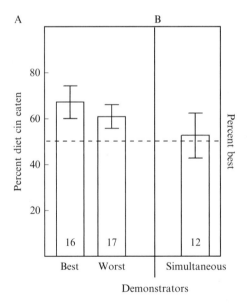

FIG. 13. Mean ± S.E. percentage demonstrator's diet eaten during testing by observers that
interacted (A) with either "best" or "worst" demonstrators and (B) simultaneously with both a
"best" and "worst" social learner. Dashed line = expected percent demonstrator's diet eaten
by observers if observers' food choices were not influenced by prior interaction with demonstrators. Numbers in histograms = N/group (Galef and Whiskin, unpublished data).

III. Conclusions

A. Overview of Results

The series of experiments discussed above was undertaken to examine predictions derived from formal models of social learning as to when animals should increase their reliance on socially learning and from whom they should learn. I hoped that examining multiple predictions from theory in a single empirical system would provide both a picture of the adequacy of current models and data of potential use in increasing their accuracy.

My students and I found that formal models had considerably greater success in predicting when rats will rely on social learning than in predicting who rats would copy (Table II). Our data were consistent with four of five "when strategies," (copy when dissatisfied, when unproductive, when uncertain, and when the environment is relatively stable), whereas only one of six "who strategies" ("copy the majority") received any empirical support, resulting in a nearly statistically reliable difference in the success of formal models in predicting who and when rats would copy (Fisher's exact probability test, $P = 0.08$; Table II). Further, as indicated in the preceding discussion of "copy the majority," (Section II.B.4) although the results of several studies indicate that both rats and other animals show a positive relationship between the proportion of demonstrators exhibiting

TABLE II

Summary of Results of Experiments Reviewed in the Present Manuscript Examining Strategies of Norway Rats Learning Socially About Foods

"When" strategies of social learning	
Copy when established behavior is unproductive	Yes
Copy when asocial learning is costly	No
Copy when uncertain	Yes
Copy when dissatisfied	Yes
Copy when the environment is stable[a]	Yes
"Who" strategies of social learning	
Copy older individuals	No
Copy kin	No!
Copy familiar individuals	No!
Copy successful individuals	No
Copy if better	No
Copy the majority	Maybe
Copy good social learners	No

Not!, the opposite of the predicted outcome.
[a]Not considered in Laland (2004).

a behavior and the probability that their observers will adopt that behavior, the support such findings offer for a "copy the majority strategy" is weak at best. Such proportional copying may reflect not a strategy of observers, but a difference in the amount of information demonstrators in the majority and minority provide to their observers.

If the data in Table II, describing the results of experiments using Norway rats' social learning about foods are analyzed, ignoring the ambiguous evidence consistent with a strategy of "copy the majority," then the difference in success of predictions of "when" and "who" strategies reaches statistical significance (Fisher's exact test, $P < 0.05$). Further evidence of the lack of success of formal models in predicting who rats will copy, if further evidence is needed, is provided by the tendency of observer rats, in contradiction to theory, to copy unfamiliar demonstrators in preference to familiar demonstrators. In general, Norway rats choosing between foods do not seem to use the "who strategies" formal theory predicts.

B.   WHY THE GREATER SUCCESS OF PREDICTIONS FROM "WHEN"
      THAN from "WHO" STRATEGIES?

Why formal models should be more successful in predicting when social learning will occur than who will serve as a model for such learning is not clear. Perhaps correlations between states of the environment and the value of reliance on socially acquired information are stronger than correlations between characteristics of potential models and the value of information that they provide. If so, natural selection for attention to the state of the environment would have been stronger than natural selection for attention to characteristics of potential informants, and the greater success of predictions of "when" than "who" strategies would be explained. However, attention to at least some characteristics of potential models would seem almost certain to have a powerful effect on the value of social leaning. For example, selection might be expected to act strongly to favor copying the behavior of healthy, successful rather than of obviously ill, unsuccessful foragers. Indeed, the failure, despite many years of attempts both in my laboratory and elsewhere, to find any evidence that rats are more likely to adopt the behaviors of healthy, conscious potential models than of unhealthy or unconscious ones remains something of a mystery.

Noble et al. (2001) have provided a model demonstrating that in environments containing exclusively lethal toxins, rats should copy the food choices of both healthy and sick individuals, though it is of course unlikely rats evolved in such an environment. Galef (1985, 1991) has proposed that, because rats may most often become ill for reasons that have nothing to do with the foods they have eaten, lost opportunity costs resulting from not eating foods ingested by unhealthy demonstrators might be greater than any benefits resulting from avoiding such foods.

Although creating both formal models (Noble et al., 2001) and informal arguments (Galef, 1985, 1991) as to why rats should not learn to avoid foods eaten by ill or unconscious conspecifics is relatively simple, such *post hoc* explanations are inherently suspect. Explanations in the literature of other failures to find evidence consistent with predictions from social-learning theory (e.g., Briggs et al., 1996; Frommen et al., 2007) are similarly *post hoc*.

1. Adaptive Specialization

Hoppitt and Laland (2008, p. 133) have recently proposed that the social enhancement of food preferences found in Norway rats is the expression of a specialized learning mechanism that evolved to implement the general adaptive strategy "eat what others eat." If so, social learning about foods might resemble taste-aversion learning, the other proposed adaptive specialization seen in rats' food selection, in restricting the range of stimuli to which rats attend when learning about foods.

As the name taste-aversion learning implies, rats learn far more easily to associate tastes than exteroceptive stimuli (e.g., sights or sounds) with subsequent aversive gastrointestinal events, a phenomenon referred to in the psychological literature as cue-to-consequence specificity (Garcia and Ervin, 1968) or preparedness (Seligman, 1970). Such preferred association of taste cues with gastrointestinal upset seems sensible in that food is tasted in the mouth and ingestion has gastrointestinal consequences.

Three of the four "when strategies" (copy when individual learning is unproductive, when dissatisfied, and when uncertain) that accurately pre-dicted rats' increased reliance on social learning each involve an animal monitoring either the consequences of its own behavior (whether that behavior was productive) or its own internal state (its level of comfort or certainty about the state of the environment). The "when strategy" (copy when predators are present) and the seven "who strategies" that were not confirmed (copy familiar individuals, older individuals, etc.) each involved monitoring features of the external environment.

As in taste-aversion learning, rats may have difficulty using information about the external environment to modulate their responses to socially acquired information about foods. If so, as Hoppitt and Laland's (2008) analogy between rats' social learning of food preferences and their taste-aversion learning suggests, then the greater success of predictions from "when" than from "who" strategies might be expected. However, why failure to attend to exteroceptive cures in social learning about foods might be adaptive is not nearly so obvious as why rats should fail to attend to such cues in individual taste-aversion learning. Consequently, positing evolution of a strategy to "eat what others have eaten," as have Hoppitt and Laland (2008) begs the question of why a strategies of "eat what healthy others have eaten" or "eat what kin have eaten" did not evolve instead.

2. *Problems with Failures to Find Evidence*

It might be argued that failure to find evidence consistent with predictions from "who strategies" is not particularly informative because, as is always the case with failures to find evidence consistent with predictions from theory, the design of failed experiments might have been inadequate to test the prediction. However, problems inherent in failures to reject null hypotheses does not explain the difference in outcomes of tests of "who strategies" and "when strategies," especially given the greater ease of designing experiments with high face validity to test the former than the latter. Convincing tests of the hypotheses that rats attend to kin, to older individuals, to the majority, etc., are far easier to design than are convincing tests of whether rats are more likely to rely on social learning when, for example, dissatisfied or engaged in unproductive behavior.

3. *Alternative Priorities*

As discussed in the sections on "copy kin or familiar individuals" (Section II.B.2) and "copy older individuals," (Section II.B.1) when individuals participate in a social interaction, the social interaction itself may be more important to participants than whatever social information might be available during the interaction. For example, Choleris et al.'s (1998) finding, in Mongolian gerbils, of an anxiety-induced failure to learn socially from unfamiliar demonstrators and Lachlan et al.'s (1998) report of young guppies preferring to feed with age mates to reduce predation risk suggest, as does our finding that rats spend more time interacting with unfamiliar than with familiar demonstrators, that considerations having nothing to do with social learning itself may be important in determining whether social learning occurs in many potential social-learning situations. More generally, characteristics of interacting individuals along dimensions orthogonal to their suitability as models for social learning, might determine the likelihood that social learning would occur during an interaction (for review, see Coussi-Korbel and Fragaszy, 1995). For example, demonstrators of high social status might be less effective than demonstrators of low social status despite the potential superiority of individuals with high social status as models, because the presence of high status individuals inhibits behavior in low-status individuals (Drea and Wallen, 1999; Nicol and Pope, 1994).

4. Where is the Problem?

The fact that results of our tests of predictions from "who strategies" of social learning were not consistent with theory suggests that there is something wrong either (1) with the theories from which the predictions derive, (2) with our methods of testing those predictions, or (3) with our choice of Norway rat's social learning about foods that makes it inappropriate for testing predictions formal theory. As discussed above, tests of copy familiar individuals, copy older individuals, etc., are fairly straightforward, so it is unlikely that methodological errors are the source of the problem. As is also discussed above, there may be some reason to question the validity of Norway rats' social learning about foods as an empirical system for examining predictions from general theory. Indeed, instances in which empirical tests of some "who strategies" have provided confirming evidence, for example, the tendency of guppies to copy the mate choices of larger and presumably older individuals, more experienced individuals (Dugatkin and Godin, 1993) is consistent with the view that Norway rats may be idiosyncratic in some way.

Last, it is of course possible that the models from which "who strategies" are derived are incomplete. In particular, as noted in Section II.B.1, results of analyses of success (Choleris et al., 1998) and of failure (Galef and Whiskin, 2008a) of predictions concerning the effects of familiarity and kinship on social learning about foods by Mongolian gerbils and Norway rats suggest that social interactions between individuals with differing characteristics that are not considered in formal models of social learning may be critical in determining whether predictions from such models are confirmed or refuted. For example, the tendency of Mongolian gerbils to attack unfamiliar, unrelated conspecifics the first time that they encounter them and of Norway rats to spend more time in olfactory investigation of unfamiliar than familiar conspecifics may interact with the processes that support social learning about foods (i.e., exposure to diet related cues carried on the breath of mammals that have recently eaten) to produce either consistent or inconsistent with predictions from social-learning theory. Thus, whether "who strategies" are confirmed or disconfirmed may depend on how the specific mechanisms resulting in social learning in any particular case are affected by the types of social interaction engaged in by potential social learners and models with various characteristics. If the social interactions elicited by the characteristics of potential models and social learners determine the likelihood of social learning occurring, then accurate prediction of the characteristics of individuals that increase the probability that they will be exploited as sources of information may require incorporation into models of social learning of variables other than those shaping the evolution of social learning itself,. Our theories may be focused on the factors affecting the evolution of reliance on socially acquired information, but our animal subjects may have priorities other than acquiring social information when they encounter potential models.

Acknowledgments

I thank the Natural Sciences and Engineering Research Council of Canada for 40 years of continuous support and 40 undergraduates and a score of graduate students who, over the decades, devoted innumerable hours to studying Norway rats' social learning about foods. I particularly thank Elaine Whiskin for her invaluable contributions during the more than 20 years that she worked with me. Her irrepressible good spirits, loyalty, and thoughtfulness were critical to whatever success our laboratory enjoyed.

References

Aoki, K., Feldman, M.W., 1987. Toward a theory for the evolution of cultural communication: coevolution of signal transmission and reception. Proc. Natl. Acad. Sci. USA 84, 7164–7168.

Beck, M., Galef Jr., B.G., 1989. Social influences on the selection of a protein-sufficient diet by Norway rats. J. Comp. Psychol. 103, 132–139.

Beck, M., Hitchcock, C., Galef Jr., B.G., 1988. Diet sampling by wild Norway rats (*Rattus norvegicus*) offered several unfamiliar foods. Anim. Learn. Behav. 16, 224–230.

Blackmore, S., 1999. The Meme Machine. Oxford University Press, Oxford.

Boyd, R., Richerson, P.J., 1985. Culture and the Evolutionary Process. Chicago University Press, Chicago.

Boyd, R., Richerson, P.J., 1988. An evolutionary model of social learning: the effects of spatial and temporal variation. In: Zentall, T.R., Galef Jr., B.G. (Eds.), Social Learning: Psychological and Biological Perspectives. Lawrence Erlbaum, Hillsdale, NJ, pp. 29–48.

Briggs, S.E., Godin, J.G., Dugatkin, L.A., 1996. Mate-choice copying under the risk of predation in the Trinidadian guppy (*Poecilia reticulata*). Behav. Ecol. 7, 151–152.

Choleris, E., Valsecchi, P., Wang, Y., Ferrari, P., Kavaliers, M., Mainardi, M., 1998. Social learning of food preferences in male and female Mongolian gerbils is facilitated by the anxiolytic chlordiazepoxide. Pharmacol. Biochem. Behav. 60, 575–584.

Chou, L.S., Richerson, P.J., 1992. Multiple models in social transmission of food selection by Norway rats. Anim. Behav. 44, 337–343.

Coolen, L., van Bergen, Y., Day, R.L., Laland, K.N., 2003. Species differences in the adaptive use of social information in sticklebacks. Proc. R. Soc. Lond. B 270, 2413–2419.

Coussi-Korbel, S., Fragaszy, D.M., 1995. On the relation between social dynamics and sSocial learning. Anim. Behav. 50, 1441–1453.

Crowley, P., Travers, S., Linton, M., Cohn, S., Sih, A., Sargent, C., 1991. Mate density, predation risk and the seasonal sequence of mate choice: a dynamic game. Am. Nat. 137, 567–596.

Dewar, G., 2004. Social and asocial cues about new food: cue reliability influences intake in rats. Learn. Behav. 32, 82–89.

Drea, C.M., Wallen, K., 1999. Low status monkeys "play dumb" when learning in mixed social groups. Proc. Natl. Acad. Sci. USA 96, 12965–12969.

Dugatkin, L.A., Godin, J.G.J., 1993. Female mate copying in the guppy (*Poecilia reticulata*): age-dependent effects. Behav. Ecol. 4, 289–292.

Enquist, M., Eriksson, K., Ghirlanda, S., 2007. Critical social learning: a solution to Roger's paradox of nonadaptive culture. Am. Anthropol. 109, 727–734.

Epstein, A.N., Stellar, E., 1955. The control of salt preference in the adrenalectomized rat. J. Comp. Physiol. Psychol. 48, 167–172.

Feldman, M.W., Aoki, K., Kumm, J., 1996. Individual versus social learning, evolutionary analysis in fluctuating environments. Anthropol. Sci. 104, 209–232.

Forkman, B., 1991. Social facilitation is shown by gerbils when presented with novel but not with familiar food. Anim. Behav. 42, 860–861.

Friedman, M.I., 2000. Too many choices? A critical essay on macronutrient selection. In: Berthoud, H.R., Seeley, R.J. (Eds.), Neural and Metabolic Control of Macronutrient Intake. CRC Press, Baton Rouge, pp. 11–18.

Frommen, J.G., Luz, C., Bakker, T.C.M., 2007. Nutritional state influences shoaling preference for familiars. Zoology 110, 369–376.

Galef Jr., B.G., 1985. Direct and indirect behavioral processes for the social transmission of f food avoidance. In: Bronstein, P., Braveman, N.S. (Eds.), Experimental Assessments and Clinical Applications of Conditioned Food aversions. New York Academy of Sciences, New York, pp. 203–215.

Galef Jr., B.G., 1986. Social interaction modifies learned aversions, sodium appetite, and both palatability and handling-time induced dietary preference in rats (*R. norvegicus*). J. Comp. Psychol. 100, 432–439.

Galef Jr., B.G., 1991. A contrarian view of the wisdom of the body as it relates to dietary self selection. Psychol. Rev. 98, 218–223.

Galef Jr., B.G., 1996. Social influences on the food preferences and feeding behaviors of vertebrates. In: Capaldi, E.D. (Ed.), Why We Eat What We Eat, second ed American Psychological Association. Washington, DC, pp. 207–230.

Galef Jr., B.G., 2002. Social learning of food preferences in rodents: A rapidly learned appetitive behavior. Curr. Protoc. Neurosci. 8.5 D1–8.5 D8, 76, 1381–1388.

Galef Jr., B.G., 2006. Theoretical and empirical approaches to understanding when animals use socially acquired information and from whom they acquire it. In: Lucas, J.R., Simmons, J. R., L, J.R. (Eds.) Essays in Animal Behaviour: Celebrating 50 Years of Animal Behaviour. Academic Press, San Diego, pp. 161–182.

Galef Jr., B.G., Stein, M., 1985. Demonstrator influence on observer diet preference: Analyses of critical social interactions and olfactory signals. Anim. Learn. Behav. 13, 31–38.

Galef Jr., B.G., Whiskin, E.E., 1995. Learning socially to eat more of one food than of another. J. Comp. Psychol. 109, 99–101.

Galef Jr., B.G., Whiskin, E.E., 2000. Demonstration of a socially transmitted flavor aversion in rats? Kuan and Colwill (1997) revisited. Psychon. Bull. Rev. 7, 631–635.

Galef Jr., B.G., Whiskin, E.E., 2004. Effects of environmental stability and demonstrator age on social learning of food preferences by young Norway rats. Anim. Behav. 68, 897–902.

Galef Jr., B.G., Whiskin, E.E., 2006. Increased reliance on socially acquired information while foraging in risky situations? Anim. Behav. 72, 1169–1176.

Galef Jr., B.G., Whiskin, E.E., 2008a. Effectiveness of familiar kin and unfamiliar non-kin demonstrator rats in altering food choices of their observers. Anim. Behav. 77, 1329–1335.

Galef Jr., B.G., Whiskin, E.E., 2008b. Use of social information by sodium- and protein-deficient rats: a test of a prediction (Boyd and Richerson 1988). Anim. Behav. 75, 627–630.

Galef Jr., B.G., Wigmore, S.W., 1983. Transfer of information concerning distant foods: a laboratory investigation of the "information-centre" hypothesis. Anim. Behav. 31, 748–758.

Galef, B.G., Yarkovsky, N., 2009. Further studies of reliance on socially acquired information when foraging in potentially risky situations. *Anim. Behav.* 77, 1329–1335.

Galef Jr., B.G., Wigmore, S.W., Kennett, D.J., 1983. A failure to find socially mediated taste-aversion learning in Norway rats (*R. norvegicus*). J. Comp. Psychol. 97, 358–363.

Galef Jr., B.G., Kennett, D.J., Wigmore, S.W., 1984. Transfer of information concerning distant foods in rats: A robust phenomenon. Anim. Learn. Behav. 12, 292–296.

Galef Jr., B.G., Kennett, D.J., Stein, M., 1985. Demonstrator influence on observer diet preference: Effects of simple exposure and the presence of a demonstrator. Anim. Learn. Behav. 13, 25–30.

Galef Jr., B.G., Mason, J.R., Preti, G., Bean, N.J., 1988. Carbon disulfide: a semiochemical mediating socially-induced diet choice in rats. Physiol. Behav. 42, 119–124.

Galef Jr., B.G., McQuoid, L.M., Whiskin, E.E., 1990. Further evidence that Norway rats do not socially transmit learned aversions to toxic baits. Anim. Learn. Behav. 18, 199–205.

Galef Jr., B.G., Beck, M., Whiskin, E.E., 1991. Protein deficiency magnifies socialinfluences on the food choices of Norway rats (*Rattus norvegicus*). J. Comp. Psychol. 105, 55–59.

Galef Jr., B.G., Dudley, K.E., Whiskin, E.E., 2008. Social learning of food preferences in'dissatisfied' and 'uncertain' rats. Anim. Behav. 75, 631–637.

Garcia, J., Ervin, F.R., 1968. Gustatory-visceral and telerectptor-cutaneous conditioning—adaptation to internal and external milieus. Commun. Behav. Biol. Part A. 1, 389–415.

Gerrish, C.J., Alberts, J.R., 1995. Differential influence of adult and juvenile conspecifics on feeding by Norway rats (*Rattus norvegicus*). J. Comp. Psychol. 109, 61–67.

Giraldeau, L.A., Valone, T.J., Templeton, J.J., 2002. Potential disadvantages of using socially acquired information. Philos. Trans. R. Soc. Lond. B 357, 1559–1566.

Grover, C.A., Kixmiller, J.S., Erickson, C.A., Becker, A.H., Davis, S.F., Nallan, G.B., 1988. The social transmission of information concerning aversively conditioned liquids. Psychol. Rec. 38, 557–566.

Higgs, P.G., 2000. The mimetic transition: a simulation study of the evolution of learning by imitation. Proc. R. Soc. Lond. B 270, 1355–1361.

Hill, S.E., Ryan, M.J., 2006. The role of model female quality in the mate choice copying behaviour of sailfin mollies. Biol. Lett. 2, 203–205.

Hile, A.G., Burley, N.T., Coopersmith, C.B., Foster, S., Stiedter, G.F., 2005. Effects of male vocal learning on female behavior in the budgerigar, *Melopsittacus undulatus*. Ethology 111, 901–923.

Hishimura, Y., 1998. Food choice in rats (*Rattus norvegicus*): the effect of exposure to a poisoned conspecific. Jpn. Psychol. J. 42, 183–187.

Hishimura, Y., 2000. Enhancement of food aversion by exposure to a poisoned conspecific in Norway rats (*Rattus norvegicus*). Jpn. Psychol. J. 40, 172–177.

Hoppitt, W., Laland, K.N., 2008. Social processes influencing learning in animals: a review of the evidence. Adv. Study Behav. 38, 105–165.

Kendal, R.L., Coolen, I., Laland, K.N., 2004. The role of conformity in foraging when personal and social information conflict. Behav. Ecol. 15, 269–277.

Kendal, J.R., 2003. An investigation into social learning: mechanisms, diffusion dynamics and evolutionary consequences. *Unpublished doctoral thesis.* University of Cambridge.

Kendal, R.L., Coolen, I., van Bergen, Y., Laland, K.N., 2005. Trade-offs in the adaptive use of social and asocial learning. Adv. Study Behav. 38, 333–379.

Kuan, L.A., Colwill, R.M., 1997. Demonstration of a socially transmitted aversion in the rat. Psychon. Bull. Rev. 4, 374–377.

Lachlan, R.F., Crooks, L., Laland, K.N., 1998. Who follows whom? Shoaling preferences and social learning of foraging information in guppies. Anim. Behav. 56, 181–190.

Laland, K.N., 2004. Social learning strategies. Learn. Behav. 32, 4–14.

Laland, K.N., Williams, K., 1997. Shoaling generates social learning of foraging information in guppies. Anim. Behav. 53, 1161–1169.

Laland, K.N., Williams, K., 1998. Social transmission of maladaptive information in guppies. Behav. Ecol. 9, 493–499.

Laland, K.N., Richerson, P.J., Boyd, R., 1996. Developing a theory of animal social learning. In: Heyes, C.M., Galef Jr., B.G. (Eds.), Social Learning in Animals: The Roots of Culture. Academic Press, San Diego, pp. 129–154.

Lefebvre, L., Giraldeau, L.A., 1994. Cultural transmission in pigeons is affected by the number of tutors and bystanders present during demonstration. Anim. Behav. 47, 331–337.

Lima, S.L., Dill, L.M., 1990. The behavioral decisions made under risk of predation- a review and prospectus. Can. J. Zool. 68, 619–640.

Nicol, C.J., Pope, S.J., 1994. Social learning in small flocks of laying hens. Anim. Behav. 52, 767–774.

Noble, J., Todd, P.M., Tuci, E., 2001. Explaining social learning of food preferences without aversions: an evolutionary simulation model of Norway rats. Proc. R. Soc. Lond. B 268, 141–149.

Nowicki, S., Searcy, W.A., Peters, S., 2002. Quality of song learning affects female response to male bird song. Proc. R. Soc. Lond. B 269, 1949–1954.

Orrock, J.L., Danielson, B.J., Brinckerhoff, R.J., 2004. Rodent foraging is affected by indirect but not direct cues of predation risk. Behav. Ecol. 15, 433–437.

Powell, F., Banks, P.B., 2004. Do house mice modify their foraging behavior in response to predator odours and habitat? Anim. Behav. 67, 753–759.

Ratcliffe, J.M., ter Hofstede, H.M., 2005. Roosts as information centres: social learning of food preference in bats. Biol. Lett. 1, 72–74.

Rogers, A., 1988. Does biology constrain culture? Am. Anthropol. 90, 819–831.

Rozin, P., 1969. Adaptive food sampling patterns in vitamin deficient rats. J. Comp. Physiol. Psychol. 69, 126–132.

Rozin, P.N., Schulkin, J., 1990. Food selection. In: Stricker, E.M. (Ed.), Handbook of Behavioral Neurobiology, vol. 10. Neurobiology of Food and Fluid Intake. Plenum Press, New York, pp. 297–321.

Real, L.A., 1990. Search theory and mate choice. Am. Nat. 136, 376–405.

Saggerson, A.L., Honey, R.C., 2006. Observational learning of instrumental discriminations in the rat: the role of demonstrator type. Q. J. Exp. Psychol. 59, 1909–1920.

Schlag, K.H., 1998. Why imitate, and if so, how? A bounded rational approach to multi-armed bandits. J. Econ. Theory 78, 130–156.

Seligman, M.E.P., 1970. On the generality of the laws of learning. Psychol. Rev. 77, 406–418.

Sih, A., 1994. Predation risk and the evolutionary ecology of reproductive behavior. J. Fish Biol. 45, 111–130.

Steiniger, von.F., 1950. Beitrage zur Soziologie und sonstigen Biologie der Wanderratte. Zeitschrift fur Tierpsycholgie 7, 356–370.

Stricker, E.M., 2000. Specific appetites and homeostatic systems. In: Berthoud, H.R., Seeley, R. J. (Eds.), Neural and Metabolic Control of Macronutrient Intake. CRC Press, Baton Rouge, pp. 3–11.

Valsecchi, P., Choleris, E., Moles, A., Guop, C., Mainardi, M., 1996. Kinship and familiarity as factors affecting transfer of food preferences in Mongolian gerbils (Meriones unguiculatus). J. Comp. Psychol. 110, 243–251.

Visalberghi, E., Fragaszy, D.M., 1995. The behavior of capuchin monkeys, Cebus apella, with novel food: the role of social context. Anim. Behav. 49, 1089–1095.

Yoerg, S.I., 1991. Social feeding reverses learned flavor aversions in spotted hyena (Crocuta crocuta). J. Comp. Psychol. 105, 185–189.

Behavior of Fishes in the Sexual/Unisexual Mating System of the Amazon Molly (*Poecilia formosa*)

Ingo Schlupp

DEPARTMENT OF ZOOLOGY, UNIVERSITY OF OKLAHOMA, NORMAN,
OKLAHOMA 73019, USA

I. Introduction

Studying unusual organisms helps us understand what appears to be more typical. The Amazon molly (*Poecilia formosa*) is such an unusual organism. Amazon mollies are of hybrid origin. They are also clonal and all-female fishes, which for an unknown reason require sperm of males of a different species to successfully reproduce. Males of several species serve as sperm donor in nature, among them the two species that were involved in the original hybridization that lead to Amazon mollies (Table I and below). This immediately raises a number of interesting questions, both ultimate and proximate. One of these questions is, for example, how the Amazon molly survives and evolves in the absence of recombination (Loewe and Lamatsch, 2008; Schlupp, 2005). This question is at the heart of a whole complex of questions trying to elucidate the maintenance of sexual recombination (Bell, 1982; Maynard Smith, 1978; West et al., 1999). As the Amazon molly is oddly sperm dependent, one can also ask what the fitness consequences are for the heterospecific males that mate with the "wrong" kind of females (Schlupp et al., 1994) or which mechanisms are in place to secure these matings from a female perspective (Schlupp et al., 1991). In a broader context, research on Amazon mollies and other organisms like it touch upon many important concepts in evolutionary biology, such as the maintenance of recombination, host–parasite dynamics, sexual selection, and communication networks. Interestingly, behavior consistently emerges as extremely important to our understanding of such sexual/asexual mating systems.

0065-3454/09 $35.00
DOI: 10.1016/S0065-3454(09)39005-1

TABLE I
SPECIES IN THE AMAZON MOLLY MATING COMPLEX

Common name	Scientific name	Remarks
Amazon molly	*Poecilia formosa*	Hybrid, mostly diploid, some triploids
Atlantic molly	*Poecilia mexicana*	Sexual host in Mexico, maternal ancestor
Sailfin molly	*Poecilia latipinna*	Sexual host in Texas, paternal ancestor
Tamesi molly	*Poecilia latipunctata*	Sexual host in Mexico

In the present review, I shall first provide some background knowledge on the origin of the Amazon molly and then focus on the contribution studies of their behavior have made to understanding this system both in terms of proximate and ultimate questions (Tinbergen, 1963). I shall further try to explain how many of these studies also have important implications for "regular" sexual species. Other aspects of this and other asexual mating systems have been reviewed elsewhere (Beukeboom and Vrijenhoek, 1998; Dawley, 1989; Schlupp, 2005; Suomalainen et al., 1987; Vrijenhoek, 1994).

II. GENERAL BACKGROUND

The Amazon molly was the first unisexual vertebrate to be described (Hubbs and Hubbs, 1932). Laura and Carl Hubbs prophetically hypothesized that Amazon mollies are hybrids, which was later confirmed multiple times using molecular methods (Avise et al., 1991; Schartl et al., 1995b; Tiedemann et al., 2005). The two species involved in this hybridization were the atlantic molly, *Poecilia mexicana* and the sailfin molly, *Poecilia latipinna* (at the time of the Hubbs's work, *P. mexicana* was not recognized as a species, but was considered *Poecilia sphenops*) (Table I). Essentially, a *P. latipinna* male is thought to have mated with a *P. mexicana* female producing unisexual hybrids (see Schlupp, 2005 for a discussion). Our current knowledge assumes a single origin, approximately 120,000 generations ago (Schartl et al., 1995b) near Tampico, Mexico. Amazon mollies since spread north to the lower Rio Grande valley and the Nueces River in Texas, USA (Costa and Schlupp, 2009; Schlupp et al., 2002) and south to the Rio Tuxpan in Mexico. Both parental species are extant and have wide distributions that reach far beyond the described distribution for Amazon mollies, providing opportunities for comparative studies with both overlapping and nonoverlapping populations (Gabor and Ryan, 2001).

Amazon mollies are not only hybrids, but also sperm dependent. All unisexual vertebrates (Dawley, 1989) and many unisexual invertebrates (Suomalainen et al., 1987) are hybrids. They were formed via mating of two well defined, sexual species, leading to instantaneous speciation. Interestingly, within vertebrates, unisexual reptiles (amniotes), like whiptail lizards (*Aspidocelis* spp.), do not require sperm to trigger embryogenesis (Dawley, 1989), while all unisexual fishes and amphibians are sperm dependent: they require sperm from heterospecific males for successful reproduction. Currently, we lack a good explanation for this pattern.

Amazon mollies are gynogenetic, in which they require sperm only to trigger embryogenesis (Schlupp, 2005). We currently know of three that species serve as sperm donor in nature: the two species involved in the original hybridization (*P. latipinna* and *P. mexicana*), and a third species, the Tamesi molly (*Poecilia latipunctata*), which had no role in the origin of the Amazon molly (Table I and Fig. 1). In the laboratory, males of a large number of species can serve as sperm donors (Schlupp et al., 2002), raising the question, what determines the natural range of the Amazon molly (see below)?

FIG. 1. Size polymorphism within males of *P. latipinna*. A US quarter with a diameter of 2.5 cm is displayed for size comparison.

Typically, male genetic information is not incorporated into the Amazon molly genome, but interestingly there are exceptions to this. In rare cases, male genes are actually incorporated and passed on (Nanda et al., 2007; Schartl et al., 1995a), providing us with extraordinary tools to study the role of ploidy changes in the evolution of these fishes (see below).

In gynogenesis, females produce unreduced eggs, which are then "pseudofertilized" by male sperm. Consequently, this mode of reproduction leads to clonal lineages in which mothers and daughters (and also sisters) are genetically extremely similar. Kallman (1962) demonstrated the same in Amazon mollies by grafting tissues between different members of a clonal lineage without eliciting an immune response (Kallman, 1962). Clonal similarity was later confirmed in several studies using some form of genetic fingerprinting (Schartl et al., 1991, 1995a; Turner et al., 1990).

The unreduced eggs of Amazon mollies are formed without meiosis (Rasch et al., 1982). They are typically diploid, but can also be triploid (see below) and in extremely rare cases even tetraploid (Lampert et al., 2007a). Gynogenesis is quite uncommon (Schlupp, 2005) in vertebrates, but because the involved clonal females depend on sperm of heterospecific males, this generates the playing field for very interesting behavioral dynamics. The broader background for this lies in the fact that two species with fundamentally different reproductive strategies are being compared. Living in the same habitat and sharing many resources, including males, sexual and clonal reproductive strategies are directly pitted against each other. Theory predicts that—all else being equal—the clonal species should outcompete the sexual species because they do not pay the twofold cost of sex (Maynard Smith, 1978): they do not produce males and they do not reduce their genome via meiosis. Since Amazon mollies are dependent on sperm, however, they do pay the costs directly associated with mating such as increased risk of predation, or transmission of sexually transmitted diseases. One of the questions that arise here is how such systems can show stable coexistence. The role of behavior in this context will be explored in the present paper.

Mollies are live-bearing fishes. Live-bearing fishes are widely used as model organisms in animal behavior and beyond (Meffe and Snelson, 1989), with the guppy being arguably one of the most studied fishes (Houde, 1997; Magurran, 2005). Males in the subfamily Poeciliinae (Hrbek et al., 2007) typically have a modified anal fin, the gonopodium, which is used as copulatory organ.

The mating sequence of the typical molly male starts with approaching the female. Once the male is close to the female he may try to make contact with his mouth with the genital region of the female (nipping). During this, males may obtain chemical information from the female. Subsequently, the male may swing his gonopodium forward, eventually seeking intromission into the female genital pore (Schlupp et al., 1991). If females do not cooperate, males may use thrusting to try to force inseminations (Schlupp et al., 2001). In some species of mollies, males may court females by swimming back and forth in front of a female. This courtship is typical for one clade of mollies, known as long-fin mollies, but not all males are courting: The small males of this species never court and rely on forced matings (Fig. 1). The sailfin molly is in this clade. A second clade, the short-fin mollies do not show courtship and all males rely only on thrusting or forced matings. Most male mollies have beautiful coloration, mainly in their fins, composed of structural colors, often blue tones, and pigment-based colors, especially yellows and reds. Males of the short-fin clade (and *P. latipunctata*, which looks like a short-fin molly, but is actually placed within the long-fin clade based on molecular evidence; Schartl et al., 1995b) can turn completely black when courting, providing very high-contrast signals with their colorful fins.

On average, females in this taxonomic group are larger than males. They form loose social groups, so-called shoals, in which numerous social interactions happen. Males make no investment into raising the offspring, other than sperm. Male size polymorphism is quite drastic: in sailfin and atlantic mollies the smallest mature males are less than 20 mm, while the largest males are more than 60 mm long (Fig. 1). In the sailfin molly, such size differences are coupled with behavioral differences (Farr et al., 1986; Travis, 1994a,b; Travis and Woodward, 1989; Trexler and Travis, 1990). The three main species discussed here seem to have relatively similar ecology. They are omnivorous feeders that take food items like small aquatic insects, but also algae and detritus. Amazon mollies form mixed schools with at least one of their sperm donor species (Schlupp et al., 1996).

III. MALE BEHAVIOR

A. MALE MATE CHOICE

Male mate choice is generally thought to be less relevant evolutionarily as compared to female choice because of the small investment males make into their gametes (Trivers, 1972) and because they can often mate many times in a short period of time. This is especially true in mating systems where males contribute nothing other than sperm, like in mollies. Male mate choice, however, can be adaptive for males, if the quality of mates differs strongly (Herdman et al., 2004; Hill and Ryan, 2006; Hoysak and

Godin, 2007; Simcox et al., 2005). Alternatively, matings might be very costly to males also selecting for male choosiness, such as in mormon crickets (Gwynne, 1981, 1984). Based on the general biology of live-bearing fishes, though, this seems very unlikely, as males make no investment into their offspring beyond sperm. Consequently, in the mating system of the Amazon molly one of the first questions that immediately comes to mind, is why males would mate with Amazon mollies? Selection should be favoring males that avoid mating with Amazon mollies, because the benefit is typically zero and there is an obvious (even if potentially small and so far undetermined) cost. Several studies have looked into this problem and many of them found that males of the host species (*P. latipinna* and *P. mexicana*) are capable of distinguishing between conspecific and hetero-specific females (e.g., Gumm et al., 2006; Hubbs, 1964; Ryan et al., 1996; Schlupp et al., 1991). This ability to discriminate, however, does not always translate into preferences and realized copulations, and several mechanisms have been reported to explain how Amazon mollies can obtain the matings they need. One example is a study by Schlupp et al. (1991), which established that Amazon molly females in a certain, "attractive" phase of their hormonal cycle are preferred by males over conspecific females that are in a different phase of their hormonal cycle. This is interesting because one would predict strong selection on Amazon mollies to evolve traits that are attractive to males—except that they are unisexual which means that they are less able to evolve such traits. In another complex with a somewhat similar mating system, the hybridogenetic *Poeciliopsis*, such a trait mimicking the sexual female has been reported (Lima et al., 1996). Unisexual females, in this case, resemble the sexual females in the pigmentation of their genital region.

Often mating preferences are studied focusing on visual cues in a binary choice test, which is a useful setup because the conditions are highly controlled and mating preferences can be carefully dissected. This can be combined with studies that allow full interactions between males and females, but the interpretation of these results is less straightforward because any mating decisions will be reflecting not only male preferences, but also female preferences and their interactions (Schlupp, 2005).

As I said earlier, in many experiments males of *P. mexicana* and *P. latipinna* have been shown to be able to discriminate between conspecific and heterospecific females. In addition to discrimination, very often males show the theoretically predicted preference for conspecific females. Male behavior should reflect a cost/benefit analysis relative to the cost of mating with females. While this seems generally a simple calculation because the benefit for males seems to be zero and any cost should favor males that mate preferentially with conspecific females, not all aspects of male mating behavior are well understood, especially not the real costs associated with matings (see below for a discussion of mate copying and its consequences). Consequently, a more complex picture has emerged, with some recent studies identifying several factors as influencing male preferences or choice. One such factor is female size. Gumm and Gabor (2005) showed that the very general male preference for larger female body size (Gabor and Page, 2003; Ryan and Keddy-Hector, 1992) can work to the Amazon molly's advantage if Amazon mollies are indeed larger, which is the case in most populations in Texas (Heubel, 2004), but it is not clear how important this phenomenon is.

Earlier studies have hypothesized that male preferences could also be relative to the male's own size. Balsano et al. (1985) had suggested that smaller males might be less discriminating because they are rejected by their conspecific females and are subordinate in the linear rank order that exists among males within this species. They also pointed out the role of "mating frenzies," in which multiple males attempt to mate with a single female, probably indicating considerable sexual conflict (Schlupp et al., 2001).

It is not clear, however, how selection would generate a pattern of weaker preferences in smaller males, because for them the payoff is thought to be zero, too, just like for larger males. Overall, there is little evidence that smaller males have clearly different preferences from larger males (Schlupp et al., 1994).

This said, it is clear that male size is important in multiple ways, influencing not only female choice, but also being critical, for example, in predation—with larger males being preferred by predators (Trexler et al., 1994)—and many more aspects of life history (Trexler et al., 1992).

B. POPULATION COMPOSITION

The composition of populations varies over time and space in many parameters, such as the frequencies of Amazons and sexual females, overall sex ratio, and the size composition of the females (Heubel, 2004). There is, for example, strong seasonal and spatial variation in population composition (Heubel et al., 2008). Interestingly, in this study, Amazon mollies seemed to increase in frequency over the breeding season, although the frequencies were almost even in the early season in Texas (Heubel, 2004). Selective winter mortality was implicated in explaining this pattern.Fischer and Schlupp (2009) found sailfin mollies to be more tolerant of cold temperatures and argued that cold spells in the winter could selectively affect Amazon mollies (Fig. 2). Amazon mollies, for example, lost motion control in a laboratory study at 8.56 °C, whereas sailfin mollies lost motion control at much lower temperatures (5.96 °C).

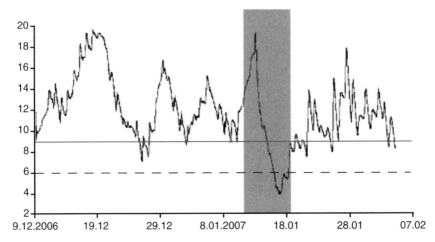

FIG. 2. Temperature profile for the winter of 2006/2007 in San Marcos, Texas. The x-axis shows time of the year, the y-axis gives temperature in C. The solid horizontal line indicates the temperature at which Amazon mollies loose motion control, the dashed line indicates the temperature at which sailfin mollies loose motion control. Sailfin mollies are much more tolerant of low temperatures. The highlighted area indicates a brief cold snap that is typical for Central Texas. See Fischer and Schlupp (2009) for details.

Temperature recordings in an actual molly habitat indicated that several times in the winter conditions existed that would selectively affect Amazon mollies, but not sailfin mollies (Fig. 2).

Over their geographic range in Texas, Heubel (2004) found that in some populations Amazon mollies dominate, whereas in other populations sailfins dominate. A similar pattern exists in Mexico (Balsano et al., 1989). The underlying reason for this is still unknown.

In Texas, mean female sizes of Amazon mollies and sailfin mollies were very dissimilar (Heubel, 2004) when compared over the whole season. Male mating preferences were reported to change seasonally with both Amazons and sailfin mollies being preferred at some time during the mating season. This pattern was relatively similar for the two populations studied. The existence of mixed groups raises the question how they arise and are maintained? Why do mollies form mixed schools? This was studied by Schlupp and Ryan (1996). They found that both Amazon mollies and sailfin mollies preferred conspecifc females when only one female of each species was present. When they titrated group size against species by presenting three heterospecific females against one conspecific female, the perceived benefits of being in a larger group trumped the preference for conspecifics.

This is in general agreement with the idea that "safety in numbers" is more important to shoaling females than species identity (Krause, 1994; Schlupp and Ryan, 1996).

Mixed groups set the stage for female/male interactions, including the heterospecific matings that Amazon mollies need to reproduce. If sexual males had an absolute preference for conspecifics, Amazon mollies would have no access to sperm. However, male choice is obviously imperfect, because Amazon mollies still exist today.

So, how do males fall for the wrong females? Several proximate mechanisms have been investigated to understand this. First, it is conceivable that Amazon mollies are under selection to make male decisions harder to reach. This points to a scenario of coevolution of sexuals and asexuals (Dawkins, 1979; Schlupp et al., 1991), but Dries (2003) argued that Amazon mollies may not evolve and in fact simply represent a "frozen F_1."

Evolution in an asexual species certainly can be slower, as compared to a sexual, but it is not less likely to happen *per se*. Interestingly, there is evidence that asexual females actively compete with sexual females over access to males (Foran and Ryan, 1994; Schlupp et al., 1992). Amazon mollies may also be similar to sexual females in their behavior and morphology, adding to male confusion. Indeed, there is relatively good evidence for such mimicry in the related taxa of asexual *Poeciliopsis*, where a unisexual topminnow appears to mimic a sexual in the coloration of the genital area (Lima et al., 1996).

As a sidebar, studies of the abiotic conditions under which signaling interactions occur can be very important. Turbidity, for example, can render decision making for males more difficult, as described by Heubel and Schlupp (2006). Under turbid conditions, males need more time to make a decision. In addition, there seems to be variation in male preferences over the mating season and based on geographic area (Heubel et al., 2008). Most importantly, sexual males living allopatrically from Amazon mollies seem to have a stronger preference for conspecifics, indicating that at least males of *P. latipinna* have evolved character displacement in response to the presence of Amazon mollies (Gabor and Ryan, 2001; Gabor et al., 2005).

Males of a third host species, *P. latipunctata* (Table I), are almost unstudied (Ptacek and Breden, 1998; Ptacek et al., 2005), but Niemeitz et al. (2002) reported that—like in other host species—males prefer conspecific females. Studies of this mating complex are rare probably because the area of overlap of *P. latipunctata* and Amazon mollies is very small (Schlupp et al., 2002; Fig. 3), and *P. latipunctata* is listed as threatened (Tobler and Schlupp, 2009). On the other hand, these areas of overlap are the only known extant situation in which Amazon mollies simultaneously have access to two species of

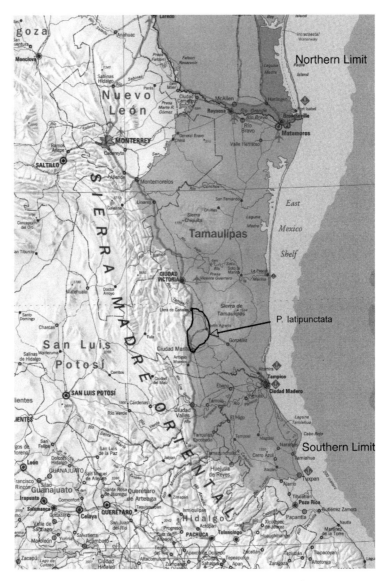

Fig. 3. Distribution map of the Amazon molly. Modified after Schlupp et al. (2002). The gray area represents the distribution of the Amazon molly (*P. formosa*). The darker gray areas in Texas and Northeast Mexico represent the principal area of sympatry with the sailfin molly (*P. latipinna*) and the lighter gray area describes sympatry with the atlantic molly (*P. mexicana*).

host males. Historically along the Gulf coast of Mexico there were several populations known in which Amazons coexisted with both *P. latipinna* and *P. mexicana* (Darnell, 1962; Darnell and Abramoff, 1968), but most of these populations have been lost (Schlupp et al., 2002), not in small part due to urban growth in the vicinity of Tampico (Fig. 3).

C. POTENTIAL SPERM LIMITATION

In recent years, the behavioral studies of male mate choice have been augmented with research looking into the role of sperm. Clearly, sperm is ultimately what males transfer and what the females need. But do males transfer the same number of sperm to conspecific and heterospecific females? A series of studies investigating sperm priming (the sperm readied for transfer) and sperm expenditure by Aspbury (2007) and Aspbury and Gabor (2004a,b) found that males prime more sperm when stimulated visually by conspecific females, as compared with Amazon mollies. It is not clear, how important this mechanism is in nature as Amazon mollies and sailfin mollies typically form mixed groups (Schlupp and Ryan, 1996). In a mixed group males are always visually stimulated by the presence of sailfin molly females and the lower sperm priming in the presence of Amazon molly females is not important. Reduced priming might be a factor, though, in cases when local populations are strongly dominated by Amazon mollies (Heubel, 2004) because then visual stimulation through conspecific females may be lacking.

Other studies of sperm transfer in this mating system found that male behavioral preferences for conspecifics match patterns of actual sperm transfer: males of *P. mexicana* preferred to mate with conspecifics and transferred more sperm to them (Schlupp and Plath, 2005).

Finally, a field study, in which females were flushed with saline solution to detect sperm in their genital tract soon after being caught in the field, revealed that more sailfin molly females had detectable sperm as compared to Amazon mollies. This could be the case for a number of reasons: One of them would be that sailfin molly females receive more matings from males as compared to the Amazon mollies. This would be in full agreement with the predictions from theory. Furthermore, among all females that had sperm (both *P. latipinna* and *P. formosa*), *P. latipinna* had more sperm on an individual basis (Riesch et al., 2008). Consequently, one could therefore argue that Amazons can be sperm limited in nature. This sparked a study by Hinz and Schlupp (unpublished data), which found that there seems to be a minimum amount of about 55,000 sperm cells needed to fertilize a full clutch of eggs. Observed values from another study were higher (Schlupp and Plath, 2005), but further research is clearly needed here. Interestingly, sperm limitation for females had already been suggested earlier by Hubbs

INGO SCHLUPP

(1964), but was rejected later by Balsano et al. (1981) based on the assumption that only very few females would be ready to be inseminated at any given time based on their hormonal sexual cycle (Parzefall, 1973). Clearly, a better understanding of the underlying mechanisms of female and male sexual behavior, such as the role of hormones, would be helpful.

D. FREQUENCY DEPENDENCY

Male mating behavior could also be negatively frequency dependent, which was suggested by McKay (1971) and Moore and Mc Kay (1971) for *Poeciliopsis*. Whenever conspecifics are rare, males should become especially choosy and strongly prefer conspecific females. According to theory, with more conspecifics around, male choosiness would decline again. However, Heubel and Schlupp (2008) found no evidence for such a pattern in a field study. Rather, male behavior showed high seasonal variation, which may be more easily explained by changes in female reproductive cycles than by changes in shoal compositions.

E. HORMONALLY INDUCED MALES OF *P. FORMOSA*

A final aspect of male behavior to consider is the behavior of the rare naturally occurring or hormonally induced (see below) males of the Amazon molly itself (Schlupp et al., 1998). Naturally occurring male-like phenotypes of the Amazon molly have been reported as a rare and odd occurrence (Hubbs, 1964; Hubbs et al., 1959), but an evolutionary significance of these "males" has never been established. The occurrence of spontaneous male phenotypes, however, indicated that the genes coding for male characteristics are still functionally intact, despite the inevitable accumulation of deleterious mutations (Schartl et al., 1991).

Several authors have used male hormones, either methyl-testosterone or 11-keto-testosterone, to force females into expressing male traits including spermatogenesis (Turner and Steeves, 1989), male morphology, coloration (Schartl et al., 1991), and behavior (Schlupp et al., 1992). These hormonally produced "males" behaved qualitatively like sexual males (Schlupp et al., 1992). Their behavior was more similar to behavior shown by *P. mexicana* (the maternal ancestor) and lacked the courtship behavior—swimming back and forth in front of a female—typical for *P. latipinna* males. The "males" studied in this project were unable to swing their gonopodium forward, because they did not develop the muscle and bony structure needed for this precopulatory behavior. The male gonopodium is a transformed anal fin that serves as a copulatory organ (Fig. 4). To inseminate a female, the male has to introduce his gonopodium into the female genital area and transfer sperm.

Fig. 4. Photograph of a male sailfin molly (*P. latipinna*) from the San Marcos River, Texas. The arrow points to the gonopodium, a copulatory organ.

In a few cases, apparently functional males spontaneously occurred in laboratory stocks. These males were triploid and had functional sperm, but were capable only of triggering embryogenesis in other Amazon mollies, but not in *P. latipinna* females (Lamatsch et al., 2000a). These findings are very intriguing, but the evolutionary significance of these unusual males is still unclear. So far, they are considered to be too rare to be of evolutionary importance. Furthermore, such "males" have not been reported from the field. Nonetheless, "male" *P. formosa* that are capable of successfully having offspring with other, unisexual Amazon mollies, could theoretically lead to the emancipation of Amazon mollies from their current, heterospecific sperm donors. There is no evidence for anything like this occurring in nature, though.

In this mating system involving a clonal and several sexual species, clearly male mate choice is a very important aspect to understanding these systems. Furthermore, studies investigating male choice in this system were among the first to highlight the importance of male mate choice in addition to female mate choice, in all mating systems.

IV. BENEFIT TO MALES: WHY MALES MATE WITH HETEROSPECIFIC FEMALES

So far, my argument has assumed that males make mistakes and would fare better if they avoided mating with Amazon mollies. This of course rests on the assumption that males face costs of mating and no compensatory or beneficial returns. Given that decision making can be costly, selection pressures would have to be very strong to produce perfect choice in males. This point was elaborated by a population-dynamical model, that examines the conditions of coexistence of Amazon mollies and their sexual hosts (but not the long-term prospects for Amazon mollies), by focusing on the role of male choice (Heubel et al., 2009). This study found that stable coexistence is possible over a fairly wide range of conditions. Based on the assumption that coexistence is unlikely given the twofold advantage of the clonal Amazon mollies, it turns out that perfect male discrimination, which could drive down the Amazon mollies, is unlikely to evolve because male choice can be costly. One currency for such a cost of male choice could be missed opportunities to mate with conspecific females (Heubel et al., 2009; Schlupp and Ryan, 1997).

A. MATE COPYING

The notion that males have mainly costs and no benefits has been challenged in studies investigating mate copying. Mate copying is a form of nonindependent mate choice in which a mating decision is influenced by the mating decisions of others (Westneat et al., 2000). Live-bearing fishes, in general and especially mollies have recently become model organisms for the study of mate copying, highlighting many different aspects of this extremely interesting behavior (Alonzo, 2008; Applebaum and Cruz, 2000; Briggs et al., 1996; Dugatkin and Druen, 2007; Dugatkin and Godin, 1993, 1998a; Dugatkin et al., 2002, 2003; Munger et al., 2004; Nordell and Valone, 1998; Witte and Massmann, 2003; Witte and Ryan, 2002; Witte and Ueding, 2003). The concept of copying has been used in economics (Bikhchandani et al., 1992), but was introduced into behavioral biology through a series of elegant experiments on guppies (Dugatkin, 1992; Dugatkin and Godin, 1992, 1993, 1998a,b). Schlupp et al. (1994) used this framework to challenge the idea that the sexual males had no benefits of mating with heterospecific females: They asked if sexual females (in this case sailfin mollies) would copy the mate choice of Amazon molly females across species barriers? The results of that study showed a strong effect of mate copying: Males that were seen by sexual females to associate with Amazon mollies were subsequently preferred by the viewing sailfin molly females (Schlupp et al., 1994). A similar finding was later reported for atlantic mollies (Heubel et al., 2008). This meant that males received an indirect benefit from mating with the Amazon mollies.

Obviously, the magnitude of this benefit of heterospecific mate copying depends on the social conditions, especially the composition of the group and the strength of conspecific mate copying relative to heterospecific mate copying. As mentioned above, Amazon mollies and their sexual hosts form mixed groups, which vary in composition. The effect of sailfin mollies

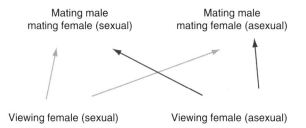

Mating male   Mating male
mating female (sexual)   mating female (asexual)

Viewing female (sexual)   Viewing female (asexual)

Fig. 5. Schematic representation of possible dyadic mate copying interactions. Note that the strength of copying varies depending on the interactions (modified after Heubel, 2004).

copying Amazon mollies, for example, on male mating patterns should be frequency dependent and influenced by how many other Amazon mollies and sailfin molly females are observing the mating interactions. A study evaluating all the possible two-way interactions (Fig. 5) was published by Heubel et al. (2008): There were substantial differences in the tendency and strength of copying, with Amazon mollies showing a weaker tendency to copy than sexual females. This means that heterospecific mate copying by sexual females can be beneficial to males, at least in populations with a balanced ratio of Amazon mollies and sexual molly females. Interestingly, the species of the interacting females influences the perceived reliability of the information provided in these sexual interactions. If, for example, the viewing female is a sailfin molly and the mating female is an Amazon molly (low quality), then the information provided would be weighted lower than if a higher quality, sexual, female were serving as the model (Hill and Ryan, 2006). More research is needed here, but a model exploring the effect of frequencies on male mating success is essential to fully understand the dynamics between model and mimic. The concept of socially influenced mate choice has already generated several theoretical papers (Agrawal, 2001; Kirkpatrick and Dugatkin, 1994; Kokko et al., 2008; Meggers, 1998; Stohr, 1998; Valone, 2007; Valone and Templeton, 2002), providing many testable hypotheses.

Interestingly, in sailfin mollies, males have also been found to imitate other males (Schlupp and Ryan, 1997), which further adds to the complexity of this mating system. The suggested adaptive value for male mate copying, which seems counterintuitive because it exposes males to sperm competition, is that males cannot afford to miss matings with any of the rare fertilizable females (Parzefall, 1973).

Overall, it seems that males prefer conspecific females, but there are apparently enough mechanisms in place for Amazon mollies to obtain matings to secure their reproductive success. Especially, the influences of the social environment have to be taken into account.

V.   Communication Networks

The numerous studies on mate copying (not only in Poeciliids) urge us to use a more complex view of animal communication. Clearly, a lot of the signaling interactions relevant to female and male choice happen in communication networks (McGregor and Peake, 2000; McGregor et al., 1999), as opposed to simple dyadic interactions. Unfortunately, signaling interactions in nature rarely happen in dyads, but have other individuals as audiences (Matos and Schlupp, 2004). Nonetheless, the dominating paradigm in studying signaling interactions is still to investigate dyads. This approach has the advantage of providing highly controlled conditions for experimentation, but this comes at the expense of biological realism.

Communication networks explicitly incorporate social interaction into the design and analysis of behavioral experiments. In the more recent attempts to provide a theoretical foundation to studying communication networks (Matos and Schlupp, 2004; McGregor and Peake, 2000; McGregor et al., 1999; Naguib et al., 2004), social interactions have been placed in a new context. If, for example, behavior is modified in the open presence of an audience (as compared to a situation where the audience is absent), we speak broadly of audience effects. The examples of mate copying mentioned above can be placed in this category.

If, however the audience is concealed, they are considered to be eavesdropping (Earley and Dugatkin, 2002; Earley et al., 2005), collecting information from social interactions. Eavesdropping has been studied using Amazon mollies as stimuli or audience in male mate choice interactions. Based on the assumption that males should prefer conspecific females, one can generally make strong predictions about the directionality of male preferences. This was used by Plath et al. (2008a) to study the effects of audiences on male mate preferences in *P. mexicana*. In this study, focal males were given a choice between a conspecific and a heterospecific female. They initially preferred the conspecific female, but the presence of a conspecific male audience altered this preference and led to a reduction in the time spent in association with the preferred female. Controls using either no audience or a different species (a swordtail) as the audience resulted in no change. A similar study using Sailfin mollies led to the same results (Schlupp et al., 2009).

The same question was then addressed again in another study, but this time allowing the focal males to interact freely with the females. As in the first study, initially the conspecific female was preferred in the absence of an audience. But surprisingly in the presence of a conspecific audience (this time the audience male was confined to a Plexiglas cylinder), the focal males now showed signs of deceptive behavior, leading the observing male away from the female the initially preferred (Plath et al., 2008b) and interacting instead with the initially not preferred Amazon molly. Again, in the control experiment males did not alter their behavior. This behavior was interpreted as an attempt to mislead the observing male and hide the "true" preference of the deceiving male. The proposed mechanism for this was the already described male mate copying (Schlupp and Ryan, 1997), which leads to nonindependent mate choice in males. This finding raises the important question of whether the males confronted with an audience can anticipate the behavior of other individuals. It should also be highlighted again, that the situation with an audience present represents the natural condition.

These studies underscore not only the importance of communication networks in many animals, but also the utility of using Amazon mollies in studying communication networks in fishes.

VI. Sexual Conflict

In numerous species, males attempt to mate with females, even if these females are apparently not willing to mate. This has been interpreted as being costly sexual harassment for females. In live-bearing fishes this phenomenon has been studied, for example, using guppies (Magurran, 2001; Magurran and Benoni, 1994), mosquitofish (Smith, 2007), and also mollies (Schlupp et al., 2001). The existence of male behavior forcing copulations has been widely interpreted as sexual conflict. An alternative explanation is that females are inviting this behavior, to test male vigor (Eberhard, 1996). Sexual conflict and sexual harassment have been studied in Poeciliids, measuring the time females spend feeding in the presence of males as compared to time spent feeding in the absence of males or in the presence of nonharrassing partners. The argument here is that reduced feeding time is costly because it could reduce fecundity in females. Furthermore, male attention might expose the otherwise cryptic females to higher levels of predation. In sailfin mollies a similar cost of reduced feeding time was detected (Schlupp et al., 2001), but in this species larger males were found to harass less than smaller males. This led to the hypothesis that the mating system might be related to the degree of harassment, with courting species showing lower levels of harassment than noncourting species. A test of this idea using nine different species of Poeciliids (Plath et al., 2007) found that female feeding times were always reduced in the presence of males. Interestingly, overall male activity determined the strength of this effect, but no differences were found between males of courting and noncourting species.

One question that arises in this context is whether sexual males would spend time and energy harassing low quality females, such as asexual females. This was addressed in a study by Heubel and Plath (2008), who found that sexual *P. mexicana* males harassed both conspecific females and Amazon mollies. Curiously, in this study using *P. mexicana*, harassment uniformly increased with male size, which is different from the findings reported by Schlupp et al. (2001) using *P. latipinna*. An obvious difference between these two species that might explain the difference is that *P. mexicana* does not show courtship (but see above).

Again, studies using Amazon mollies can serve as templates to advance our knowledge of the behavior of sexual species and provide an interesting comparison with "regular" species.

VII. FEMALE BEHAVIOR: CHOOSY ASEXUALS?

Female behavior, especially female choice, is among the most intriguing behaviors of all. Do preferences of Amazon mollies in this system simply represent the frozen condition of the hybridization a long time ago or have Amazon molly preferences evolved after the original formation? Only a few scenarios seem plausible. Firstly, the current state of female behavior could be unaltered from the state of the original hybridization. Since the hybridization was about 100,000 generations ago, comparing Amazon mollies to freshly formed, *de novo* hybrids from laboratory crossings, is of limited value because the ancestral species have undergone many generations of independent evolution (Dries, 2003; Schlupp, 2005). Nonetheless, studies viewing Amazon mollies as frozen hybrids have been very useful in detecting male traits that have been perpetuated in Amazon mollies, despite the apparent lack of selection maintaining these traits (Schartl et al., 1991; Schlupp et al., 1992, 1998; see above). Male traits expressed under hormonal masculinization, such as coloration and the gonopodium, provided a glimpse at the evolutionary fate of seemingly neutral traits: many male traits were astonishingly intact despite the lack of stabilizing selection.

Secondly, female behavior could be altered due to genetic changes via mutation or introgression (Schlupp, 2005). This might result from the accumulation of deleterious mutations, potentially resulting in more variable behavior in Amazon mollies. Thirdly, if no evolution happens, female behavior across Amazon molly clones should be uniform (or decaying slowly, but relatively uniformly), and show no specific differences related to their current host. In other words, there should be no behavioral differences between Amazon mollies from areas of sympatry with one host species when compared with Amazon mollies from sympatry with another host. Again, this pattern might be altered through the influence of introgression (see below). Surprisingly, little work has been done along those lines, most likely because it is difficult to derive testable hypotheses.

Sexual females of the sailfin molly and the atlantic molly, as well as Amazon mollies have more or less similar preferences for larger male body size (Marler and Ryan, 1997; Schlupp and Plath, 2005; Schlupp and Ryan, 1997). This could be due to phylogenetic inertia, or still reflect the ancestral state from the original hybridization, but such a preference is not necessarily predicted. One alternate prediction would be that Amazon mollies evolve to utilize and prefer to interact with the small males of both species that are being rejected as mating partners by the sexual females—of course assuming that those males would mate with the Amazon mollies.

While no differences in preferences for male size were found so far, Amazon mollies and the sexual sailfin molly differ in their preference for shoaling partners: in an experiment addressing shoaling behavior, both sailfin mollies and Amazon mollies initially preferred conspecific females, and switched over to heterospecific shoaling as the heterospecifics outnumbered the conspecifics (Schlupp and Ryan, 1996). Interestingly, the switching point was different in the two species, with Amazon mollies switching over to heterospecific shoaling when two heterospecific sailfin mollies were titrated against one conspecific Amazon molly. Sailfin mollies switched when the ratio was 1–3.

Amazon mollies and sailfin mollies also differed in their preference for a spontaneously occurring new ornament found in a sailfin molly male (Schlupp et al., 1999). Interestingly, this ornament was a brightly orange tumor found in the dorsal fin of one *P. latipinna* male. The sexual sailfin molly females preferred the novel ornament, showing a preexisting bias (Endler and Basolo, 1998), whereas the Amazon mollies showed no preference. Several potential explanations are possible to explain this finding, but what is relevant in the context of this review is that there were differences at all.

Another difference that may be meaningful is that Amazon mollies avoid males parasitized by Black Spot Disease. This disease is caused by trematode larvae, which are encapsulated in the skin of a fish. The fish responds to being parasitized by producing a black, melanin-rich, spot around the parasite. This indicator of parasitization is highly visible and occurs in many species, including most Poeciliids. In a study investigating the response of females to males visibly infected by Black Spot Disease, Tobler et al. (2006) found that the two sexual species *P. latipinna* and *P. mexicana* did not show avoidance (Tobler et al., 2006), although Amazon mollies did. The authors suggested that avoidance of infected males might provide some (unknown) direct benefit to females. Interestingly, Amazon mollies in nature do not have more parasites as compared to Sailfin mollies (Tobler and Schlupp, 2005, 2008), as would be predicted by the Red Queen Hypothesis. Obviously, only very few differences were detected so far between Amazon mollies and either *P. mexicana* or *P. latipinna*. It does not seem as if selection is favoring females that differ.

Future studies could aim at finding adaptive changes in Amazon mollies between different populations. In this context, the roles of learning, development (Körner et al., 1999; Landmann et al., 1999), and plasticity need to be explored.

VIII. BEHAVIOR AND PLOIDY

One important motor of evolution in both plants and animals are ploidy elevations, often via genome duplications. This has long been recognized for many taxa such as gymnosperms (Soltis et al., 2007), animals in general (Crow and Wagner, 2006), and especially fishes (Le Comber and Smith, 2004; Leggatt and Iwama, 2003). While most cases of ploidy elevation are genome duplications leading to autopolyploid organisms, in unisexuals added genomes mostly originate from the unusual sperm–egg interaction and represent added parental genomes. The evolutionary consequences of the added genomes in unisexuals are poorly understood and it is not clear if they—as in sexual organisms—lead to rapid evolution.

It is important in this context to realize that despite their clonal mode of reproduction, unisexuals show some genetic variation on the population level. This variation can have a number of sources: Firstly, different clones (or lineages) may go back to different hybridization events. Such a pattern is known, for example, from another live-bearing fish, *Poeciliopsis* (Vrijenhoek, 1994). In this complex, several independent hybridizations at different times led to the current diverse clonal structure. Amazon mollies, by contrast, are thought to have originated from a single hybridization event (Möller, 2001). The original hybrid was apparently formed between an atlantic molly female and a sailfin molly male and was diploid. Still today, diploids are most common among Amazon mollies, but triploids have been described both from the laboratory and the field (see below). A second source of variation is mutation. Amazons should suffer the same mutation rate as other organisms (and there is no evidence that mutation rates would differ), leading to genetically different clones every generation. These differences would, of course, be minimal. Two further sources of clonal variation are mitotic recombination (Tiedemann et al., 2005) and introgression (Schartl et al., 1995a). Mitotic recombination or homologous recombination is the genetic exchange between homologous DNA sequences during mitosis. This process can homogenize the genome (Helleday, 2003).

Introgression can happen in two independent ways. First, the whole genome of the sperm can be added to the Amazon germline, leading to triploid clones (Balsano et al., 1989; Lamatsch et al., 2000a,b), which also are gynogenetic and clonal. Triploids are known from laboratory studies and from nature where they seem to have had a single origin (Lampert et al., 2005). Recently, a tetraploid individual was reported (Lampert et al., 2008). Furthermore, astounding mosaics have been described (Lampert et al., 2007b). However, these later phenomena seem to be too rare to be meaningfully explored in behavioral studies.

Based on the variation generated by the mechanisms outlined here, selection or random phenomena will lead to differential survival between individuals and clones, leading to structured populations. Behavioral differences between clones may then be studied in the laboratory and the field, but unfortunately not much is known. A recent study, though found that triploid Amazons are outcompeted by diploids in group tanks in the laboratory (Lamatsch et al., 2009). In another study, triploids were also found to be behaviorally different from diploids: Triploid females were significantly faster at finding a food source (Schlupp et al., 2009).

IX. SENSORY ECOLOGY

For a better understanding of signaling interactions, it is important to understand the sensory ecology of the study organism in question. To fully appreciate the significance and evolution of signaling interactions this should include studies of both the receiver side (sensory systems), sender side (signaling structures), and the environment through which signals must travel (Bradbury and Vehrencamp, 1998). Fishes, including mollies have a number of potential signaling channels, but as in most organisms only a few of these have been studied, leading to a bias in the literature (Coleman, 2009) and large gaps in our understanding of signaling. Chemical communication, for example, is known to be important in live-bearing fishes for several behavioral interactions. This ranges from species recognition in swordtails (Crapon de Caprona and Ryan, 1990) and mollies (Zeiske, 1968), to mate choice in swordtails (Fisher and Rosenthal, 2006; Fisher et al., 2006).

Although clearly important, chemical communication has been barely studied in the Amazon molly mating system yet. One study (Aspbury et al., in press) asked if chemical signals played a role in species recognition by letting sailfin molly males choose between Amazon mollies and sailfin molly females, but failed to establish a role of chemical communication. Since much of the behavioral work has focused on visual communication, studies addressing the sensory ecology of these mollies have focused on this area, too. On the receiver side of communication interactions it was important to characterize the visual pigments of mollies using microspectrophotometry (MSP) (Körner et al., 2006). This study included Amazon mollies, sailfin mollies and atlantic mollies. All three species turned out to be very similar in their visual pigments. Other than humans, mollies (like many fishes) have four visual pigments, which are relatively evenly spread from UV to yellow. Finding a UV-sensitive class of cones in the retina was unsurprising, but lead to the realization that color manipulations are conceptually difficult (Oliveira et al., 2000a,b), because whatever may appear to have a certain color to humans will likely be perceived very differently by mollies. A similar logic can be applied to using video playback in behavioral studies. While these techniques are very powerful because of the opportunities to manipulate traits, their utility in manipulating color is limited because available playback techniques are matched for human vision, not fish vision (Schlupp, 2000). Nonetheless, video playback has been successfully used in mollies to investigate preexisting biases for swords in sailfin mollies (Witte and Klink, 2005), preferences for healthy males (Tobler et al., 2006), ontogeny of sexual preferences in Amazon mollies (Landmann et al., 1999), and species recognition in combination with sexual preferences for host species in Amazon mollies (Körner et al., 1999).

Studies of the sender side of signaling in mollies and evolution of signal design are still absent, but a few studies have addressed the environmental conditions under which signaling occur. For example, mollies live under a wide range of turbidity conditions, ranging from very clear water in springheads like Comal Springs in Central Texas, to extremely turbid water in some drainage ditches in South Texas (Heubel, 2004). How do these differences affect visual communication? Turbidity is known to affect many aspects of fish behavior, such as foraging (Booth, 1985) and mating (Engstrom-Ost and Candolin, 2007). Human-induced changes in turbidity have also been implicated in the reversal of speciation in a species flock in African rift valley lakes (Seehausen et al., 1997) and sticklebacks (Wong et al., 2007). One study by Heubel and Schlupp (2006) addressed potential effects of turbidity in the Amazon molly mating system and asked how decision making by males is influenced by turbidity. They were able to show that high turbidity slows down decision making, thereby probably raising the cost of decision making for males. One question resulting from this kind of research is should males of the sailfin molly adjust their mating behavior plastically to local conditions? Clearly, more experimental work is needed to follow up on this and other findings. In a mating system like this, where visual communication seems to be very important more research looking at the effects and evolutionary consequences of abiotic conditions is needed.

It seems obvious that it is very helpful to include knowledge of the sensory ecology of study organisms into experimental design (Cummings and Mollaghan, 2006; Cummings et al., 2003), just as ignoring the sensory ecology of the test animal can weaken the conclusions presented (Endler, 1978; Endler et al., 2005).

Quite often studying the unusual is providing us with unique insights. Looking at the behavior, ecology, and evolution of the unisexual Amazon molly seems to be such a case. In the Amazon molly mating system, male mate choice is clearly very important. By mating with Amazon mollies (or not) males can drive this system. If male mating with heterospecific females is selected against, why do males still do it? One of the surprising answers had to do with mate copying, a form of nonindependent mate choice, providing an example for how indirect benefits might be offsetting male costs of mating with a heterospecific female. Male choice in this system is juxtaposed with the role of females probably competing over males (and sperm), in the mixed groups which provide the backdrop for the complex, multispecies interactions found in this mating system. Studying Amazon mollies was especially fruitful as it can be combined with studies looking at behavior like shoaling or sexual conflict also in the two known parental species. Indeed, the Amazon molly mating system has been used to try to implement a research program as suggested by Tinbergen (1963). Based on a known phylogeny, both questions of proximate (like studying visual pigments) and ultimate (like the adaptive significance of male choice) nature have been addressed. Only the ontogeny of behavior is still an open field.

Overall, the behavior of Amazon mollies is amazingly rich and can be used in the future in many meaningful ways to address questions of broad interest, ideally by employing a comparative approach. But of course, studying the behavior of one of the rare fishes that is all-female, yet has to mate with males of a different species, is fascinating in its own right!

Acknowledgments

I am very grateful to Michael J. Ryan, Manfred Schartl, Jakob Parzefall, Katja Heubel, Martin Plath, Michael Tobler, Rudy Riesch and Ralph Tiedemann for long-time collaborations. Many students, both graduate and undergraduate, worked with me. Without them I would have accomplished nothing. Funding was mainly provided by the University of Oklahoma, the German Academic Exchange Service, and the Deutsche Forschungsgemeinschaft. Rudy Riesch kindly commented on a draft of this manuscript. A special thanks goes to Jane Brockman for careful and patient editing.

References

Agrawal, A.F., 2001. The evolutionary consequences of mate copying on male traits. Behav. Ecol. Sociobiol. 51, 33–40.

Alonzo, S.H., 2008. Female mate choice copying affects sexual selection in wild populations of the ocellated wrasse. Anim. Behav. 75, 1715–1723.

Applebaum, S.L., Cruz, A., 2000. The role of mate-choice copying and disruption effects in mate preference determination of *Limia perugiae* (Cyprinodontiformes, Poeciliidae). Ethology 106, 933–944.

Aspbury, A.S., 2007. Sperm competition effects on sperm production and expenditure in sailfin mollies, *Poecilia latipinna*. Behav. Ecol. 18, 776–780.

Aspbury, A.S., Espinedo, C., Gabor, C.R., In press. Lack of species discrimination based on chemical cues by male sailfin mollies, *Poecilia latipinna*. Evol. Ecol.

Aspbury, A.S., Gabor, C.R., 2004a. Differential sperm priming by male sailfin mollies (*Poecilia latipinna*): effects of female and male size. Ethology 110, 193–202.

Aspbury, A.S., Gabor, C.R., 2004b. Discriminating males alter sperm production between species. Proc. Natl. Acad. Sci. USA 101, 15970–15973.

Avise, J.C., Trexler, J., Travis, J., Nelson, W.S., 1991. *Poecilia mexicana* is the recent female parent of the unisexual fish *Poecilia formosa*. Evolution 45 (6), 1530–1533.

Balsano, J.S., Kucharski, K., Randle, E.J., Rasch, E.M., Monaco, P.J., 1981. Reduction of competition between bisexual and unisexual females of *Poecilia* in northeastern Mexico. Environ. Biol. Fishes 6, 39–48.

Balsano, J.S., Randle, E.J., Rasch, E.M., Monaco, P.J., 1985. Reproductive behavior and the maintenance of all-female *Poecilia*. Environ. Biol. Fishes 12, 251–264.

Balsano, J.S., Rasch, E.M., Monaco, P.J., 1989. The evolutionary ecology of *Poecilia formosa* and its triploid associate. In: Meffe, G.K., Snelson, F.F. (Eds.), Ecology and Evolution of Livebearing Fishes (Poeciliidae). Prentice Hall, New Jersey, pp. 277–298.

Bell, G., 1982. The Masterpiece of Nature: The Evolution and Genetics of Sexuality. University of California Press, Berkeley.

Beukeboom, L.W., Vrijenhoek, R.C., 1998. Evolutionary genetics and ecology of sperm-dependent parthenogenesis. J. Evol. Biol. 11, 755–782.

Bikhchandani, S., Hirshleifer, D., Welch, I., 1992. A theory of fads, fashion, custom, and cultural change as informational cascades. J. Polit. Econ. 100, 992–1026.

Booth, D.J., 1985. Prey detection by the blue-eye *Pseudomugil signifer* (Atherinidae) analysis of field behavior by controlled laboratory experiments. Aust. J. Mar. Freshw. Res. 36, 691–700.

Bradbury, J.W., Vehrencamp, S., 1998. Principles of Animal Communication. Sinauer, Sunderland.

Briggs, S.E., Godin, J.G.J., Dugatkin, L.A., 1996. Mate-choice copying under predation risk in the Trinidadian guppy (*Poecilia reticulata*). Behav. Ecol. 7, 151–157.

Coleman, S.W., 2009. Taxonomic and sensory biases in the mate-choice literature: there are far too few studies of chemical and multimodal communication. Acta Ethol. 12, 45–48.

Crapon de Caprona, M.D., Ryan, M.J., 1990. Conspecific mate recognition in swordtails, *Xiphophorus nigrensis* and *X. Pygmaeus* (Poeciliidae): olfactory and visual cues. Anim. Behav. 39, 290–296.

Crow, K.D., Wagner, G.P., 2006. What is the role of genome duplication in the evolution of complexity and diversity? Mol. Biol. Evol. 23, 887–892.

Cummings, M., Mollaghan, D., 2006. Repeatability and consistency of female preference behaviours in a northern swordtail, *Xiphophorus nigrensis*. Anim. Behav. 72, 217–224.

Cummings, M.E., Rosenthal, G.G., Ryan, M.J., 2003. A private ultraviolet channel in visual communication. Proc. R. Soc. Biol. B 270, 897–904.

Darnell, R.M., 1962. Fishes of the Rio Tamesi and related coastal lagoons in east central Mexico. Pub. Inst. Mar. Sci. Univ. Tex. 8, 299–365.

Darnell, R.M., Abramoff, P., 1968. Distribution of the gynogenetic fish, *Poecilia formosa*, with remarks on the evolution of the species. Copeia 1968, 354–361.

Dawkins, R., 1979. Arms races between and within species. Proc. R. Soc. Lond. B 205, 489–511.

Dawley, R.M., 1989. An introduction to unisexual vertebrates. In: Dawley, R.M., Bogart, J.P. (Eds.), Evolution and Ecology of unisexual vertebrates, The New York State Museum, Albany, New York, pp. 1–19.

Dries, L.A., 2003. Peering through the looking glass at a sexual parasite: are Amazon mollies red queens? Evolution 57, 1387–1396.

Dugatkin, L.A., 1992. Sexual selection and imitation females copy the mate choice of others. Am. Nat. 139, 1384–1389.

Dugatkin, L.A., Druen, M., 2007. Mother-offspring correlation and mate-choice copying behavior in guppies. Ethol. Ecol. Evol. 19, 137–144.

Dugatkin, L.A., Godin, J.G.J., 1992. Reversal of female mate choice by copying in the guppy (*Poecilia reticulata*). Proc. R. Soc. Lond. B Biol. Sci. 249, 179–184.

Dugatkin, L.A., Godin, J.G.J., 1993. Female mate copying in the guppy (*Poecilia reticulata*): age-dependent effects. Behav. Ecol. 4, 289–292.

Dugatkin, L.A., Godin, J.G.J., 1998a. Effects of hunger on mate-choice copying in the guppy. Ethology 104, 194–202.

Dugatkin, L.A., Godin, J.G.J., 1998b. How females choose their mates. Sci. Am. 278, 56–61.

Dugatkin, L.A., Lucas, J.S., Godin, J.G.J., 2002. Serial effects of mate-choice copying in the guppy (*Poecilia reticulata*). Ethol. Ecol. Evol. 14, 45–52.

Dugatkin, L.A., Druen, M.W., Godin, J.G.J., 2003. The disruption hypothesis does not explain mate-choice copying in the guppy (*Poecilia reticulata*). Ethology 109, 67–76.

Earley, R.L., Dugatkin, L.A., 2002. Eavesdropping on visual cues in green swordtail (*Xiphophorus helleri*) fights: a case for networking. Proc. R. Soc. Lond. B Biol. Sci. 269, 943–952.

Earley, R.L., Druen, M., Dugatkin, L.A., 2005. Watching fights does not alter a bystander's response towards naive conspecifics in male green swordtail fish, *Xiphophorus helleri*. Anim. Behav. 69, 1139–1145.

Eberhard, W.G., 1996. Female control: Sexual selection by cryptic female choice. Princeton University Press, 501pp.

Endler, J.A., 1978. A predator's view of animal colour patterns. Evol. Biol. 11, 319–363.

Endler, J.A., Basolo, A.L., 1998. Sensory ecology, receiver biases and sexual selection. Trends Ecol. Evol. 13, 415–420.

Endler, J.A., Westcott, D.A., Madden, J.R., Robson, T., 2005. Animal visual systems and the evolution of color patterns: sensory processing illuminates signal evolution. Evolution 59, 1795–1818.

Engstrom-Ost, J., Candolin, U., 2007. Human-induced water turbidity alters selection on sexual displays in sticklebacks. Behav. Ecol. 18, 393–398.

Farr, J.A., Travis, J., Trexler, J.C., 1986. Behavioral allometry and interdemic variation in sexual-behavior of the sailfin molly, *Poecilia latipinna* (Pisces, Poeciliidae). Anim. Behav. 34, 497–509.

Fisher, H.S., Rosenthal, G.G., 2006. Female swordtail fish use chemical cues to select well-fed mates. Anim. Behav. 72, 721–725.

Fisher, H.S., Wong, B.B.M., Rosenthal, G.G., 2006. Alteration of the chemical environment disrupts communication in a freshwater fish. Proc. R. Soc. B Biol. Sci. 273, 1187–1193.

Fischer, C., Schlupp, I., 2009. Differences in thermal tolerance in coexisting sexual and asexual mollies (*Poecilia*, Poeciliidae, Teleostei). J. Fish Biol. 74, 1662–1668.

Foran, C.M., Ryan, M.J., 1994. Female–female competition in a unisexual/bisexual complex of mollies. Copeia 1994, 504–508.

Gabor, C.R., Page, R., 2003. Female preference for large males in sailfin mollies, *Poecilia latipinna*: the importance of predation pressure and reproductive status. Acta Ethol. 6, 7–12.

Gabor, C.R., Ryan, M.J., 2001. Geographical variation in reproductive character displacement in mate choice by male sailfin mollies. Proc. R. Soc. Lond. B Biol. Sci. 268, 1063–1070.

Gabor, C.R., Ryan, M.J., Morizot, D.C., 2005. Character displacement in sailfin mollies, *Poecilia latipinna*: allozymes and behavior. Environ. Biol. Fishes 73, 75–88.

Gumm, J.M., Gabor, C.R., 2005. Asexuals looking for sex: Conflict between species and mate-quality recognition in sailfin mollies (*Poecilia latipinna*). Behav. Ecol. Sociobiol. 58, 558–565.

Gumm, J.M., Gonzalez, R., Aspbury, A.S., Gabor, C.R., 2006. Do I know you? Species recognition operates within and between the sexes in a unisexual-bisexual species complex of mollies. Ethology 112, 448–457.

Gwynne, D.T., 1981. Sexual difference theory—mormon crickets show role reversal in mate choice. Science 213, 779–780.

Gwynne, D.T., 1984. Sexual selection and sexual differences in mormon crickets (Orthoptera, Tettigonidae, *Anabrus simplex*). Evolution 38, 1011–1022.

Helleday, T., 2003. Pathways for mitotic homologous recombination in mammalian cells. Mutat. Res. 532, 103–115.

Herdman, E.J.E., Kelly, C.D., Godin, J.G.J., 2004. Male mate choice in the guppy (*Poecilia reticulata*): do males prefer larger females as mates? Ethology 110, 97–111.

Heubel, K.U., 2004. Population Ecology and Sexual Preferences in the Mating Complex of the Unisexual Amazon Molly *Poecilia formosa* (GIRARD, 1859). Dissertation, University of Hamburg.

Heubel, K.U., Plath, M., 2008. Influence of male harassment and female competition on female feeding behaviour in a sexual–asexual mating complex of mollies (*Poecilia mexicana*, *P. formosa*). Behav. Ecol. Sociobiol. 62, 1689–1699.

Heubel, K.U., Rankin, D.J., Kokko, H., 2009. How to go extinct by mating too much: population consequences of male mate choice and efficiency in a sexual-asexual species complex. Oikos 118, 513–520.

Heubel, K.U., Schlupp, I., 2006. Turbidity affects association behaviour in male *Poecilia latipinna*. J. Fish Biol. 68, 555–568.

Heubel, K.U., Hornhardt, K., Ollmann, T., Parzefall, J., Ryan, M.J., Schlupp, I., 2008. Geographic variation in female mate-copying in the species complex of a unisexual fish, *Poecilia formosa*. Behaviour 145, 1041–1064.

Hill, S.E., Ryan, M.J., 2006. The role of model female quality in the mate choice copying behaviour of sailfin mollies. Biol. Lett. 2, 203–205.

Houde, A.E., 1997. Sex, Color, and Mate Choice in Guppies. Princeton University Press, Princeton and Oxford.

Hoysak, D.J., Godin, J.G.J., 2007. Repeatability of male mate choice in the mosquitofish, *Gambusia holbrooki*. Ethology 113, 1007–1018.

Hrbek, T., Seckinger, J., Meyer, A., 2007. A phylogenetic and biogeographic perspective on the evolution of poeciliid fishes. Mol. Phylogenet. Evol. 43, 986–998.

Hubbs, C., 1964. Interactions between bisexual fish species and its gynogenetic sexual parasite. Bull. Texas Mem. Mus. 8, 1–72.

Hubbs, C.L., Hubbs, L.C., 1932. Apparent parthenogenesis in nature in a form of fish of hybrid origin. Science 76, 628–630.

Hubbs, C., Drewry, G.E., Warburton, B., 1959. Occurence and morphology of a phenotypic male of a gynogenetic fish. Science 129, 1227–1229.

Kallman, K.D., 1962. Gynogenesis in the teleost *Mollienesia formosa*, with a discussion of the detection of parthenogenesis in vertebrates by tissue transplantation. J. Genet. 58, 7–21.

Kirkpatrick, M., Dugatkin, L.A., 1994. Sexual selection and the evolutionary effects of copying mate choice. Behav. Ecol. Sociobiol. 34, 443–449.

Kokko, H., Heubel, K.U., Rankin, D.J., 2008. How populations persist when asexuality requires sex: the spatial dynamics of coping with sperm parasites. Proc. R. Soc. B Biol. Sci. 275, 817–825.

Körner, K.E., Lütjens, O., Parzefall, J., Schlupp, I., 1999. The role of experience in mating preferences of the unisexual Amazon molly. Behaviour 136, 257–268.

Körner, K.E., Schlupp, I., Plath, M., Loew, E.R., 2006. Spectral sensitivity of mollies: comparing surface- and cave-dwelling Atlantic mollies, *Poecilia mexicana*. J. Fish Biol. 69, 54–65.

Krause, J., 1994. Shoal choice in the banded killifish (*Fundulus diaphanus*, Teleostei, Cyprinodontidae): effects of predation risk, fish size, species composition and size of shoals. Ethology 98, 128–136.

Lamatsch, D.K., Nanda, I., Epplen, J.T., Schmid, M., Schartl, M., 2000a. Unusual triploid males in a microchromosome-carrying clone of the Amazon molly, *Poecilia formosa*. Cytogenet. Cell Genet. 91, 148–156.

Lamatsch, D.K., Steinlein, C., Schmid, M., Schartl, M., 2000b. Noninvasive determination of genome size and ploidy level in fishes by flow cytometry: detection of triploid *Poecilia formosa*. Cytometry 39, 91–95.

Lamatsch, D.K., Lampert, K.P., Fischer, P., Geiger, M., Schlupp, I., Schartl, M., 2009. Diploid Amazon mollies (*Poecilia formosa*) show a higher fitness than triploids in clonal competition experiments. Evol. Ecol. (online first DOI: 10.1007/s10682-008-9264-2).

Lampert, K.P., Lamatsch, D.K., Epplen, J.T., Schartl, M., 2005. Evidence for a monophyletic origin of triploid clones of the Amazon molly, *Poecilia formosa*. Evolution 59, 881–889.

Lampert, K.P., Lamatsch, D.K., Fischer, P., Epplen, J.T., Nanda, I., Schmid, M., et al., 2007a. Automictic reproduction in interspecific hybrids of Poeciliid fish. Curr. Biol. 17, 1948–1953.

Lampert, K.P., Steinlein, C., Schmid, M., Fischer, P., Schartl, M., 2007b. A haploid-diploid-triploid mosaic of the Amazon molly, *Poecilia formosa*. Cytogenet. Genome Res. 119, 131–134.

Lampert, K.P., Lamatsch, D.K., Fischer, P., Schartl, M., 2008. A tetraploid Amazon molly, *Poecilia formosa*. J. Hered. 99, 223–226.

Landmann, K., Parzefall, J., Schlupp, I., 1999. A sexual preference in the Amazon molly, *Poecilia formosa*. Environ. Biol. Fishes 56, 325–331.

Le Comber, S.C., Smith, C., 2004. Polyploidy in fishes: Patterns and processes. Biol. J. Linn. Soc. 82, 431–442.

Leggatt, R.A., Iwama, G.K., 2003. Occurrence of polyploidy in the fishes. Rev. Fish Biol. Fish. 13, 237–246.

Lima, N.R.W., Kobak, C.J., Vrijenhoek, R.C., 1996. Evolution of sexual mimicry in sperm-dependent all-female forms of *Poeciliopsis* (Pisces: Poeciliidae). J. Evol. Biol. 9, 185–203.

Loewe, L., Lamatsch, D.K., 2008. Quantifying the threat of extinction from Muller's ratchet in the diploid Amazon molly (*Poecilia formosa*). BMC Evol. Biol. 8, 88.

Magurran, A.E., 2001. Sexual conflict and evolution in Trinidadian guppies. Genetica 112, 463–474.

Magurran, A.E., 2005. Evolutionary Ecology. The Trinidadian Guppy. Oxford University Press, Oxford.

Magurran, A.E., Benoni, H.S., 1994. A cost of sexual harassment in the guppy, *Poecilia reticulata*. Proc. R. Soc. Lond. B 258, 89–92.

Marler, C.A., Ryan, M.J., 1997. Origin and maintenance of a female mating preference. Evolution 51, 1244–1248.

Matos, R., Schlupp, I., 2004. Performing in front of an audience—signalers and the social environment. In: McGregor, P.K. (Ed.), Animal Communication Networks. Cambridge University Press, Cambridge.

Maynard Smith, J., 1978. The Evolution of Sex. Cambridge University Press, Cambridge.

McGregor, P.K., Peake, T.M., 2000. Communication networks: social environments for receiver and signaller behaviour. Acta Ethol. 2, 71–81.

McGregor, P.K., Otter, K., Peake, T.M., 1999. Communication networks: receiver and signaller perspectives. In: Espmark, Y., Amundsen, T., Rosenqvist, G. (Eds.), Animal Signals: Signalling and Signal Design in Animal Communication. Tapir Academic Press, Trondheim, pp. 405–416.

McKay, F.E., 1971. Behavioral aspects of population dynamics in unisexual-bisexual *Poeciliopsis* (Pisces: Poeciliidae). Ecology 52, 778–790.

Meffe, G.K., Snelson, F.F., 1989. An ecological overview of poeciliid fishes. In: Dawley, R.M., Bogart, J.P. (Eds.). Ecology and Evolution of Livebearing Fishes (Poeciliidae). Prentice Hall, Englewood Cliffs, New Jersey.

Meggers, B.J., 1998. Mate copying and cultural inheritance. Trends Ecol. Evol. 13, 240.

Möller, D., 2001. Aspekte zur Populationsgenetik des eingeschlechtlichen Amazonenkärpflings *Poecilia formosa* (GIRARD 1859) unter Beru_cksichtigung der genetischen parentalen Arten, dem Breitflossenkärpfling *Poecilia latipinna* (LESUEUR 1821) und dem Atlantikkärpfling *Poecilia mexicana*, STEINDACHNER 1863. Dissertation, University of Hamburg.

Moore, W.S., Mc Kay, F.E., 1971. Coexistence in unisexual–bisexual breeding complexes of *Poeciliopsis* (Pisces: Poeciliidae). Ecology 52, 791–799.

Munger, L., Cruz, A., Applebaum, S., 2004. Mate choice copying in female humpback limia (*Limia nigrofasciata*, family Poeciliidae). Ethology 110, 563–573.

Naguib, M., Amrhein, V., Kunc, H.P., 2004. Effects of territorial intrusions on eavesdropping neighbors: communication networks in nightingales. Behav. Ecol. 15, 1011–1015.

Nanda, I., Schlupp, I., Lamatsch, D.K., Lampert, K.P., Schmid, M., Schartl, M., 2007. Stable inheritance of host species-derived microchromosomes in the gynogenetic fish *Poecilia formosa*. Genetics 177, 917–926.

Niemeitz, A., Kreutzfeldt, R., Schartl, M., Parzefall, J., Schlupp, I., 2002. Male mating behaviour of a molly, *Poecilia latipunctata*: a third host for the sperm-dependent Amazon molly, *Poecilia formosa*. Acta Ethol. 5, 45–49.

Nordell, S.E., Valone, T.J., 1998. Mate choice copying as public information. Ecol. Lett. 1, 74–76.

Oliveira, R.F., McGregor, P.K., Schlupp, I., Rosenthal, G.G., 2000a. Video playback techniques in behavioural research. Acta Ethol. 3, 1.

Oliveira, R.F., Rosenthal, G.G., Schlupp, I., McGregor, P.K., Cuthill, I., Endler, J.A., et al., 2000b. Considerations on the use of video-playback as visual stimuli: the Lisbon workshop consensus. Acta Ethol. 3, 61–65.

Parzefall, J., 1973. Attraction and sexual cycle of poeciliids. In: Schröder, J.H. (Ed.), Genetics and Mutagenesis of Fish. Springer, Berlin, pp. 177–183.

Plath, M., Makowicz, A.M., Schlupp, I., Tobler, M., 2007. Sexual harassment in live-bearing fishes (Poeciliidae): comparing courting and noncourting species. Behav. Ecol. 18, 680–688.

Plath, M., Blum, D., Schlupp, I., Tiedemann, R., 2008a. Audience effect alters mating preferences in a livebearing fish, the Atlantic molly, *Poecilia mexicana*. Anim. Behav. 75, 21–29.

Plath, M., Richter, S., Tiedemann, R., Schlupp, I., 2008b. Male fish deceive competitors about mating preferences. Curr. Biol. 18, 1138–1141.

Ptacek, M.B., Breden, F., 1998. Phylogenetic relationships among the mollies (Poeciliidae: *Poecilia: Mollienesia* group) based on mitochondrial DNA sequences. J. Fish Biol. 53, 64–81.

Ptacek, M.B., Childress, M.J., Kittell, M.M., 2005. Characterizing the mating behaviours of the Tamesi molly, *Poecilia latipunctata*, a sailfin with shortfin morphology. Anim. Behav. 70, 1339–1348.

Rasch, E.M., Monaco, P.J., Balsano, J.S., 1982. Cytomorphometric and autoradiographic evidence for functional apomixis in a gynogenetic fish, *Poecilia formosa* and its related, triploid unisexuals. Histochemistry 73, 515–533.

Riesch, R., Schlupp, I., Plath, M., 2008. Female sperm limitation in natural populations of a sexual/asexual mating complex (*Poecilia latipinna*, *Poecilia formosa*). Biol. Lett. 4, 266–269.

Ryan, M.J., Keddy-Hector, A.C., 1992. Directional patterns of female mate choice and the role of sensory biases. Am. Nat. 139 (Suppl.), 4–35.

Ryan, M.J., Dries, L.A., Batra, P., Hillis, D.M., 1996. Male mate preferences in a gynogenetic species complex of Amazon mollies. Anim. Behav. 52, 1225–1236.

Schartl, M., Schlupp, I., Schartl, A., Meyer, M.K., Nanda, I., Schmid, M., et al., 1991. On the stability of dispensable constituents of the eukaryotic genome—stability of coding sequences versus truly hypervariable sequences in a clonal vertebrate, the Amazon molly, *Poecilia formosa*. Proc. Natl. Acad. Sci. USA 88, 8759–8763.

Schartl, M., Schlupp, I., Schartl, A., Meyer, M.K., Nanda, I., Schmid, M., et al., 1995a. Incorporation of subgenomic amounts of DNA as compensation for mutational load in a gynogenetic fish. Nature (London) 373, 68–71.

Schartl, M., Wilde, B., Schlupp, I., Parzefall, J., 1995b. Evolutionary origin of a parthenoform, the Amazon molly *Poecilia formosa*, on the basis of a molecular genealogy. Evolution 49, 827–835.

Schlupp, I., 2000. Are there lessons from negative results in studies using video playbacks? Acta Ethol. 3, 9–13.

Schlupp, I., 2005. The evolutionary ecology of gynogenesis. Annu. Rev. Ecol. Evol. Syst. 36, 399–417.

Schlupp, I., Plath, M., 2005. Male mate choice and sperm allocation in a sexual/asexual mating complex of *Poecilia* (Poeciliidae, Teleostei). Biol. Lett. 1, 169–171.

Schlupp, I., Ryan, M.J., 1996. Mixed-species shoals and the maintenance of a sexual-asexual mating system in mollies. Anim. Behav. 52, 885–890.

Schlupp, I., Ryan, M.J., 1997. Male sailfin mollies (*Poecilia latipinna*) copy the mate choice of other males. Behav. Ecol. 8, 104–107.

Schlupp, I., Parzefall, J., Schartl, M., 1991. Male mate choice in mixed bisexual unisexual breeding complexes of *Poecilia* (Teleostei, Poeciliidae). Ethology 88, 215–222.

Schlupp, I., Parzefall, J., Epplen, J.T., Nanda, I., Schmid, M., Schartl, M., 1992. Pseudomale behaviour and spontaneous masculinization in the all-female teleost *Poecilia formosa* (Teleostei, Poeciliidae). Behaviour 122, 88–104.

Schlupp, I., Marler, C., Ryan, M.J., 1994. Benefit to male sailfin mollies of mating with heterospecific females. Science 263, 373–374.

Schlupp, I., Parzefall, J., Epplen, J.T., Schartl, M., 1996. *Limia vittata* as host species for the Amazon molly: no evidence for sexual reproduction. J. Fish Biol. 48, 792–795.

Schlupp, I., Nanda, I., Döbler, M., Lamatsch, D.K., Epplen, J.T., Parzefall, J., et al., 1998. Dispensable and indispensable genes in an ameiotic fish, the Amazon molly *Poecilia formosa*. Cytogenet. Cell Genet. 80, 193–198.

Schlupp, I., Waschulewski, M., Ryan, M.J., 1999. Female preferences for naturally-occurring novel male traits. Behaviour 136, 519–527.

Schlupp, I., McKnab, R., Ryan, M.J., 2001. Sexual harassment as a cost for molly females: Bigger males cost less. Behaviour 138, 277–286.

Schlupp, I., Parzefall, J., Schartl, M., 2002. Biogeography of the Amazon molly, *Poecilia formosa*. J. Biogeogr. 29, 1–6.

Seehausen, O., vanAlphen, J.J.M., Witte, F., 1997. Cichlid fish diversity threatened by eutrophication that curbs sexual selection. Science 277, 1808–1811.

Simcox, H., Colegrave, N., Heenan, A., Howard, C., Braithwaite, V.A., 2005. Context-dependent male mating preferences for unfamiliar females. Anim. Behav. 70, 1429–1437.

Smith, C.C., 2007. Independent effects of male and female density on sexual harassment, female fitness, and male competition for mates in the western mosquitofish *Gambusia affinis*. Behav. Ecol. Sociobiol. 61, 1349–1358.

Soltis, D.E., Soltis, P.S., Schemske, D.W., Hancock, J.F., Thompson, J.N., Husband, B.C., et al., 2007. Autopolyploidy in angiosperms: have we grossly underestimated the number of species? Taxon 56, 13–30.

Stohr, S., 1998. Evolution of mate-choice copying: a dynamic model. Anim. Behav. 55, 893–903.

Suomalainen, E., Saura, A., Lokki, J., 1987. Cytology and Evolution in Parthenogenesis. CRC Press, Boca Raton, FL.

Tiedemann, R., Moll, K., Paulus, K.B., Schlupp, I., 2005. New microsatellite loci confirm hybrid origin, parthenogenetic inheritance, and mitotic gene conversion in the gynogenetic Amazon molly (*Poecilia formosa*). Mol. Ecol. Notes 5, 586–589.

Tinbergen, N., 1963. On aims and methods of ethology. Z. Tierpsychol. 20, 410–433.

Tobler, M., Schlupp, I., 2005. Parasites in sexual and asexual mollies (*Poecilia*, Poeciliidae, Teleostei): a case for the Red Queen. Biol. Lett. 1, 166–168.

Tobler, M., Schlupp, I., 2008. Expanding the horizon: the Red Queen and potential alternatives. Can. J. Zool. 86, 765–773.

Tobler, M., Schlupp, I., 2009. Threatened fishes of the world: *Poecilia latipunctata* Meek, 1904 (Poeciliidae). Environ. Biol. Fishes 85, 31–32.

Tobler, M., Plath, M., Burmeister, H., Schlupp, I., 2006. Black spots and female association preferences in a sexual/asexual mating complex (*Poecilia*, Poeciliidae, Teleostei). Behav. Ecol. Sociobiol. 60, 159–165.

Travis, J., 1994a. Evolution in the sailfin molly: the interplay of life-history variation and sexual selection. In: Real, L.A. (Ed.), Ecological Genetics. Princeton University Press, New Jersey, pp. 205–232.

Travis, J., 1994b. Size-dependent behavioral variation and its genetic control within and among populations. In: Boake, C.R.B. (Ed.), Quantitative Genetic Studies of Behavioral Evolution. University of Chicago Press, Chicago, pp. 165–187.

Travis, J., Woodward, B.D., 1989. Social context and courtship flexibility in male sailfin mollies *Poecilia latipinna* (Pisces: Poeciliidae). Anim. Behav. 38, 1001–1011.

Trexler, J.C., Travis, J., 1990. Phenotypic plasticity in the sailfin molly, *Poecilia latipinna* (Pisces: Poeciliidae). I. field experiments. Evolution 44, 143–156.

Trexler, J.C., Travis, J., McManus, M., 1992. Effects of habitat and body size on mortality rates of *Poecilia latipinna*. Ecology 73, 2224–2236.

Trexler, J.C., Tempe, R.C., Travis, J., 1994. Size-selective predation of sailfin mollies by two species of heron. Oikos 69, 250–258.

Trivers, R.L., 1972. Parental investment and sexual selection. In: Campbell, B. (Ed.), Sexual selection and the descent of Man. Aldine, Chicago, pp. 139–179.

Turner, B.J., Steeves, H.R.I., 1989. Induction of spermatogenesis in an all-female fish species by treatment with an exogeneous androgen. In: Dawley, R.M., Bogart, J.P. (Eds.), Evolution and Ecology of Unisexual Vertebrates. University of the State of New York, Albany, NY, pp. 113–122.

Turner, B., Elder, J., Jr., Laughlin, T., Davis, W., 1990. Genetic variation in clonal vertebrates detected by simple-sequence DNA fingerprinting. PNAS 87, 5653–5657.

Valone, T.J., 2007. From eavesdropping on performance to copying the behavior of others: a review of public information use. Behav. Ecol. Sociobiol. 62, 1–14.

Valone, T.J., Templeton, J.J., 2002. Public information for the assessment of quality: a widespread social phenomenon. Philos. Trans. R. Soc. Lond. B Biol. Sci. 357, 1549–1557.

Vrijenhoek, R.C., 1994. Unisexual fish—model systems for studying ecology and evolution. Annu. Rev. Ecol. Syst. 25, 71–96.

West, S.A., Lively, C.M., Read, A.F., 1999. A pluralist approach to sex and recombination. J. Evol. Biol. 12, 1003–1012.

Westneat, D.F., Walters, A., McCarthy, T.M., Hatch, M.I., Hein, W.K., 2000. Alternative mechanisms of nonindependent mate choice. Anim. Behav. 59, 467–476.

Witte, K., Klink, K.B., 2005. No pre-existing bias in sailfin molly females, *Poecilia latipinna*, for a sword in males. Behaviour 142, 283–303.

Witte, K., Massmann, R., 2003. Female sailfin mollies, *Poecilia latipinna*, remember males and copy the choice of others after 1 day. Anim. Behav. 65, 1151–1159.

Witte, K., Ryan, M.J., 2002. Mate choice copying in the sailfin molly, *Poecilia latipinna*, in the wild. Anim. Behav. 63, 943–949.

Witte, K., Ueding, K., 2003. Sailfin molly females (*Poecilia latipinna*) copy the rejection of a male. Behav. Ecol. 14, 389–395.

Wong, B.B.M., Candolin, U., Lindström, K., 2007. Environmental deterioration compromises socially enforced signals of male quality in three-spined sticklebacks. Am. Nat. 170, 184–189.

Zeiske, E., 1968. Prädispositionen bei *Mollienesia sphenops* (Pisces, Poeciliidae) für den Übergang zum Leben in subterranen Gewässern. Z. Vgl. Physiol. 58, 190–222.

Alternative Mating Tactics in Acarid Mites

Jacek Radwan

INSTITUTE OF ENVIRONMENTAL SCIENCES, JAGIELLONIAN UNIVERSITY,
UL. GRONOSTAJOWA 7, 30-387 KRAKOW, POLAND

I. Alternative and Conditional Strategies

Understanding the evolution of complex adaptations is one of the major aims of evolutionary biology. Studying discontinuous phenotypic variation within species can be particularly revealing as it allows for comparisons between phenotypes which differ only in the trait of interest and share much of the genetic background. Alternative mating tactics provide a good example of complex adaptations in which behavioral variants are often characterized by specialized morphologies. Alternative mating tactics occur when individuals of one sex (usually males) use distinct ways to gain access to sexual partners (reviewed in Brockmann, 2001; Gross, 1996; Oliveira et al., 2008). In a typical case, one type of male engages in open intersexual contests (e.g., territorial behaviors), whereas the other uses various ways of obtaining mates without confronting rivals (sneaker behaviors; e.g., Brockmann, 2002; Emlen, 1997a; Gross, 1991; Shuster and Wade, 1991; Tomkins and Brown, 2004). Behavioral alternatives may often be associated with differences in morphology where, for example, territorial males bear structures such as horns that are useful in fights (Eberhard, 1982; Emlen, 1997a).

Why should selection maintain alternative mating tactics within populations rather than establishing a single, optimal tactic? Game-theoretical analyses of conflicts over resources (such as conflicts between males over access to females) have demonstrated the possibility of two basic scenarios (Maynard Smith, 1982). The first leads to the maintenance of genetic polymorphism at the locus responsible for the expression of the tactic, whereas the second assumes that alternative tactics are distinct phenotypically, but not necessarily genetically. The latter scenario seems especially likely if the success of a given tactic is conditional on some environmental factor (Maynard Smith, 1982). Below, I will summarize results obtained

185

0065-3454/09 $35.00
DOI: 10.1016/S0065-3454(09)39006-3

from these models and discuss their limitations. In particular, the complex interactions between genetic and environmental factors affecting morph expression make the scope of classification based on genetic monomorphism/polymorphism limited. Some of these complexities are taken into account in more recent models of the evolution of alternative mating tactics which I summarize at the end of this section.

Maynard Smith and Price (1973) considered a simple scenario of two types of behavior that can be performed in a situation of conflict: aggressive and submissive. The first behavioral type, which they called the hawk strategy, would fight for access to territories or mates, whereas the alternative dove strategy would withdraw when faced with aggression from hawks, or share the resource with other doves.

In the simple hawk–dove model, the outcome of the contest depended only on the behavior of the opponent. Consequently, average fitness of a strategy depended on the relative frequencies in the population of strategists playing hawks and doves. In a version of the models where costs of an aggressive contest exceeded the benefit of gaining access to the resource, fitness of hawks and doves were negatively frequency-dependent: hawks thrived in a population of doves, because they gained resources without paying the price of fighting, whereas the high cost of fights made their fitness lower in hawk-dominated populations. Such negative frequency dependence leads to a stable equilibrium where both strategies coexist in the population at frequencies yielding equal fitness to each. This so-called mixed Evolutionarily Stable Strategy (ESS) could be achieved in two ways: alternative strategies could reflect genetic differences between strategies, or a population could be genetically homogeneous, but with individuals adopting alternative behaviors at random, at the appropriate ESS frequency (Maynard Smith, 1982). According to terminology adopted later, the polymorphic case represents two alternative strategies, the strategy being defined as a genetically determined decision rule, resulting in the adoption of particular behavioral phenotypes, called tactics (Dominey, 1984; Gross, 1996). The case where the behavioral tactics were adopted at random represents a single "mixed" strategy.

The two features of the ESS models of mixed and alternative strategies (negative-frequency dependence and equal fitness of alternative strategies at equilibrium), were, according to Maynard Smith, the features distinguishing them from another set of models, asymmetric games, which also could account for stable coexistence of alternative variants. In an extension of the hawk–dove model, Maynard Smith considered asymmetry in the ability to win contests, such as might result from differences in body mass. The so-called Assessor strategy, behaving as a hawk when the opponent is weaker, and as a Dove when faced with a stronger competitor, was shown to be evolutionarily stable when competing with pure Hawk and pure Dove strategies (Maynard Smith, 1982). Assessor represents a so-called conditional strategy, expressing two alternative tactics depending on the resource-holding potential (RHP) or, more generally, status (Gross, 1996). Unlike the case of mixed and alternative strategy-ESSs, the fitness of alternative tactics need not be equal (Maynard Smith, 1982; Tomkins and Hazel, 2007). In the Assessor game, stronger individuals will gain access to resources more often than weak individuals, and will thus achieve a higher fitness on average, even though for low RHP individuals the dove strategy yields higher fitness than the hawk strategy (Fig. 1).

Environmentally induced differences between individuals may force them to "make the best of a bad job" in a similar way. For example, in some horn-dimorphic beetles, individuals with nutritionally determined low body mass develop tiny horns and adopt sneaky behaviors to obtain matings (Eberhard, 1982; Emlen, 1997b). Such conditional strategies can thus be considered a case of a broader phenomenon of polyphenisms, where alternative phenotypes arise in response to some environmental factor (Hazel et al., 1990; Roff, 1996; Tomkins and Hazel, 2007).

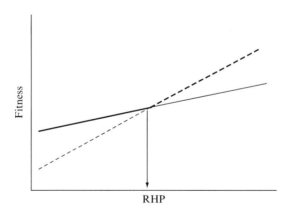

Fig. 1. An illustration of status dependence of alternative mating tactics. Fitness of males increases with the increase in resource-holding potential (RHP), irrespective of the tactic assumed. However, above a certain threshold of RHP (arrow), higher fitness is gained by individuals assuming a hawk strategy (broken line) than those assuming a dove strategy (solid line). Selection could be expected to favor genotypes which switch between phenotypes depending on the RHP. The optimal switch point should be close to the threshold. Consequently, we should mostly observe high RHP hawks and low RHP doves (thick lines); after Gross and Repka (1998), modified.

The classification put forward by Maynard Smith specified that genetic polymorphism is a feature of alternative strategies coexisting at an ESS frequency in the population, whereas when tactic is adjusted to an individual's RHP, a so-called "monomorphic" conditional strategy evolves. Although ESS models did not make explicit assumptions about genetics underlying alternative strategies, the terms monomorphism and polymorphism refer to a single locus. However, heritable differences between alternative tactics may not conform to a single-locus model (Radwan, 1995; Tomkins et al., 2004). For example, body mass, likely to impact RHP, need not be purely environmentally determined, as it is often heritable. Therefore, even in a population fixed for a single conditional strategy, mating tactics can be heritable due to heritability of RHP (Gross and Repka, 1998).

Furthermore, there is no reason to assume that mating tactics need to be determined at a single locus, and the term "monomorphism" may not be an accurate reflection of the genetic underpinnings of conditional strategies (Hazel et al., 2004; Shuster and Wade, 2003). There may be genetic variation with respect to the switchpoint between alternative mating tactics (i.e., the threshold value of individual's state delimiting expression of alternative phenotypes, Fig. 1), as assumed by the environmental threshold (ET) models (Hazel et al., 2004; Tomkins and Hazel, 2007). There are multiple sources of genetic variation for switchpoint location, including variation in the level of hormones mediating development of alternative traits and behaviors, or in the number or sensitivity of receptors of such hormones (Emlen, 2008). Clearly, genetic variation may concern not only pure strategies, but also conditional strategies differing in the location of the switchpoint. As shown by the ET models, assuming quantitative genetic variation for the switchpoint and searching for a stable equilibrium, fitnesses of alternative mating tactics may or may not be equal under parameter values favoring evolution of conditional strategies (reviewed in Tomkins and Hazel, 2007). Thus, traditional delimitations of alternative and conditional strategies (genetic/nongenetic; fitness equal/not equal; see Gross, 1996) are unlikely to accurately reflect natural variation. Distinguishing cases where alternative phenotypes represent genetically distinct "pure" alternative strategies, from conditional strategies, where genetic differences may represent quantitative genetic variation concerning an individual's status or the norm of reaction, requires the study of the genetic architecture of alternative mating tactics.

The optimal choice between alternative mating tactics may be determined not only by individual status (determined by both genes and environment), but also by the environment in which the tactics are to be performed (Gross, 1996; Radwan, 1993; Tomkins and Hazel, 2007).

An adaptive response to environmental cues, known from many other forms of polyphenism (Roff, 1996), can also be considered a form of conditional strategy. Unlike individual status, the external environment affecting tactic payoffs is usually not inherited (but see Kotiaho et al., 2003). Nevertheless, sensitivity to environmental cues can be heritable (Fairbairn and Yadlowski, 1997; Roff, 1996; Unrug et al., 2004) rendering tactics heritable as well.

The evolutionary outcome of selective pressures on alternative mating tactics may thus depend on complex interactions between different sources of genetic and environmental variation. As I will show below, acarid mites represent a variety of such outcomes, and are thus an ideal model to study the evolution of alternative mating tactics. Their short generation time and straightforward rearing methods make them highly suitable to quantitative genetic, and experimental evolution studies.

II. Andropolymorphism Among Acarids

Mites of the family Acaridae are among those lineages of the order Astigmata which underwent an early radiation in the nests of birds and mammals (OConnor, 1982). At present, representatives of the family live in such habitats as stored food products, nests of bees and ants, decaying organic matter, or bulbs of tubers of various plants. In several species of at least three genera of the mite family Acaridae (Astigmata), two male morphs (andropolymorphism) exhibit different ways of securing mating partners (Hughes, 1976). Heteromorphic males can be distinguished by a massively thickened and sharply terminated third pair of legs, whereas homeomorphic males possess slender legs, similar to those of females (Fig. 2). Andropolymorphic species are found in genera *Sancassania* (syn. *Caloglyphus*), *Rhizoglyphus*, and *Schwiebia*, belonging to the subfamily *Rhizoglyphinae*, characterized by a preference for wet habitats (decaying organic matter, bulbs, tubers; OConnor, 1982). These three genera also contain species where heteromorphic males have not been described (Hughes, 1976; Woodring, 1969a). In species where sexual dimorphism is marked by longer dorsal setae in males than in females, homemorphs and heteromorphs are sometimes referred to as bimorphs and pleomorphs, respectively (Hughes, 1976).

The thickened legs are used in intrasexual contests to puncture the cuticle of the rival. Such aggressive behavior, associated with mortality of the successfully punctured opponents, was first reported by Woodring (1969b) for *Sancassania anomalus*, and later reported also for other species (Timms et al., 1980a) and genera (Radwan et al., 2000). Homeomorphic males, on

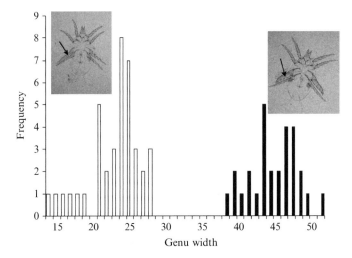

Fɪɢ. 2. Alternative male morphs in Arideae. Fighter males (right, black bars) are character-ized by thickened and sharply terminated third legs, whereas in scramblers (left, white bars) the third pair of legs is similar to the fourth pair. The distribution of leg thickness (measured at base of the second segment, *genu*, indicated with arrow) is discontinuous.

the other hand, engage in aggressive interaction much less frequently and were not reported to be capable of killing other males (Radwan et al., 2000; Timms et al., 1980a). In *Rhizoglyphus robini*, aggressive behavior of males was more often observed in the presence of females, which is consistent with earlier reports suggesting that killing rivals is a way to obtain exclusive access to females (Radwan, 1993). For simplicity, and following earlier literature, I will refer to males possessing thickened legs (i.e., heteromorphs or pleomorphs) as fighters, and those with unmodified legs (homoeomorphs or bimorphs) as scramblers.

III. MORPH DETERMINATION: GENETIC AND ENVIRONMENTAL IMPACTS

Theoretical work has identified several selective forces that should favor either genetic or environmental determination of alternative mating tactics. If success of the tactic depends on some environmental factors (such as the level of nutrition affecting RHP or population density affecting mating skew) and if the future environment can be predicted from reliable cues, a response to such cues should be selected for, resulting in environmental morph determination (Lively, 1986; Maynard Smith, 1982; Moran, 1992).

If the reliability of cues is low, genetic polymorphism for mating tactics can be maintained, particularly if there are costs to plasticity and if competition between tactics for resources (e.g., mates) is intense (Hazel et al., 2004; Plaistow et al., 2004). Acarid mites seem well suited to test predictions of these models, because, as I will summarize below, both environmental and genetic factors are known to affect tactic expression.

Foa (1919) was the first to study determination of male morphs in the acarids. She concluded from crosses using both morphs that the morph is heritable in *Rhizoglyphus echinopus* and suggested that it is due to a single-locus polymorphism. Woodring (1969a) divided andropolymorphism in acarids into two categories: primary and secondary. Species exhibiting primary andropolymorphism (exemplified, according to Woodring, by *Sancassania berlesei*) show, under a specified temperature and humidity, a regular ratio of fighters to scramblers, whereas in species with secondary andropolymorphism, fighter morph is normally absent, but it is induced when larvae are developing in isolation or in very small groups. Further research by other students confirmed both environmental and genetic influences on morph expression, although some results of early studies were not always confirmed (e.g., Radwan, 2001), possibly due to incorrect species assignment resulting from taxonomic confusion in early acarological literature (e.g., Manson, 1972), or due to actual intraspecific variation (see below).

As first reported by Woodring, expression of thickened legs is indeed modulated by demographic conditions during larval development in some species. Larvae and nymphs exposed to volatiles emanating from dense colonies were found to express predominantly or exclusively the scrambler morph in *S. beresei* (Radwan et al., 2002; Timms et al., 1980b; unlike reported by Woodring, 1969a), and in *R. echinopus* (Radwan, 2001). However, no impact of population density was detected in *R. robini* (Radwan, 1995).

Male morph is also influenced by factors which impact body mass, such as diet (Radwan, 1995) or temperature (Radwan, 2001; Woodring, 1969a). Poor diet or low temperature during development cause a decrease in the proportion of fighters emerging, suggesting that status-dependence may be widespread among acarids. Indeed, Radwan et al. (2002) found in *S. berlesei* that on average, fighters emerge from heavier nymphs than nonfighters.

The impact of volatile chemicals and of nymphal mass may sometimes be confounded, as colony density during development is negatively related to adult body size, probably because of the accumulation of detrimental waste products in the environment (Radwan, 1992). However, when nymphs are exposed to only volatiles, without sharing the environment, the body size they achieve is not significantly different from that of unexposed nymphs, indicating that the fighter-suppressing effects of volatiles are independent of the effects of body mass (Radwan et al., 2002).

Considerable variation is found in the degree of genetic variation underlying morph expression. A high heritability, estimated from parent–offspring regression, was found in *R. robini*, but no significant correlation between father and son morph was detected in *S. berlesei* (Radwan, 1995) or *R. echinopus* (Radwan, 2001). However, a study of another population of *S. berlesei* showed a significant effect of father morph on the proportion of scramblers in progeny (Tomkins et al., 2004). This indicates that heritability of male morph may differ between populations within species. Interestingly, a population started from mites found near Krakow (Poland) studied by Radwan (1995) yielded 97% fighters emerging from nymphs reared individually, whereas this proportion was only 78% in a population derived from Stirling (UK) studied by Tomkins et al. (2004). The latter population thus appears similar to *R. robini*, where some males do not appear to be capable of expressing the fighter morph even under optimal conditions. Unlike *R. robini*, however, expression of fighter morphs was completely suppressed at high density in the Stirling population.

Thus, rather than fitting the simple distinction between alternative and conditional strategies, acarids show a range of genetic and environmental factors impacting morph expression. Disentangling genetic architecture of morph determination and selective pressures that have led to this variation remains a considerable challenge.

IV. GENETIC ARCHITECTURE OF MORPH DETERMINATION

In order to test the predictions stemming from theoretical models of the evolution of alternative mating tactics, an understanding of the mechanisms of morph determination is needed. Consider an example of a species in which the male morph is found to be heritable. Predictions of which model should we test using this system? The answer depends on the details of the genetic architecture of morph determination. If the tactic is determined at a single locus, the system might be described in terms of alternative strategies (Maynard Smith, 1982). However, if heritability of the tactic results from heritability of status (e.g., body mass), then conditional strategy models would be relevant (Gross and Repka, 1998; Hazel et al., 2004).

Genetic variation underlying determination of alternative phenotypes may consist of three layers. First, a population may consist of individuals polymorphic for mating strategy, such that different genotypes express different mating tactics, as reported for some systems (Lank, 1995; Shuster and Sassaman, 1997; Zimmerer and Kallman, 1989). Second, alternative tactics may represent the same conditional strategy, but individuals may differ heritably in status, resulting in tactic heritability (Gross and Repka, 1998). Third, individuals may differ in the threshold of response to status, or to environmental cues (Fig. 3), such that there may be genetic variation with respect to conditional strategy (Emlen, 2008; Hazel et al., 1990; Roff, 1996), as documented earlier in the context of environmentally cued crypsis (Hazel and West, 1982), or migratory polymorphism (Fairbairn and Yadlowski, 1997). All three layers seem to occur among Acarids.

The heritability of male morph can be estimated using the liability model developed for threshold traits (Falconer, 1989). The model assumes that expression of all-or-none characters depends on quantitative genetic variation in an underlying variable, called liability. The expression takes place if liability exceeds a certain threshold value (Fig. 3). Such a protocol, applied to the data on the proportion of fighters among progeny of *R. robini* males of both morphs, yielded an estimate of heritability exceeding one (1.5 from progeny of scramblers 0.98 from progeny of fighters). Values of heritability that exceed 1.0 value suggest that the assumptions of the liability model, relying on polygenic variation underlying fighter morph expression, are not met, possibly because of the impact of a gene of large effect (Falconer, 1989)

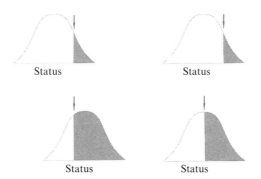

Fig. 3. Two scenarios of the response of a status-dependent trait to selection. Ancestral population (upper graphs) is characterized by normally distributed status. Individuals above the threshold value of the status (arrow) express fighter phenotype (shaded part). Liability model assumes polygenic variation in the underlying trait (here: status). Selection for the fighter phenotype shifts distribution of status (bottom left). Alternatively, if there is additive genetic variation for switchpoints, selection for fighters may cause the shift in the population threshold without changing the distribution of the status (bottom right). If status is determined environmentally, this is the only way to respond to selection. If additive genetic variation exists for both status and switchpoints, both may simultaneously respond to selection (not shown).

or sex linkage (Houde, 1992). The proportion of morphs within families did not, however, conform to any simple model of single-locus inheritance (Radwan, 1995). Thus, the most likely scenario is that the effect of a putative major gene is obscured by additional genetic and environmental impacts on morph expression, such as those resulting from status-dependence documented by diet manipulation in this species (Fig. 4). Morph determination in *R. robini* exemplifies the distinction between genotypic determination and genotypic influence, stressed by (West-Eberhard, 2003): despite strong influence of the genotype, it is not the only factor that determines expressed phenotype. A selection experiment carried out on a different population of *R. robini* confirmed the heritability of male morph in this species (Radwan, 2003). The response to 10 generations of selection (Fig. 5) was asymmetrical and faster during the first few generations than later on, which is consistent with a scenario of a gene of large effect segregating in the population (Falconer, 1989). However, heritability estimates were lower in this population compared to result obtained earlier (Radwan, 1995), possibly reflecting interpopulation differences in the relative roles of genetic and environmental impacts.

High heritability for alternative phenotypes was also found in the Stirling population of *S. berlesei* (Tomkins et al., 2004). The value was in this case less than one (0.81 for fighter progeny and 0.90 for scrambler progeny). A part of this genetic variation for male morph could be explained by heritability of status: sires which were heavier at the tritonympal stage (the last nymphal instar) had more fighters in their progeny. The effect of father morph, however, remained significant after accounting for his tritonymphal mass (Tomkins et al., 2004), indicating that some other genetic

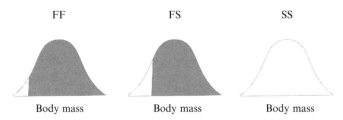

FIG. 4. A hypothetical model of morph determination in *Rhizoglyphus robini*. A single gene with two alleles (F and S) has a major effect on morph determination. However, genetically and/or environmentally determined body mass (a measure of status) causes genetic fighters that achieve small size to develop scrambler phenotype (white part of the distribution). The model reconciles indications of the presence of a gene of major effect in *R. robini* with status-dependence, which is one of possible reasons for deviation of morph rations from Mendelian proportions. Gray area: fighters, white area: scramblers.

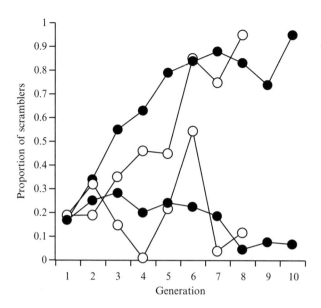

F<small>IG</small>. 5. Response of *R. robini* to selection on male morph. At each generation, only one male type (scramblers of fighters) was selected as sires. Two replicates (white and black circles) were run in each direction. Heritability estimates in upward direction (toward scramblers) were higher (0.79 and 0.83) than in downward direction (0.19 and 0.39) (modified from Radwan, 2003, with permission).

factor, independent of status, impacts male morph. This could be due to genetic variation in the sensitivity to volatiles produced by conspecifics, or to a major effect gene.

Unrug et al. (2004) documented genetic variation for status dependence in *S. berlesei*. They selected the Stirling population for increased proportion of either fighter, or scrambler morph under conditions where both morphs were expressed; larvae were reared in groups, resulting initially in 24% of fighters emerging. After seven generations they found a highly significant divergence between lines, with the proportion of fighters increasing to 68–83% in upselected replicates, and decreasing to 6–16% in downselected lines. The response, however, was not due to a change in status, as the lines selected in different directions did not differ in the mass at the tritonymphal stage. On the other hand, Unrug et al. (2004) showed that the threshold where males had a 50% chance of becoming either morph differed between selection regimes. Thus, the response to selection resulted from genetic variation for the location of the switchpoint leading to fighter expression (Fig. 3). A common-garden experiment on three populations of *S. berelesei* has shown that there exists interpopulation variation in the switchpoint (Tomkins et al., 2004), demonstrating that the underlying genetic variation could be subject to variable selective pressures under different ecological conditions. Similar variation between populations was also reported for male-dimorphic beetles (Moczek et al., 2002) and earwigs (Tomkins and Brown, 2004). This variation seems to be driven by interpopulation differences in intensity of sexual selection (Moczek, 2003). Intensity of sexual selection could thus be a factor shaping relative fitness functions of alternative mating tactics (Tomkins and Brown, 2004).

The response to selection on male morph in the Unrug et al.'s (2004) study could also be due to a change in sensitivity to environmental cues. Indeed, Tomkins et al. (2004) found in a common-garden experiment that populations differ in their sensitivity to the fighter-suppressing effect of group rearing. They reared larvae of *S. berlesei* derived from three different populations either singly, or in groups of four different sizes, and found that the proportion of fighters decreased with group size in all populations. However, the rate of a decrease differed, with a population derived from Germany maintaining an overall higher proportion of fighters than two other populations, derived from two different locations in Scotland. Thus, apart from natural variation in status dependence, there appears to be interpopulation variation in sensitivity to cues produced by conspecifics.

Finally, the response could be due to pure strategies replacing conditional strategies. As discussed in the previous section, a fraction of male genotypes (22%) in the Stirling population were found incapable of fighter morph expression under optimal feeding conditions, and when unsuppressed by volatiles from the colony. The response to selection could thus partly result from a change in the proportion of such males between the lines. This was indeed the case, as the proportion of fighters that developed from unsuppressed nymphs was significantly higher in fighter-selected lines (range: 87–100%) than in scrambler-selected lines (range: 63–81%). It is not clear, however, whether males not capable of expressing the fighter morph represent a pure scrambler strategy determined by a single locus, or by an extreme value from a distribution of conditional strategies differing in sensitivity to volatiles produced by conspecifics (Hazel et al., 2004). It is theoretically possible that such extreme values might result in suppression of fighter production by one's own pheromone. Further, genetic analyses are needed to distinguish between these mechanisms.

Summarizing, all three possible levels of genetic variation underlying heritability of alternative mating tactics are represented in acarids, although species, and populations within species, differ in relative impacts of these levels. This variation makes acarids an ideal system for uncovering selective pressures shaping the evolution of alternative mating tactics.

V. Identifying Selection Pressures on Alternative Mating Tactics

Key selective pressures acting on alternative mating tactics include frequency dependence and status/environment dependence. The dependence of tactic success on status or environment, coupled with appropriate cues, favors conditional strategies (Hazel et al., 2004; Lively, 1986; Maynard Smith, 1982). When the environment is unpredictable, or differences in fitness across environments are small, frequency dependence arising from competitive interactions between males appears to favor the maintenance of pure strategies (Hazel et al., 2004; Lively, 1986; Plaistow et al., 2004). The evolution of alternative mating strategies will also be affected by evolutionary tradeoffs, preventing the development of well-performing generalist phenotypes independent of status/environment (Moran, 1992). In this section, I review the evidence for these pressures operating on male morphs among acarids.

A. Frequency Dependence

Gross (1996) lists frequency dependence as one of the defining features of alternative mating strategies. Frequency-dependence could thus be expected to maintain morph heritability in *R. robini*, where an impact of a gene of large effect is suspected (Radwan, 1995). Radwan and Klimas (2001) created a range of populations of *R. robini* differing in morph ratio (from 0.1 to 0.9 fighters), but no indication of frequency dependence of male mating success was found (Fig. 6). While factors maintaining morph heritability in *R. robini* remain to be determined, this result suggests that the maintenance of alternative mating strategies may not necessarily require frequency dependence resulting from social interactions.

B. Status Dependence

A simple Assessor game (Maynard Smith, 1982) predicted that if individuals differ in RHP and are capable of assessing this difference, tactics conditional on RHP should evolve. In species where tactics are chosen for life (which facilitates evolution of morphological adaptations supporting alternative behaviors), body mass at the outset of the final life stage is likely to affect the decision (Maynard Smith, 1982). Indeed body mass is perhaps the most universal factor affecting morph expression in acarids, being documented by both experimental manipulation with diet (Radwan, 1995), and by correlation between tritonymphal mass and fighter morph expression (Radwan et al., 2002; Tomkins et al., 2004).

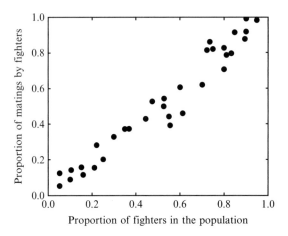

Fig. 6. Association between frequency of fighters and their relative mating success in populations of 42 mites. The slope of regression of mating success on the proportion of fighters in a population was not significantly different from one, providing no support for frequency dependence (from Radwan and Klimas, 2001, with permission).

C. Environmental Impacts

Apart from determining individual RHP, the environment may directly impact the fitness of alternative mating tactics. In *S. berlesei*, population parameters were shown to have an important impact on relative finesses of male morphs (Radwan, 1993). This possibility was inferred from the fact that volatiles produced by conspecifics, which are likely to carry reliable information about current population size and density, have strong suppressing effects on fighter morph expression in this species. Indeed, fighters were demonstrated to be able to kill all rival males in small populations (consisting of a dozen adults), which gives them exclusive access to females and, consequently, greater average reproductive success compared to scramblers (Radwan, 1993). In *S. berlesei* monopolization took place in 51% of such small populations. If a local population consists of hundreds of adults, monopolization is not possible. Under such circumstances, fighters became involved in combats about five times as often as scramblers, which caused higher mortality among fighters, making their average reproductive success lower than that of scramblers (Fig. 7). Differential survival seems to be the most important cause of differential reproductive success of male morph in populations of different size, as fighters and scramblers had the same per-individual copulation frequency (Radwan, 1993). Apart from

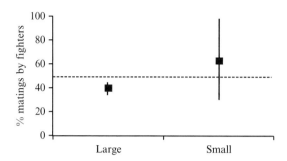

FIG. 7. Mating success (mean ± range) of fighter males of *Sancassania berlesei* in populations of two sizes: large (120 individuals) and small (10 individuals). Initial proportions of both morphs were even, such that the null expectation was 50% of matings achieved by fighters (broken line). In large populations fighters suffered higher mortality, and their mating success was always lower than that of scramblers (mean and upper range below the null expectation of 50%). In small colonies, mating success was more variable and depended on whether a fighter male was able to kill all rivals and monopolize females. In cases of early monopolization mating success of fighters approached 100%. As monopolization occurred in over half of small colonies, average mating success of fighters exceeded that of scramblers (Radwan, 1993).

avoiding contests, scramblers may owe their better survival in large colonies to higher motility (third legs of fighters apparently hinder male movements in *S. berlesei*, personal observations).

S. berlesei is commonly found is debris containing poultry feces. Such a patchy and structured habitat may indeed allow monopolization of local small populations, but fast reproductive rates of this species are likely to result in rapid increases in population size, making monopolization no longer possible. Furthermore, species of *Sancassania* are phoretic on beetles (OConnor, 1982): a migratory deuteronymph, called hypopus, induced by overcrowding and food shortage, attaches to the body of an insect and can thus be transported to new patches. Dead insects were reported to host small colonies of mites that emerged from hypopi (Chmielewski and Lipa, 1967; OConnor, 1982). Such situations provide an opportunity to exterminate all rivals. Radwan (1993) speculated that timing of sensitivity to colony volatiles, which is at the early tritonymphal stage (the stage following hypopus) may be an adaptation allowing perception of an opportunity for female monopolization in the newly established subpopulation.

Interestingly in *R. robini*, in which fighters are not suppressed by colony volatiles, fitness functions of alternative morphs do not seem to cross between populations of different size (Radwan and Klimas, 2001). Like in *S. berlesei*, a single fighter was sometimes able to monopolize females by killing all rivals in a small population, although monopolization occurred less frequently in *R. robini* (15% in small populations). Unlike in *S. berlesei*, however, fighters did not seem to pay a high price of their aggression in large populations, where they still survived better than scramblers. Indeed, when field-derived populations are brought to the laboratory and reared under standard conditions, including >1000 adults at high density, the proportion of fighters increases to near fixation (personal observations).

The reasons for the difference in morph fitness functions between species remain unclear. Like in *S. berlesei*, fighters of *R. robini* do not seem to avoid attacking other fighters, and aggression between pairs of fighters was observed more often than that between fighter-scrambler pairs (Radwan et al., 2000). It thus appears that once attacked, scramblers suffer higher mortality than fighters, which may result from lower average RHP of scramblers. If, as in *Sancassania*, fighters emerge from heavier nymphs, then they may be more difficult to kill than smaller scramblers. Indeed, poor diet decreases body mass and drastically decreases the proportion of fighters emerging in *R. robini*, and these fighters tend to be heavier than scramblers, although under optimal conditions male morphs do no differ in body mass (Radwan, 1995). However, higher vulnerability of scramblers does not explain why fighters do not pay the price of aggression in large colonies, as is the case in *S. berlesei*. The likely explanation lies in the general lower effectiveness of *R. robini* in killing rivals compared to *S. berlesei*, leading to lower monopolization success in small colonies on one hand, but higher survival in large colonies on the other hand. As a consequence, neither fighter survival, nor reproductive success, was found to be significantly related to local population size (Radwan and Klimas, 2001). The lower killing efficiency might result from lower motility of *R. robini* compared to larger, long-legged *S. berlesei*.

It would be important to see if other species showing fighter morph suppression under high colony density (e.g., *R. echinopus*) show crossing of fitness functions in populations of different size similar to that found in *S. berlesei*, and if the opposite is true for density-insensitive species. This would show if the differences in response to population cues evolve as a result of variation in relative fitness functions of male morphs.

Apart from demographic environment, habitat complexity may be a factor influencing the shape of fitness factions. Complex habitat may facilitate formation of small, locally isolated subpopulations, enabling monopolization of females by killing rival males. Indeed, Lukasik et al. (2006) found that the killing of rivals occurred more frequently in *S. berlesei* populations placed in a complex, spatially subdivided environment. Yet another, so far unexplored factor, may be ambient temperature, which would affect motility and perhaps monopolization efficiency. Perhaps temporal and spatial variation in such environmental factors can explain the maintenance of male dimorphism in *R. robini* which could not be attributed to either demographic factors, or frequency dependence.

D. TRADEOFFS

Fitness functions of alternative male tactics may be mediated by tradeoffs associated with male reproductive phenotypes. Investment in weapons, for example, may come at the cost of other structures (Emlen, 2001). Such tradeoffs may foster phenotypic divergence of alternative tactics, each phenotype achieving fitness in its own, specialized way. Some species with alternative mating tactics were found to differ in relative investment in postcopulatory sexual selection. Facing increased sperm competition risk, individuals adopting sneaker strategies may be expected to invest more resources in sperm production, especially since they often save resources that would otherwise have been spent on weapons. Increased investment in sperm competitive ability by sneakers was indeed reported in beetles (Simmons et al., 2007). However, scramblers were not found to differ significantly from fighters in sperm competition success either in *S. berlesei* (Radwan, 1991, 1993), or in *R. robini* (Radwan, 1997; Radwan and Bogacz, 2000). This result is not unexpected. Because of the small size of these animals, the difference in gamete size between the sexes is not as prominent as in larger-bodied species. As a consequence, males copulating frequently may limit female fecundity by providing insufficient sperm numbers (Radwan, 1991, 1993, 1997). Because fighter males that succeed in killing all rivals will often have access to several females simultaneously, they will be selected to produce enough sperm to assure full fecundity of females, even though the risk of sperm competition will be low. Thus, selection for high sperm production rates in Acaridae is expected in both morphs.

Apart from increased risk of injury, assuming the fighter tactic seems to be associated with physiological and life-history costs. Although in *S. berlesei* fighters emerge from heavier tritonymphs, they loose more body mass between this final nymphal stage and the adult stage than do scramblers (Radwan et al., 2002). This indicates that there is a physiological cost of producing the fighter morphology. Life-history costs were detected in *R. robini*: when reared only with a single female (i.e., excluding fights between males), fighters lived, 20% shorter than scramblers (Radwan and Bogacz, 2000). However, as male reproductive potential decreases with age, the impact of this tradeoff on the relative fitness of male morphs may not be significant. No cost of developing fighter morphology in terms of increased development time was detected in either *R. robini* or *S. berlsesei* (Radwan, 1993; Radwan and Bogacz, 2000).

VI. Future Directions

As it is clear from this review, in terms of identifying the selective pressures that could explain the remarkable intraspecific variation in proximate factors affecting the expression of alternative mating tactics found among acarids, we have only scratched the surface. Identifying these pressures remains an important goal of future research. Selection will shape the genetic architecture underlying the expression of phenotypic alternatives, but, conversely, the genetic architecture will also impact on the response to selection (Schluter, 1996). The classical quantitative genetic methods used so far could usefully be supplemented by molecular methods, allowing precise analysis of genes underlying alternative mating tactic expression. Comparative work (aided by molecular phylogenies) should make use of interspecific variation in expression of alternative mating tactics among Acarids to answer questions about their evolution.

A. Explaining Variation

The question that has not been addressed so far is why male dimorphism evolved in some species, but not in others. The fact that closely related species may differ in possessing dimorphic males (e.g., fighter morphs have not been reported in several species of *Rhizoglyphus* and *Sancassania*; Hughes, 1976) offers the possibility of comparative work to address this question. The two genera containing as least several male-dimorphic species, *Sancassania* and *Rhizoglyphus*, are currently known to contain 75 and 47 species, respectively (Klimov and Oconnor, 2003 and references therein). For such comparative work to be possible, much more background work is necessary. Reports on the lack of male dimorphism are often based on small sample sizes. Furthermore, if cultures were reared at high density, the fighter morph might not be expressed. Thus, the occurrence of alternative male morphs should be studied systematically in more species. Once interspecific variation in the occurrence of alternative male phenotypes is confirmed, we can start to explore ecological factors explaining this variation.

Theoretical work indicates that alternative phenotypes evolve under disruptive selection if a generalist phenotype, able to cope with both roles or environments, cannot develop due to functional constraints, or is costly to maintain (Moran, 1992). Future work should thus attempt to identify selective pressures causing disruptive selection. Work on *Sancassania* shows that environmental factors causing disruptive selection include variation in population size (Radwan, 1993), and in habitat complexity (Łukasik et al., 2006). An as yet unexplored factor, known to affect the evolution of alternative mating tactics in other systems (Tomkins and Brown, 2004; Moczek, 2003) is the intensity of intersexual competition.

Comparative analyses should also provide insights into factors explaining variation in the mode of determination of alternative male morphs, both within and between species. As discussed above (see Section V), if environment/status has little impact on tactic success or if cues to future environments are unreliable, genetic rather than environmental morph determination can be favored. The failure to detect any effect of population size on tactic success in *R. robini* was suggested to explain the lack of sensitivity of this species to colony volatiles, suppressing fighter expression in other acarid species (Radwan and Klimas, 2001). Comparative work involving more acarid species would enable rigorous verification of this hypothesis.

On a shorter evolutionary timescale, interpopulation variation may be used to identify factors affecting expression of alternative tactics. For example, populations of *S. berlesei* were found to differ in the threshold of response to both tritonymphal mass, and to demographic conditions during development, but the causes of these differences remain unclear. Genetic variation within populations at all possible levels that could affect morph expression makes it possible to apply experimental evolution as a tool to uncover these causes. This approach has so far not been applied to study the evolution of alternative mating tactics directly, but was applied to explore consequences of relaxed sexual selection in *R. robini* (Tilszer et al., 2006). Tilszer et al. maintained replicate lines for 37 generations either under monogamy or polygamy. The proportions of fighters, high at the outset of the experiment, remained similarly high in both types of lines. This was not unexpected, as the cost of fights was not born under monogamy, and so there was probably no strong selection against fighter morphology in this treatment. However, fighters from monogamy lines were less aggressive at the end of the experiment (although the difference was marginally nonsignificant), possibly because aggressive disposition made males more harmful to females (an impact that would be strongly selected against under monogamy).

This last result highlights the need to pay more attention to behavioral variation associated with alternative morphologies. As life-history costs of fighter morphology are apparently not very high (see above), aggression-associated mortality appears a major cost of the fighter tactic. Selection against expression of this tactic could, at least initially, act on male aggressiveness more strongly than on morphology.

Apart from withholding aggression, a way to avoid attack by other males is female mimicking, observed in some species with alternative mating tactics (e.g., Shuster and Wade, 1991). Indeed in the absence of females, scrambler males of *R. robini* were mounted by both types of males, who assumed a typical copulatory position (Radwan et al., 2000). This suggests that scramblers may mimic females, perhaps chemically, to avoid aggression from other males. Alternatively, aggressive fighters might counterattack approaching males, thus preventing mounting. The issue of female-mimicking deserves further exploration in acarid mites.

Persistence of genetically distinct, alternative strategies is more likely if there is a cost of plasticity (Plaistow et al., 2004). The costs may include developmental errors. In acarids, males which possess thickened legs on one side of the body only (so-called intermorphs) occur at low frequencies (Tomkins et al., 2004). Intermorphs are likely to have lower fitness than either morph (they are inefficient fighters, but are likely to pay most of the costs associated with this tactic) and their occurrence can thus be considered a cost of plasticity: maintaining alternative phenotypic options open until late in development seem to result in a risk of developmental errors.

In the simple scenario of the Assessor game, fitness payoffs are determined by frequencies of alternative mating tactics. More realistic models allow for variation in payoffs to be dependent on other factors, such as mating skew (Plaistow et al., 2004) or environmental factors (Hazel et al., 2004; Lively, 1986). Under such scenarios, coexistence of pure (or alternative) and conditional strategies, or even predominance of the former, is possible. The case of the Stirling population of *S. berlesei* may possibly conform to this scenario. As discussed above, some individuals (22%) do not express fighter morph even if unexposed to pheromones and fed a high-quality diet (Tomkins et al., 2004 see above). These individuals might represent a pure scrambler strategy, while the remaining part of the population, capable of expressing either morph depending on the concentration of colony volatiles, represents a conditional strategy. Acarids seem well suited to test these new models of evolution of alternative mating tactics.

B. UNCOVERING MECHANISMS

Studying genetic and environmental factors impacting morph determination, using the classical methods described above, will be necessary to obtain more data for comparative analyses. Future work should also explore genetic correlations between morph and behavior. While many observations indicate that scramblers are less aggressive than fighters, there is only a single study which supported this observation with formal analysis (Radwan et al., 2000). Evolution should favor integration of behavior and morphology (Pigliucci and Preston, 2004; West-Eberhard, 2003), for example, by subjecting expression of genes responsible for integrated traits to the same developmental switches. A search for such developmental switches would be an exciting task, made possible by recent advances in genomic studies of nonmodel organisms (Ellegren, 2008). Large variation in modes of male determination may possibly be explained by a relatively small number of master switches. For example, a change in dependence of morph expression on some environmental variable may be due to a change in sensitivity of genes that turn on a set of integrated traits specific to alternative tactics, to specific signals. In some species, the signal may be derived from environmental cues, whereas in other species it can be some internal signal (Emlen, 2008; Emlen and Nijhout, 1999; Suzuki and Nijhout, 2006). For example, a transcription factor may require some external co-factor (such as pheromone) to suppress fighter expression, but a mutation of the transcription factor may cause it to induce morph expression without the cofactor. Alternatively, spatial or temporal change in the expression pattern of receptors binding pheromones produced by conspecifics may make them sensitive to self-produced pheromones. Polymorphism with respect to pheromone production or sensitivity to the pheromone may in turn lead to single-locus control of the expression of alternative tactics. Thus, multiple ways in which conditional strategies may evolve into genetic polymorphisms and back are theoretically possible. Acarid mites, with a large number of species within genera characterized by male dimorphism, and striking variation in the mode of determination of these tactics, are a promising system with which to explore whether these possibilities are actually realized, whether such multiple reversals did occur, and the nature of the ancestral form of andropolymorphism.

Acknowledgments

I thank Jane Brockmann, Leigh Simmons, Joe Tomkins, and an anonymous Referee for their comments on earlier versions of this manuscript. I was supported by the Fundation for Polish Science, professor subsidy 9/2008.

References

Brockmann, H.J., 2001. The evolution of alternative strategies and tactics. Adv. Stud. Behav. 30, 1–51.
Brockmann, H.J., 2002. An experimental approach to altering mating tactics in male horseshoe crabs (*Limulus polyphemus*). Behav. Ecol. 13, 232–238.
Chmielewski, W., Lipa, J.J., 1967. Biological and ecological studies on *Caloglyphus* mite (Acarina: Acaridae) associated with Scarabaeid. Acta Parasitol. Pol. 14, 179–190.

Dominey, W.J., 1984. Alternative mating tactics and evolutionarily stable strategies. Am. Zool. 24, 385–396.

Eberhard, W.G., 1982. Beetle horn dimorphism: making the best of a bad lot. Am. Nat. 119, 420–426.

Ellegren, H., 2008. Sequencing goes 454 and takes large-scale genomics into the wild. Mol. Ecol. 17, 1629–1631.

Emlen, D.J., 1997a. Alternative reproductive tactics and male-dimorphism in the horned beetle *Onthophagus acuminatus* (Coleoptera:Scarabaeidae). Behav. Ecol. Sociobiol. 41, 335–341.

Emlen, D.J., 1997b. Diet alters male horn allometry in the beetle *Onthophagus acuminatus* (Coleoptera: Scarabaeidae). Proc. R. Soc. Lond. B 264, 567–574.

Emlen, D.J., 2001. Costs and the diversification of exaggerated animal structures. Science 291, 1534–1536.

Emlen, D.J., 2008. The roles of genes and environment in the expression and evolution of alternative mating tactics. In: Oliveira, R.F., Taborsky, M., Brockmann, H. (Eds.) Alternative Reproductive Tactics, Cambridge University Press, Cambridge, pp. 85–107.

Emlen, D.J., Nijhout, H.F., 1999. Hormonal control of male horn length dimorphism in the dung beetle *Onthophagus taurus* (Coleoptera: Scarabaeidae). J. Insect Physiol. 45, 45–53.

Fairbairn, D.J., Yadlowski, D.E., 1997. Coevolution of traits determining migratory tendency: correlated response of a critical enzyme, juvenile hormone esterase, to selection on wing morphology. J. Evol. Biol. 10, 495–513.

Falconer, D.S., 1989. Introduction to Quantitative Genetics. 3rd ed. Longman, Harlow.

Foa, A., 1919. Studio del polimorfismo unissessuale del *Rhizoglyphus echinopus*. Memeoria Accad. Pontificia Nuovi Lincei Roma 12, 3–109.

Gross, M.R., 1991. Evolution of alternative reproductive strategies: frequency-dependent selection in male bluegill sunfish. Philos. Trans. R. Soc. Lond. B 332, 59–66.

Gross, M.R., 1996. Alternative reproductive strategies and tactics: diversity within sexes. Trends Ecol. Evol. 11, 92–98.

Gross, M.R., Repka, J., 1998. Stability with inheritance in the conditional strategy. J. Theor. Biol. 192, 445–453.

Hazel, W.N., West, D.A., 1982. Pupal colour dimorphism in swallowtail butterflies as a threshold trait: selection in *Eurytides marcellus* (Cremer). Heredity 59, 449–455.

Hazel, W.N., Smock, R., Johnson, M.D., 1990. A polygenic model for evolution and maintenance of conditional strategies. Proc. R. Soc. Lond B 242, 181–187.

Hazel, W., Smock, R., Lively, C.M., 2004. The ecological genetics of conditional strategies. Am. Nat. 163, 888–900.

Houde, A.E., 1992. Sex-linked heritability of a sexually selected character in a natural population of *Poecilia reticulata*. Heredity 69, 229–235.

Hughes, A.M., 1976. The Mites of Stored Food and Houses. Technical Bulletin of Ministry of Agriculture, Fisheries and Food (9), London.

Klimov, P.B., Oconnor, B.M., 2003. Phylogeny, historical ecology and systematics of some mushroom-associated mites of the genus *Sancassania* (Acari: Acaridae), with new generic synonymies. Invert. Syst. 17, 469–514.

Kotiaho, J.S., Simmons, L.W., Hunt, J., Tomkins, J.L., 2003. Males influence maternal effects that promote sexual selection: a quantitative genetic experiment with dung beetles Onthophagus taurus. Am. Nat. 161, 852–859.

Lank, D.B., 1995. Genetic polymorphism for alternative mating behaviour in male ruff *Philomachus pugnax*. Nature 378, 59–62.

Lively, C.M., 1986. Canalizatoin versus developmental conversion in a spatially variable environment. Am. Nat. 128, 561–572.

Lukasik, P., Radwan, J., Tomkins, J., 2006. Structural complexity of the environment affects the survival of alternative male reproductive tactics. Evolution 60, 399–403.

Manson, D.C.M., 1972. A contribution to the study of the genus *Rhizoglyphus* Claparede 1869 (Acarina: Acaridae). Acarologia 13, 621–650.

Maynard Smith, J., 1982. Evolution and the Theory of Games. Cambridge University Press, Cambridge.

Maynard Smith, J., Price, G.R., 1973. The logic of animal conflict. Nature 246, 15–18.

Moczek, A.P., 2003. The behavioral ecology of threshold evolution in a polyphenic beetle. Behav. Ecol. 14, 841–854.

Moczek, A.P., Hunt, J., Emlen, D.J., Simmons, L.W., 2002. Threshold evolution in exotic populations of a polyphenic beetle. Evol. Ecol. Res. 4, 587–601.

Moran, N., 1992. The evolutionary maintenance of alternative phenotypes. Am. Nat. 139, 971–979.

OConnor, B.A., 1982. Evolutionary ecology of astigmatid mites. Annu. Rev. Entomol. 27, 385–409.

Oliveira, R.F., Taborsky, M., Brockmann, H., 2008. Alternative Reproductive Tactics. Cambridge University Press, Cambridge.

Pigliucci, M., Preston, K., 2004. Phenotypic Integration: Studying Ecology and Evolution of Complex Phenotypes. Oxford University Press, Oxford.

Plaistow, S.J., Johnstone, R.A., Colegrave, N., Spencer, M., 2004. Evolution of alternative mating tactics: Conditional versus mixed strategies. Behav. Ecol. 15, 534–542.

Radwan, J., 1991. Sperm competition in the mite *Caloglyphus berlesei*. Behav. Ecol. Sociobiol. 29, 291–296.

Radwan, J., 1992. The influence of crowded environment on the size of males of *Caloglyphus berlesei* (Acari: Acaridae). Int. J. Acarol. 18, 67–68.

Radwan, J., 1993. The adaptive significance of male polymorphism in the acarid mite *Caloglyphus berlesei*. Behav. Ecol. Sociobiol. 33, 201–208.

Radwan, J., 1995. Male morph determination in two species of acarid mites. Heredity 74, 669–673.

Radwan, J., 1997. Sperm precedence in the bulb mite, *Rhizoglyphus robini*: context-dependent variation. Ethol. Ecol. Evol. 9, 373–383.

Radwan, J., 2001. Male morph determination in *Rhizoglyphus echinopus* (Acaridae). Exp. Appl. Acarol. 25, 143–149.

Radwan, J., 2003. Heritability of male morph in the bulb mite, *Rhizoglyphus robini* (Astigmata, Acaridae). Exp. Appl. Acarol. 29, 109–114.

Radwan, J., Bogacz, I., 2000. Comparison of life-history traits of the two male morphs of the bulb mite, *Rhizoglyphus robini*. Exp. Appl. Acarol. 24, 115–121.

Radwan, J., Klimas, M., 2001. Male dimorphism in the bulb mite, *Rhizoglyphus robini*: Fighters survive better. Ethol. Ecol. Evol. 13, 69–79.

Radwan, J., Czyż, M., Konior, M., Kołodziejczyk, M., 2000. Aggressiveness in two male morphs of the bulb mite *Rhizoglyphus robini*. Ethology 106, 53–62.

Radwan, J., Unrug, J., Tomkins, J., 2002. Status-dependence and morphological trade-offs in the expression of a sexually selected character in the mite, *Sancassania berlesei*. J. Evol. Biol. 15, 744–752.

Roff, D.A., 1996. The evolution of threshold traits in animals. Q. Rev. Biol. 71, 3–35.

Schluter, D., 1996. Adaptive radiation along genetic lines of least resistance. Evolution 50, 1766–1774.

Shuster, S.M., Sassaman, C., 1997. Genetic interaction between male mating strategy and sex ratio in a marine isopod. Nature 388, 373–377.

Shuster, S.M., Wade, M.J., 1991. Equal mating success among male reproductive strategies in a marine isopod. Nature 350, 608–610.

Shuster, S.M., Wade, M.J., 2003. Mating Systems and Strategies. Princeton University Press, Princeton, NJ.

Simmons, L.W., Emlen, D.J., Tomkins, J.L., 2007. Sperm competition games between sneaks and guards: a comparative analysis using dimorphic male beetles. Evolution 61, 2684–2692.

Suzuki, Y., Nijhout, H.F., 2006. Evolution of a polyphenism by genetic accommodation. Science 311, 650–652.

Tilszer, M., Antoszczyk, K., Salek, N., Zajac, E., Radwan, J., 2006. Evolution under relaxed sexual conflict in the bulb mite *Rhizoglyphus robini*. Evolution 60, 1868–1873.

Timms, S., Ferro, D.N., Emberson, R.M., 1980a. Selective advantage of pleomorphic male *Sancassania berlesei* (Michael). (Acari: Acaridae). Int. J. Acarol. 6, 97–102.

Timms, S., Ferro, D.N., Waller, J.B., 1980b. Suppression of production of pleomorphic males in *Sancassania berlesei* (Michael). (Acari: Acaridae). Int. J. Acarol. 6, 91–96.

Tomkins, J.L., Brown, G.S., 2004. Population density drives the local evolution of a threshold dimorphism. Nature 431, 1099–1103.

Tomkins, J.L., Hazel, W., 2007. The status of the conditional evolutionarily stable strategy. Trends Ecol. Evol. 22, 522–528.

Tomkins, J., LeBas, N., Unrug, J., Radwan, J., 2004. Testing the status-dependent ESS model: population variation in fighter expression in the mite *Sancassania berlesei*. J. Evol. Biol. 17, 1377–1388.

Unrug, J., Tomkins, J., Radwan, J., 2004. Alternative phenotypes and sexual selection: can dichotomous handicaps honestly signal quality? Proc. R. Soc. Lond. B 271, 1401–1406.

West-Eberhard, M.J., 2003. Developmental Plasticity and Evolution. Oxford University Press, Oxford.

Woodring, J.P., 1969a. Environmental regulation of andropolymorphism in Tyroglyphids (Acari). In: Evans, G.O. (Ed.), Proceedings of the 2nd International Congress of Acarology, Akademiai Kiado, Budapest, pp. 433–440.

Woodring, J.P., 1969b. Observations on the biology of six species of acarid mites. Annu. Entomol. Soc. Am. 62, 102–108.

Zimmerer, E.J., Kallman, K.D., 1989. Genetic bais for alternative reproductive tactics in the pygmy swordtail *Xipohorus nigrensis*. Evolution 43, 1289–1307.

Index

G

H

U

Unfamiliar flavor, 126

V

Vasopressin, 91
Vocalization, 25

W

Welfare problems, 79
Whiptail lizards, 155
Wild chimpanzees, 50
Wild dogs, 11
Wild European rabbits, 4
Wild gorillas, 51
Wild vervet monkeys, 56
Win contests, 186

Wolf(ves), 11, 82
  autonomous problem-solving
    behavior of, 92
  behavioral homology, between dog
    and, 90
  comparative background, 82
  convergent skills of extant dogs
    from, 82
  divergence of dog from, 84
  gazing plays, role in, 102
  human-related social behavior of
    dogs and, 86
  puppies socialized by, 90
  shared and distinctive traits, 86

Y

Yellow baboons, 10, 20

Contents of Previous Volumes

g225CONTENTS OF PREVIOUS VOLUMES 225